C00 44387911

EDINBURGH LIBRARIES

the 52 Seductions

D1390616

Betty Herbert lives by the sea with her husband and much-adored cat, Bob. In real life, she's been a PA, a marketing consultant, a teacher, a writing tutor, a cultural producer and a director of a literary festival that never quite happened. She likes sea-swimming, cocktails, Stevie Wonder and holidaying in Devon.

the 52 Seductions

Betty Herbert

WITHDRAWN

headline

Copyright © Betty Herbert 2011

The right of Betty Herbert to be identified as the Author of
the Work has been asserted by her in accordance with the
Copyright, Designs and Patents Act 1988.

First published in 2011
by HEADLINE PUBLISHING GROUP

1

Apart from any use permitted under UK copyright law, this publication
may only be reproduced, stored, or transmitted, in any form, or by
any means, with prior permission in writing of the publishers or, in
the case of reprographic production, in accordance with the terms of
licences issued by the Copyright Licensing Agency.

Every effort has been made to fulfil requirements with regard to
reproducing copyright material. The author and publisher will be
glad to rectify any omissions at the earliest opportunity.

Cataloguing in Publication Data is available from
the British Library

ISBN 978 0 7553 6252 3

Typeset in Palatino by Palimpsest Book Production Limited,
Falkirk, Stirlingshire

Printed and bound in Great Britain by
Clays Ltd, St Ives plc

Headline's policy is to use papers that are natural,
renewable and recyclable products and made from wood
grown in sustainable forests. The logging and manufacturing
processes are expected to conform to the environmental
regulations of the country of origin.

HEADLINE PUBLISHING GROUP
An Hachette UK Company
338 Euston Road
London NW1 3BH

www.headline.co.uk
www.hachette.co.uk

For C, with love

EDINBURGH LIBRARIES	
C0044387911	
Bertrams	19/07/2011
	£12.99
CH	HQ21

Prologue

I realise how prudish I am about to sound, but that's not the case at all.

No, I am not prudish; I have just been married for ten years. There is a difference, although I suspect that if I drew a Venn diagram in which one circle represented 'prudishness' and one represented 'having been married for ten years', there would be considerable overlap. I mention this to Herbert, and he says, 'A vulva-shaped overlap.' This is how bad things have got. It's way past Freudian.

Look, see, I am not prudish. There, in the paragraph above, I freely used the word 'vulva' without a care in the world. Oh, I can talk good sex, me. Just watch me down the pub on a Saturday night. I'll be the one cracking bawdy jokes in the corner, making the rest of the table howl with embarrassment.

I am, however, all talk. I'm expert in conversationally faking it. In real life, in the bedroom, I am about as sexually enlightened as Mary Whitehouse. Actually, scrub that. I have no right to cast aspersions on Mary's erotic drive. For all I know, she could have been a bit of a goer.

The point is, I am not naturally uptight. I was not brought up in sexually repressed circumstances (quite the opposite – my mother's sheer enthusiasm for sex would put Samantha Jones to shame), and I do not in any way disapprove of sex. It's just that I've come to feel a bit icky about it involving me.

We started off on great form, Herbert and I. We could

barely put each other down. But that was fifteen long years ago now, and I was just eighteen. Now, at thirty-three, sex seems so far away from me that I struggle to remember the point of it. We rarely do it at all, and when we do, it's usually out of a sense of obligation. *How long's it been? A month? Well, I guess we really ought to have a shag then. Hang on, I'll go and shave my legs first.*

It feels, sometimes, as though all of my desire has run away. It's just not there any more. Desire used to creep up on me and set my body and my imagination ablaze. It used to be triggered by the most intangible things: the smell of warm skin on a summer afternoon, a shared glance. Nowadays, even when I look for it, it's strangely absent. I remember it well, and it seems that this should be enough to conjure it up at will. But no. Instead, I feel as though I'm calling after a lost cat. Everything tells me that something should come running, but I am shouting into an empty backyard.

This isn't a book about the dying of love. Herbert and I adore each other and are extremely, smugly happy. We don't have any children to exhaust us or get in the way of our sex life. It's just that the fireworks ceased in the bedroom long ago. In their place, we have developed something resembling embarrassment.

Surely a loving relationship should encourage experimentation? In my experience, it does not. Herbert is my best friend, my confidante, my scaffolding. He is the person who takes care of me, whether or not I'm sick. He knows what makes me sad and what makes me angry. He knows what makes me happy. The sense of safety that has built up between us is the most valuable thing in the world.

But this safety is a death-blow to desire. The modern

marriage is just too damned fraternal. Who wants to compromise all that wonderful security by asking for sex? We share the cooking and the cleaning, we talk about our feelings, and we do our best to support each other through life's trials. Where's the sex in that? Where's the mystery? Where's the erotic frisson?

In the clean, new world of the modern marriage, sex is the nefarious toad lurking at the bottom of the garden. We're secretly afraid of it, but we know we ought to find it fascinating. We couldn't bring ourselves to actually kill it, so we just hope it will die of its own accord. It is an inconvenient reminder of the state of nature we think we've designed out of our lives.

Even if, suddenly, I was seized by a fit of passion and wanted to ravish Herbert, I wouldn't know where to start. We just don't have the language for sex any more, verbally or physically. We've lost our sexual imaginations. It would pain me to admit to Herbert that I found a film, picture or outfit sexy. It would just seem too ridiculous. I am his stable, sensible wife. It's not that he would disapprove; it's just that he would be so surprised that we would both become snared in self-consciousness. Sex is like a secret I'm keeping from myself.

I would have hated to admit it when I was eighteen, but I was inexperienced. Somehow, by staying with the same partner since then (and both of us have been utterly faithful, I'm sure of that), I have retained the sexuality of an eighteen-year-old. Less saucy than it sounds, I can assure you, particularly without the benefits of a teen-ager's firm midriff.

If you'd have asked me back then what sex with Herbert was like, I would have said, quite truthfully, mind-blowing. But the problem is, we kept having that same sex over and over again. Devaluation occurred. Mind-blowing at eighteen, if it doesn't develop, translates to boring at thirty-three. And we are strangely content to look back fondly on memories of our past sexual exploits rather than generating new ones. How I envy my friends who sailed through dozens of partners in their twenties! They have a whole rainbow of experience that I just can't access.

Yet something has changed. For a start, we managed to have sex after a particularly long break, even by our standards. This may have been due to the fact that we found ourselves staying in a hotel room with its own Jacuzzi and a supply of lube in the cupboards. This is what happens when you get upgraded to the Honeymoon Suite. It would have been a shame not to make full use of the facilities. But more to the point, the sex was bloody good. So good, in fact, that (after we'd stopped reeling with surprise) we did it again. Three times in one weekend. Quite something for us, I can assure you.

It was like being hit by a revelation. What a perfect, complete idiot I've been. What a bloody waste! So many women of my age are out embarking on sexual adventures but craving The One. I found The One years ago, and wasted him. My sexuality is my own responsibility. What's the point in sacrificing it to my own, very English, sense of embarrassment? Fifteen years together should lead to some sort of expertise; in our case, it has led to a kind of blind, dumbfounded ignorance. Even if I wanted to, I would have no idea how to turn Herbert on. I have no idea of his erotic tastes and preferences, let alone my own. I have made a habit of saying no even before the question is asked, and it's time that stopped.

Nervously, I sidle up to H in the kitchen and make a proposition. 'We're never going to be the couple who have sex every day,' I say, 'so let's be more realistic. What if we book a date for sex once a week, but with a twist? We take it in turns to arrange a seduction for each other every week for the next year.'

I am surprised how readily he agrees – in fact, a lovely smile spreads over his face. 'Okay,' he says.

'We have to stick to it, though,' I say. 'Both of us. It'll take a bit of effort.'

'I think I can manage that.'

'When we were first together, part of the reason the sex was so good was because we'd looked forward to it all day. We could do with a little more of that anticipation.'

'Fine,' he says; 'good. Great! So long as it doesn't have to be too elaborate, always.'

'No, not elaborate. Just interesting. Just *intended*.'

'And that doesn't mean to say that we can't have sex at other times too.'

'Don't push your luck.'

This is how the seductions begin.

I wake up the next morning and think: *Oh God, I actually said that aloud*. It was a lovely idea floating around in my head, and I've gone and ruined it by turning it into some bizarre sex pact. I now have to imagine – and own up to – twenty-six seductions over the next year, and be open-minded about the twenty-six that Herbert throws at me. Inside, I am already curling up with embarrassment.

It's alright, I think. I don't expect Herbert will say anything if we just let the idea drop. It wouldn't be the first time, after all. But Herbert is breezing around the kitchen, actually whistling.

'Seeing as it's your idea, I think it's only fair that you do the first seduction,' he says.

'Um, yes. Right. Probably.' I can't really argue with his logic, and I don't suppose he's any keener than I am to be the first to suggest something.

'Friday then?'

'Friday.'

Trapped in the confines of my imagination, a seduction seemed like such a fun, thrilling thing. Out in the open, it has taken on an air of menace. A seduction is an expression of your personal sexual taste, an invitation to share a pleasure. If you're not sure what you like any more, that's a terrifying prospect.

In desperation, I do as any sane woman would: I type 'seduction' into Google.

My goodness, there's a lot out there. I'm scared of clicking on something I don't want to see. I'm even more scared of clicking on a link that opens infinite windows, or decimates my hard drive altogether. Exactly how do you navigate this world and sort the good from the bad? What am I even looking for?

I am relieved to see a national newspaper near the top of the listings. Gingerly, I click on their 'Ten Best Sex Toys' guide. Ribbon handcuffs, a quilted spanking paddle, a 'hot and cold ceramic dildo'. Steady on. I have to go and pour myself a glass of wine. Is this normal? Is everyone doing this?

I follow their links, hoping for something a bit more beginner-level. The first URL has clearly fallen victim to the recession, and its contents have been replaced by something much dodgier-looking. I close down the window post-haste.

I reject the next site simply for its poor aesthetics. Too many pictures of pumped-up blondes make me think of nylon knickers, I'm afraid. I may be putting my whole sense of self on the line here, but I see no reason to compromise my good taste. Or give myself thrush, for that matter.

Worse, the higher-end stuff prices me out of the market. The newspaper directs me to what looks like a knuckle-duster ('worn on the middle finger of one's strongest hand'), which costs £560 from Coco de Mer. I mean, really. I struggle to imagine the circumstances in which I would pay that much for a quick session of mutual masturbation, assuming that's what you do with it. In truth, its applications are entirely mysterious to me.

Coco de Mer has already scared me off, anyway, with their leather dog mask (£220-worth of 'utilitarian bondage chic', apparently) and 300-quid knickers which are gorgeous but out of my league. I wonder, shamefaced, if I'm not more of an Ann Summers girl, at least in terms of price range, if not ambition.

Coco de Mer at least features arty photos of women with meat on their thighs and non-Brazilianed pubic hair. Insinuate's site is full of porny young women offering their thin bodies up to the male gaze. I wonder how many men buy their stuff and are disappointed when they see their partners' bodies in it. We can't possibly live up to that. I nevertheless consider a pair of Bridgette spanking briefs – until I see the back of them. I'm just not sure that my arse crack merits its own window. Probably the fact that I'm calling it my arse crack tells you all you need to know.

Ann Summers it is then. I'm expecting a proliferation of ruching, sateen and cheap lace, all in the obligatory red. I'm not entirely wrong, but to be honest, most of it wouldn't look out of place in M&S these days. This simultaneously depresses and comforts me. By this point I am anyway in a state of utter despair. I click disconsolately through the site, wondering if saucy underwear is really what I need. It's not as if I've surrendered to five-pack pants and greying bras. I like to think that my underpinnings are rather well maintained actually; you never know when you are going to be run over by that bus.

I sense a revolt brewing. Why do I have to buy something to be sexy? And when did we develop this notion that we must accessorise in order to have sex at all? You can buy vibrating cock rings in Boots these days, for heaven's sake. I can't help but feel that we are losing the core of our sexuality under this deluge of frills and numbing vibration.

Thus resolved, I shut down my laptop, wondering what on earth I am going to do if I have to rely on my imagination alone.

December

Seduction #1
The First Date

The day of the first seduction arrives, and I find myself considering wearily how the special events of life, like birthday presents and keeping in touch with old friends, are always my responsibility. Why do I have to invent the first seduction? Perhaps we could just have a nice discussion about it tonight, and maybe make a wall chart together or something. You know where you are with a wall chart.

But then, at some point along the way (and in fact this is at about 5 p.m., with Herbert due home in an hour), I realise how mean-minded I'm being. The spirit of the thing is not to measure tit against tat, to drag the same old, petty irritations into this. A seduction is an act of generosity, a gesture of goodwill. The resistance I'm feeling is rooted in fear rather than any genuine sense of grievance.

I practically hurl myself into the bath, managing to

shave my legs and underarms without a great deal of bloodletting. It's a good (if unusual) omen. I may not have a seduction ready, but I shall at least be utterly lovely when he arrives home. I spray a bit of perfume around and consider putting on the rather hot red dress I wore to a party last Christmas. No, I think, I will not dress up as someone else tonight; I will dress as myself. I want to feel relaxed and at my ease, not trussed up like a ridiculous turkey. There's more than a faint whiff of suburban housewife in that. After a bit of light deliberation, I put on a pair of seamed stockings with knee-high socks over the top, my best frilly knickers, a denim skirt and a stripy jumper. Looking at myself in the mirror, I feel relieved that I look much like normal, if slightly improved.

It is only when I'm putting on my make-up (lots of black eyeliner, in tribute to Herbert's rather unfortunate crush on Gwyneth Paltrow in *The Royal Tenenbaums*) that an idea arrives. What if we start all over again?

When I first met Herbert, I was still living with my mother, so I stayed at his house on weekends. I used to pack up my overnight things in a small, brown vintage suitcase and meet him at the pub. H has since commented, misty-eyed, that he knew his luck was in whenever he saw me with that case. The real McCoy has long since disintegrated, having been walked home in the rain too many times, but I do have a small, blue vanity case, bought recently in a charity shop, that might do the job. It will be useless, of course, if I don't take it out of the house. I must meet Herbert at the pub to get that whole 'first date' feeling.

I rather wish I had thought of this before six o'clock. Praying for Friday night traffic to delay H, I rush around the house, searching for the bloody blue case. When, eventually, I find it (stuffed down the side of the sofa, obviously), it is full of books. I tip these out on to the living-room floor and then immediately tidy them up again, realising that there's nothing remotely seductive about coming home to a bombsite (although this may actually have served to replicate the state of Herbert's house when I first met him). I deposit my purse, phone and keys into the case, throw on my lovely new black and white brogues, and nearly run out of the door, hoping that I won't bump into him walking up the road.

What actually happens is that our cat, Bob, follows me nearly all the way to the pub, wailing for my attention. H, however, is nowhere to be seen. I manage to palm off the cat on a passing woman with a toddler and slip into the pub, where I buy myself a steadying vodka and tonic. On a whim, I ask the barman if I can get a table in their upstairs restaurant a little later.

This will be a much more grown-up date than when we first met then. That happened in a gay bar on Christmas Eve 1995. I had been taken there by another man, who promptly left without me. I couldn't drive, the buses had stopped running and my mother couldn't pick me up for another two hours. There was no choice but to sit on my own and hope someone was willing to talk to me. Luckily, that person was Herbert. As soon as he sat down next to me, I felt like I'd been caught in a tractor beam. I went home to my family and told them I'd fallen in love.

In the here and now, I realise I'm surprisingly nervous. It all feels like a bit of a risk. I hope he's not disappointed. As I carry my drink to a table, I notice that a couple of men by the bar actually check me out. This has not happened in a very, very long time. It must have something to do with my look of intent; or maybe it's just that I'm a woman on my own on a Friday night. I text H: *For my first seduction, I'm taking you on a date. When you're ready, meet me in the pub.*

No reply. I gulp at my V&T, thinking that he almost certainly has a flat battery. It is ever thus with Herbert's phone. Fifteen minutes later, I get a text in return saying, *Groovy. On my way.*

I am reduced to drinking the melted ice in the bottom of my glass when Herbert arrives in his best shirt, looking more scared than I do. What a ridiculous pair we are. He goes to the bar and buys me a Cosmopolitan, which I drink gratefully. 'Look,' I say, 'I've brought my little case with me, just like old times,' and he looks baffled for a few beats and then laughs and says, 'What have you got in it?'

'Oh,' I say, 'just my keys, I'm afraid. And my wallet.'

But we're a bit more relaxed after this. We chat happily and he puts his hand on my knee. I feel quite splendid – sort of excited to be with him. He normally thinks it's pointless going to the pub on our own, but tonight it means that we have to pay each other some attention, rather than crashing out in front of the telly for a few hours before falling asleep. 'I wondered if I should put my suit on before I came out,' he admits after a while. I'm pleased that he felt like it was potentially that important, but glad he decided against it.

To cut a long story short, we have a couple more drinks and a very nice dinner (I have to swap starters with Herbert, who is rather alarmed by the rareness of his roast veal), and then we retire home and to bed. I draw a veil over the proceedings at this point, not through modesty, but because my memory is a little hazy after two cocktails, a vodka and tonic and half a bottle of wine. I have a vague notion that it involved the Reverse Cowgirl, but I can say no more than that. I can divulge, however, that we also had (entirely unscheduled) sex the next afternoon.

Our first seduction probably looks fairly tame for a couple who have fundamentally had sex before, but you have to bear in mind that we're starting from a pretty low base.

Apart from the very beginning of our relationship, Herbert and I have never had the most frequent sex life. It has never really been a major part of our identity as a couple. This is not to say that we don't enjoy sex; it's just that, quite often, neither of us can be bothered. However, over the last eighteen months, this has got particularly bad for a very specific reason.

I have been on a more or less continuous period for eighteen months. Last July, I had my contraceptive implant removed. Big mistake. It seems that my body has forgotten how to regulate itself without synthetic hormones. I am an emotional, hormonal and physical mess, all migraines, nausea, swollen ankles and mysterious aches that seem to spread from my belly to my wrists on bad days. If you pull my eyelids back, they're pure white inside. I'm permanently exhausted.

My error was to mention to my GP that we were considering trying for a baby. That seems a long time ago now; the desire to reproduce seeped out of me with the last dregs of my energy. But somewhere on my records there must be a note of it, because whenever I ask what can be done, she offers to refer me for IVF. I don't want IVF. I just want to feel better.

In April, I got sick of being told to 'wait four months and see if it settles down'. I didn't feel like there would be any of me left by then. I asked for a mini coil to be fitted, because it had stopped my periods altogether when I'd used one before. My GP looked appalled, and asked if I understood that I couldn't get pregnant with a coil in. I felt like I was breaking a taboo, saying that perhaps I didn't mind whether or not I had children. It was as if a whole set of cultural assumptions had fallen into place the minute a thirty-something woman entered the surgery. At my age, I was supposed to prioritise my ability to reproduce over my health.

I had to wait two months for the coil to be fitted. In the meantime, ironically, I had an early miscarriage. I had no idea I was pregnant, because the bleeding hadn't stopped. In any case, the coil made no difference at all. When I went back after two months for my check-up, I was told to wait for another two months to see if it settled down. It didn't.

In October, I returned to my GP.

'Come back in four months,' she said. At this point, I'm afraid I cried right there in her office. I'm not much of a crier normally, but I was beyond desperate. 'I can't keep waiting for months,' I said. 'Nothing changes.'

'Well, what do you want me to do?' she asked, somewhat defensively.

'Give me something to stop the bleeding and refer me to a gynaecologist.'

'Okay,' she said. I hadn't realised she was waiting for me to give her instructions. She prescribed me the mini-Pill, and after three weeks it seemed to have calmed down the worst of the bleeding. With a referral, I was able to use my health insurance to bring the gynaecologist appointment forward.

He widened his eyes in horror when I told him my story. He then gave me a proper examination. My cervix, he said, was red-raw, with an overgrowth of tissue on the outside, and was bleeding profusely at the merest touch. 'Has no one looked at this up until now?' he said. 'It's obviously not right.'

That was last week. Within a couple of days, he had arranged for me to have another scan (this time a transvaginal one, administered with the help of a comedy ultrasound dildo), and, next week, a colposcopy (looking at my cervix with a magnifying camera) and biopsy.

For three days after seeing him, I grinned like a smug cat, delighted to finally have the chance to get to the bottom of my problems. Then, I suddenly realised what it all might mean. I am having a test next week for cervical cancer. I can't even bring myself to think about what it might mean if it's positive.

Seduction #2
Surrender

We book our second seduction – Herbert's turn – for Saturday afternoon.

I work in education, helping teachers to be more creative, and I'm delivering a residential training course on the Friday night. This means I have plenty of time to wonder what on earth he will plan – and indeed whether he will manage to plan anything at all – while I struggle to entertain a group of people I don't know, all of whom are apparently a bit shocked that the restaurant of a four-star hotel doesn't serve food in gutbuster portions.

My residential finishes at lunchtime on Saturday, and I text Herbert: *Home in about forty-five. Shall we get some lunch?*

His reply pings straight back: *Seduction first.*

Wow. I experience what I think might be termed an

erotic frisson. I push back the pernicious thought that it had better be quick, as I'm starving.

Driving home, I mentally rehearse an advance apology for the state of my bikini line (my waxing lady can't wax, allegedly, when her car is broken down), and wonder if I can sneak into the bathroom to floss my teeth before it all kicks off.

I am really quite nervous by the time I open the front door. The house is completely quiet. There is a note in the middle of the hall floor that says, 'Seduction'. I put down my bags and open it up.

Go up to the bedroom and undress. There is a scarf on the bed – put it on as a blindfold and lie down. It should be nice and warm in there.

When you're ready, I will come in. I won't talk to you. I will tie up your hands with the dressing-gown cord, and then I will stimulate you. If you don't feel comfortable at any point, just say.

Well. I first think, *Oh fuck*, and then I feel slightly delighted. Boy, has he called my bluff. I can immediately see that this all relates directly to a conversation we had a couple of weeks ago, in which I said that sometimes I want to just take whatever pleasure he's giving me and not have to worry about returning it. I am also trying hard not to giggle at the specification of a dressing-gown cord rather than, say, something less mundane. Silken rope, maybe? No, a dressing-gown cord. Let's not overreach, eh?

Herbert, then, must be sitting in the spare room waiting for me. This in itself is somehow quite exciting. I take off my clothes and fold them up on the chest of drawers, and then sit down on the bed. My paisley scarf is draped across the pillow. I tie it around my eyes and then lie back, wondering how much he can tell from listening through the walls.

He's obviously listening very carefully; I don't have to wait long. He comes in and I giggle, just slightly. I think I want to send out a signal to him that I'm pleased rather than terrified. He resists saying hello, as I expect him to. Instead, I hear him come towards me. He gently picks up my right hand, kisses it, and then ties the cord around my wrist. He is being, I realise, deliberately reassuring – the cord is a soft, familiar thing, not tied too tight, entirely escapable. He does the same to the other hand.

Already, my senses are working in an entirely different way from usual. Without sight and without being able to actively touch, the world feels more spacious somehow. I am conscious of the pauses between Herbert's touches, not knowing what will happen next. My sense of smell is activated too; I catch a scent of something unfamiliar on him, and wonder if he's worn aftershave just to fool me (he usually approaches aftershave as if it's some kind of affront to his status as a natural man). I think, on reflection, that this wasn't the case. I think I was just encountering everything differently.

Later that afternoon, he tells me that he wondered if I would question whether it was him at all, but in fact the effect was the opposite – I realised how many ways I knew him other than sight and sound. It was odd to not be able to move, adjust or touch back; I felt everything much more intensely than usual, and I quite enjoyed the thought that I was handing over my body to H, surrendering all control over what he did or saw. With the blindfold on, I felt more anonymous too, more able to accept what was given to me. I was able to gasp and moan – in fact, this was more necessary than usual, being our only means of communication.

Interestingly, though, despite it all being intensely pleasurable, I struggled to orgasm until he finally untied me and I could move around a little more. I think H was more bothered by this than I was (he was driven to bringing the electric toothbrush into the equation at one point, until it began to bleep frantically in defence of its depleted batteries).

For me, being finally untied felt like the wonderful opening of the floodgates, especially seeing as he had refrained from kissing me until that moment. I can honestly say that that first kiss was one of the most delicious kisses we've ever shared.

When we broke our dry spell in the hotel Jacuzzi, we hadn't had sex for four months. The last time we'd even tried had led to a nuclear row. There is something particularly dangerous about adding sex to a dispute. It's like adding a peppermint to a can of Coke – the resulting explosion is almost unimaginably disproportionate. The blandest comment can take a crowbar to your entire sense of sexual worth.

It's hard to recount a row without making one or both of you sound bullying and unreasonable. I'm the natural picker of fights in our household; H prefers to turn the other cheek, to an infuriating degree, and then suddenly break into a Hulk-angry rage. This reflects our basic perspectives on these matters. I see arguments as largely harmless bouts of blowing off steam, a chance to clear the air. H, meanwhile, sees them as potentially life-threatening. He will go to nearly any lengths to avoid them, and then behaves like a riled bear when he can stand it no longer.

I give this background, I suppose, as a means of explaining just how odd this particular argument was. For once, I was not picking at Herbert; I was doing my absolute best to be kind and gentle and open-minded. This, most likely, is what particularly pissed him off. He probably saw it as an attempt to wrong-foot him.

We had just come downstairs from a sorry and frankly distracted attempt at sex. I don't honestly remember whether it had eventually come to a satisfactory conclusion for either party, but both of us were quiet. In my memory, H is bustling around the cooker. It is early evening, and dusk. He's in his dressing gown.

'Honey,' I say, as gently as possible, 'I noticed you were finding it hard to concentrate there.'

'Was I?' he says.

'Yes. I think I understand why. Are you feeling a bit, you know, put off by all that's going on, the bleeding and that?'

H looks horrified. 'No. Not at all. I'm not put off. It's all fine.'

'But it isn't, though, is it?'

'I don't see that, no.'

'Herbert, I think we both know that you've been . . . struggling . . . to keep an erection.'

Silence. 'No. I can't say I've noticed that.'

'Herbert.' This is exasperating. I thought he might get cross, but I never expected him to deny it altogether.

Nothing.

'Herbert, I'm trying to put this as delicately as possible, but what I mean to say is that I can understand why you might be finding this hard. You must worry about all sorts of things. There's no wonder it would have an effect on you.'

No answer again.

'Herbert,' I say, 'I need you to at least reply.'

He turns towards me. 'Well, if you're going to make me say it, there's nothing wrong with my dick. It's you. You're just not tight enough any more.'

I will leave you to imagine the scale of the row that ensued. For a while, I try to argue the toss. I fully accept that my vagina is not the paradise it used to be, I say (although this may well have expressed itself as, 'My cunt is the Slough of Despond! What do you want me to do about that?' I have a special talent for literary swearing), but a soft dick is an objectively existent thing. You can't deny it's happening. It just is.

H is having none of it. It is like something has broken

in him. He has spent a year being the supportive, patient, turn-a-blind-eye husband. He has sympathised and consoled and, sometimes, mopped up the blood. He has tolerated my occasional need to change the sheets before the cleaner comes, and then to let her change them all over again so that she doesn't guess something is wrong. He has held earnest conversations with our friends about my problems without ever retreating into masculine embarrassment. He's damned if he's going to be accused of any of this stopping him from fancying me, even if this means him saying something far more offensive. He's fought hard to behave perfectly through all of this.

Four months later, I still have no idea if he'd noticed the waning erections or not. I suppose it's entirely possible that he'd pushed them out of his mind; he must have been pushing so much else out of his mind already. Either way, I ended up in a grieving puddle on the floor. I felt like the most disgusting, foetid thing that existed. 'I wish you would just go and find someone else to have sex with,' I kept saying. 'I can't offer you that any more.' H just held on to me and whispered, 'I'm so sorry,' over and over again into my hair.

Arguments are an odd, altered state of being. Psychologists talk about the 'flooding' of chemicals in the bloodstream that occurs when we are angry, which may even disable our rational control of our actions. All I know is that it's perfectly possible to say one thing during an argument, and to deeply, sincerely mean it, and then, an hour later, to realise you don't mean it at all. It's like you've been dragged along by the argument's own logic, and no longer know which way up you are. Herbert was mortified that he'd refused to take any responsibility for his part in the death of our sex life; and I didn't really want him to go off and sleep with someone else. Neither of us was right to say what we said, but then one of the mysterious privileges of being in a committed relationship is that you can express your darkest thoughts and still be forgiven.

That said, you'll understand why neither of us so much as mentioned sex for the next four months. We just didn't know where to start from again.

Seduction #3
Enter the Boudoir

The ball's back in my court this week. And after Herbert's rather surprising first seduction, I feel that the stakes have been raised – or rather, that it is no longer enough to simply be willing to have sex with him, as I'd hoped.

Despite this, I spend most of the week dithering. We have made a date for Friday night; on Friday morning, I am still considering my options. I just can't escape a sense of intimidation. There's no way I can live up to the kinkiness of Herbert's last seduction. Half of me feels obliged to raise the stakes a little, but the other, noisier, half is strongly petitioning to forget about the whole seduction thing and watch *QI* in our pyjamas instead.

I head into town to see if I can shop my way out of this dilemma. Over a bowl of soup and a soothing latte, I come to a kind of compromise. There's no point in stretching my comfort zone so far that I'm filled with dread. I need to work with what I've got. My offer is different from Herbert's – a more feminine approach, perhaps, but also a more organised one. My seduction will be to turn our bedroom into a boudoir.

Now, our bedroom has issues. I can't even tell you why. I am not ashamed to say that the rest of the house looks rather splendid, but our bedroom seems impervious to my decorative charms. It contains a gorgeous new heavy wood bed, fabulous Neisha Crosland wallpaper, the best bed linen I could raid from TK Maxx, and some lovely curtains made by my own fair hands, but still somehow manages to retain the air of a Premier Inn. This is a mystery to me; it stubbornly resists all my advances. I fill it with lovely things, and it wilfully remains considerably less than the sum of its parts.

Perhaps this is our problem; perhaps our bedroom is so resolutely unsexy that it actively counteracts any saucy thoughts we might be having. It probably does not help that I get insanely hot and dry-mouthed overnight, and so like to keep it at a temperature that some might call 'refrigerated'.

I zoom around the shops looking for a few things to make it slightly more inviting. In M&S, I buy Prosecco, finger-food and a bunch of roses. In Fenwick, I buy geranium massage oil. In WHSmith, I hunt for a 'How To' sex guide, and settle on Em & Lo's *Sex: How To Do Everything*, which I select on the basis of the rather graphic photos. I also pick up a copy of *Cosmopolitan*, hoping for a few extra tips.

Once home, I turn up the heating in the bedroom, light candles on every surface, strew the bed with rose petals and bring my Dansette record player upstairs. I must say, the room looks rather lovely with its hotel-room formality disrupted, but I want to encourage some serious lounging, so I also bring a huge stack of cushions upstairs from the living room and pile them at the head of the bed. I then put on some nice underwear, a pair of socks to keep my feet warm, and my slightly-more-glamorous dressing gown (my usual one is grey with a hood; not really the thing). Then I set about waiting for Herbert to arrive.

He's gone to the gym. Fine. I flick through *Cosmo*, coming to the uncomfortable conclusion that it's aimed at women far younger than me. Its 'best-ever sex tip to send him wild', signalled on the front page, turns out to be 'look really into it'. Thanks, *Cosmo*. I hadn't worked out that he was expecting me to look like I was actually enjoying myself.

Anyway, I will not harp on about how late home Herbert is, or how he's not bothered to shower at the gym. (Him: 'I didn't know what we'd be doing.' Me: 'Nothing – ever – that wouldn't require you to shower first.')

I will say, instead, that the boudoir idea is a wonderful one. We loll about, getting tipsy and listening to boogaloo records. It feels slow-paced, comfortable, flirtatious. With both of us semi-clothed, we can linger over the stroking and snogging; there's no rush. I give H his first massage in years, and then slide my naked body up and down his back. He doesn't seem to mind this at all.

Finger-food is just right for a Friday night, although I can officially state that M&S mini beef Wellingtons are horrid. Em & Lo's sex guide receives rolled eyes from H, who seems to think he is something of a sexpert; the pictures that I considered to be a bit racy are declared tame by him. But the Prosecco cocktails keep us warm and enthusiastic and the candlelight is delicious.

I will, however, not be strewing the bed with rose petals ever again. After spending most of the evening picking them out of various crevices, I then have to spend a considerable time the next morning sweeping them out from under the bed. Despite these efforts, I find three of them lined up on the windowsill after the cleaner has visited on Monday, just so I know she's found them.

Things are changing around here. Three times this week, Herbert has slapped me hard on the behind, once while we were having sex. This is unprecedented.

The old, staid Betty would not have liked it, but I am resolved to confront it with an open mind. On reflection, it's rather sweet, a bit like being a waitress in a *Carry On* film. Not that I would approve of Herbert doing the same thing to waitresses, but I can, I suppose, harbour no objection to him doing it to me. It doesn't really hurt, and it's done in that spirit of appreciation that I have long sought to foster in this relationship.

Being a creature of absolutely no subtlety at all, though, I cannot just let this lie. After the third incident (in the kitchen, while I am cooking dinner), I am compelled to say, with great delicacy, 'Oi, you keep slapping my bum!'

'Yes,' says Herbert, 'I quite like it.'

Now this may not seem to be much to crow about, but believe me, H is not the most forthcoming of beasts, and it delights me to think that he likes any part of my body at all. Not that he particularly dislikes any part of it either, you understand; it is more that he is not given to rhapsodising. If pushed, I suspect he'd name 'vagina' and 'mouth' as his two favourite parts of me. Functional. Effective.

H has never been one for sexual aesthetics. Hence, when showing him a website of saucy underwear this week in the hope of an 'impromptu' gift or two, I eventually have to concede defeat.

'You're not really bothered about underwear, are you?'

'Not really, no.'

'Is there nothing that would even slightly interest you?'

A heavy sigh. 'Naked?'

'You see me naked all the time.'

'Yes, that's the problem.'

Thanks, Herbert. I try to explain that this is the point of lingerie – it exoticises the mundane. Herbert shrugs. 'Yeah, maybe. It's more for you than for me.'

This is where he has a point. Sex, for me – and I think for other women too – is only 25 per cent mechanics. The rest is imagination, inclination, anticipation, performance. For example, the only way I can get any pleasure from a quickie is if I'm tickled by the idea of having a quickie. The quickie itself is simply not enough. Sex, for me, is about being in the mood.

This week, I've made an effort to be a little bit more foxy, a little bit less everyday. Despite there being absolutely no call for it in my professional life, I have avoided wearing jeans all week, and have instead ventured into skirts and shoes with heels (only small ones, you understand). My standard Birkenstock clogs are feeling a little under-loved. I have, most days, worn stockings. I rather like stockings, incidentally – not for any particularly kinky reason, but for what they don't do, which is make you feel like you've kept your genitals in a Tupperware container all day, as I find with tights. The added benefit is that they make your legs look quite lovely.

Herbert's right: it's all made me feel a little better. If I can manage to continuously appear, well, at least presentable, then I'm more likely to be in the mood for sex when the opportunity arises. That's the theory, anyway.

When I first met Herbert, I was known as a bit of a dresser. I used to raid the charity shops for lovely things and spend hours getting ready. It would have appalled me to wear the same outfit twice, let alone to dress casually. I didn't even own a pair of jeans.

That all changed when I realised that other women

hated me for it. They thought I was competing. I was not; I just really, really liked clothes. All the same, I compromised. And now, when I look around at my friends, I see that we all look the same. We layer on two T-shirts at a time; we put leggings under our skirts and jeans under our dresses. We are a little bit scandalised when we see cleavage. More and more, we dress like the toddlers that accompany most of us.

Of course, we dress for comfort – and amen to that – but I think we're also sending out a deliberate signal. In our smocks and our Crocs, we are sexless and we are safe. We are not going to steal anyone's husband, or indeed stray from our own. We are good girls, and we are dressing like playgroup attendants to prove it.

In the last few weeks, I've found myself looking for a third way. I'm seeking a casual womanliness, and the kind of sexy that doesn't involve pinched toes and squeezed-in breasts. I don't want to scare the horses or compromise my feminist values; I just want to feel a little bit less neutered. Similarly, I am not 'spicing up' my sex life. Rather, I am reforming it. 'Spicing up' is just too desperate for me. It puts me in mind of low-cut nurses' uniforms and, frankly, swinging. I yearn for a middle way between sex bomb and Boden, between spicing it up and leaving it to rot.

Perhaps my problem in general is that I just don't see sex as remotely spicy. It is a normal thing that normal people do, with many well-documented variations and predilections. I have always taken orgasms as my birthright, and not something that I may, occasionally, be blessed with, given a prevailing wind and a great deal of concentration. I don't feel at all embarrassed about sex (only really about the lack of it in my life, until recently), and I don't have any guilty notions that it should be procreational. I understand the bodily processes behind it, and I understand how to achieve these for myself, without the help of a man.

Yet so much of the sexual literature out there insists on clinging to the idea that sex is somehow naughty, that one must rely on a giddy sense of guilt and transgression to ratchet up the excitement. I just don't get it.

So here I am, betwixt and between. I'm pretty sure I'm not the only one who feels like this. And, frankly, those of us for whom sex is not a forbidden thing, for whom pleasure is an entitlement, need to put our heads together. It's almost like we're inventing it anew.

Seduction #4
La Vie Parisienne

O ur Christmas present to each other is a trip to Paris, city of romance and, let's face it, sauciness. 'We won't bother organising a seduction while we're there, will we?' says Herbert before we leave. 'We'll just see what inspires us.' I agree; we've always had sex on holiday, even in our driest years. I suppose it's because we've got the time, but I also think that it's because sex is on the (unstated) agenda. We're both expecting to have sex on holiday, so we do. It's a lesson for the rest of life.

There's something transformative about being on holiday. You drop all thoughts about work and obligations for a while, and you're allowed to feel like a different type of person entirely. What is it about ordinary, everyday married life that makes you feel desire isn't allowed?

On the first day, we walk down from our hotel through the Marais, browsing through the gorgeous boutiques and stopping for the occasional hot chocolate. It's bitterly cold;

there are still patches of snow piled at the sides of the pavement from the flurries the day before. I buy a bottle of saffron perfume, and I enjoy letting Herbert smell it on my wrist every few minutes as it settles into the background scent of my own skin. Later, when we get back to our room, he pushes me on to the bed as soon as the door is shut, and whispers in my ear, 'You smell gorgeous.'

This is all I want: to be desired. That's enough to turn me on forever. But it's hard to keep desiring the same person, over and over again. Desire is a fickle beast; she demands constant change to maintain her interest.

The next day, we edge our way around a crowded sex shop populated mainly by teenage girls. I'm rarely comfortable in places like this – and this one is a modern, brightly lit affair, half kitsch emporium, half Day-Glo dildo store. I don't object to sex toys in and of themselves, but they seem to me to often represent the death of desire, a kind of sensory inflation. A lot of the toys seem to be an addendum to sex itself, as if the sensations our bodies produce aren't quite exquisite enough. They speak of the boredom that many of us feel, I suppose, the sense that sex needs to progress across the lifetime of our relationship to keep us interested. More often than not, it contracts rather than progresses, retreating into a disinterested clump of the safe and the uncontroversial.

I once owned a rabbit vibrator that I found entirely boring, so I'm not all that interested in the shop, but Herbert seems keen to bring something home, so we settle on a little jelly contraption with one loop that stretches round the penis, one that goes round the balls, and two vibration units that sit above and below the penis. The idea is that we would both get a bit of extra 'buzz' during sex.

H puts it on when we get home. The effect is like

stretching a rubber band over his testicles – they are forced into a tight balloon, looking really quite uncomfortable (though he assures me it feels fine). It also has a disgusting plasticky smell that doesn't do much to heighten the mood. I gamely climb on top of him, and spend the next ten minutes trying to position myself so that the damned thing actually makes contact with my clitoris. In the end, I only really manage intermittent service, but even this has a strange effect on me: I can feel the vibrations, but not the other more usual sensations. I am completely unable to tell whether H is inside me or not. It is as if my vagina is distracted. I have to concentrate very hard to enjoy it at all. In the end we take it off, as I'm getting bored and feeling a bit alienated by it. To my mind, the feelings it produces are inferior to normal sex.

So what do we learn from this? Well, maybe that the sex is good enough already, when it happens. I'm lucky, I suppose. I enjoy the simple elements of sex: the eye contact, the kisses and the touches. I've never had a very great problem accessing an orgasm, and, on the occasions when I can't quite get there, I can rest safe in the knowledge that I can always achieve one on my own. So perhaps I can afford to be dismissive of these little devices that replace those sensations with vibration. Or perhaps I've not yet encountered one of sufficient quality to take me that extra mile.

But more than this, I learned about desire: how the encounter is equally important to anything else that happens. Given the option, I would always take H throwing me on the bed over small, pink vibrating devices. Desire, I think, is stronger than the most expensive vibration. The question is, how can we keep feeling that desire, year in, year out?

January

My cat, Bob, taught me all I know about playing hard to get.

Bob is a very beautiful cat, a velvety tortoiseshell. Passing strangers in the street find her irresistible, and so do I. I almost physically long for her – not just her soft fur, but the smell of her, the feeling of her tail wrapping around my hand in greeting.

But she mostly shuns me. She prefers, it seems, the ministrations of passing schoolchildren to mine. This is an utter, abject misery to me. I just can't understand it. I lavish her with the best of my attention and it only seems to drive her away, usually with an appalled look on her face. It wasn't like this when she was a kitten; then, she couldn't get enough of me. Now, it seems, I have served my purpose. She doesn't want me any more.

I shudder when I think how similar this sounds to the way I've been treating Herbert. Here am I, yearning ridiculously for Bob, whilst until recently I was denying my own husband the same affections.

There must have been a point in our relationship when sex got pushed off the agenda. I can't put my finger on an exact moment, but I remember an era when sex moved from being a compulsive, luxurious indulgence to an unwanted demand on my time. I'm pretty sure the transition came earlier for me than for Herbert, because I can remember a sense of dread that his hand would reach over to me, that little bit too deliberately to be acting in simple affection. I remember, too, learning to avoid kisses and cuddles, lest they segued into an attempt at something more. Either way, Herbert was too polite to question it, or perhaps he lacked the language. After a while, rather than rail against this rejection, he adjusted his desire downwards to match mine.

It's a pattern of behaviour that Bettina Arndt describes vividly in her book *The Sex Diaries*. One partner goes off sex, and the other is left with a bewildered sense of rejection, wondering where it all went wrong. The erotic terminator is most often a woman, but certainly not in all cases.

In relationships, a 'no' too often outweighs a 'yes'. I have always viewed my ability to say no to sex as an unquestionable veto. Herbert never consented to this state of affairs, and I never asked his opinion. I just withdrew sex unilaterally.

Of course, women must have the inalienable right to say no to sex, whether or not they are in a relationship with the partner they are refusing. But what if we always say no? What if we say no to lovers who are kind and attentive, who have promised to be faithful to us and stuck to it, who know they could offer us pleasure if only we'd let them? What must our lovers do then?

I realise now that I became the quartermaster of sex, rationing out sexual favours as if we were under siege. I'm not even sure how it happened. I suppose, like many women, I came to see men's all-encompassing desire for sex as a weakness, an inability to gain control. By the time I settled into a long-term relationship, I was sick to the teeth of the intrusiveness of male sexual desire. To be a teenage girl is to be groped, coerced, begged, harassed and tricked by men of varying levels of appeal. When, at eighteen, I met Herbert, I'd already run out of sympathy. And, vitally, I'd learned to equate the desire to have sex with power. I was determined to be on the winning team.

As time went by, I noticed my friends withdrawing from the sexual world too. Once we settled down into couples, talking about our sex lives became taboo, a breach of the monogamous pact. Then, a few years later, the wary confessions came. *We don't really do it any more*. The standard conversational tack was that we were mildly relieved at this; we'd rather have a good night's sleep. We never actually know what goes on behind our friends' closed bedroom doors, but I wonder how many of us really believe this. I found myself publicly declaring my gratitude for the death of my sex life, and privately mourning it. I felt as though I'd be breaking ranks to do otherwise. I played my part in shoring up the unsexy sisterhood. It was a different sort of power-play, one that wanted to ensure that no one else was having more fun than I was.

In the present tense, sex is beginning to seem like an easy, simple pleasure again, something that gives as much to me as it does to Herbert. It may be hard to extract sex from power, but that power doesn't have to be oppositional. It can be the power of two people working together for the same thing; not a battle, but an augmentation. Why couldn't I see that before?

The only answer I can offer is this: women have a hierarchy of loves, and sexual love is at the bottom of it. We think, foolishly, that we can simply transcend sexual love once it passes into something deeper and put it to one side.

Men understand something different – that it's all the same thing. They see love as a cumulative process that gathers all its previous incarnations together to make a greater, deeper whole. Understood this way, sex isn't the poor relation of love: it is an ongoing practice that rehearses all the wonderful things about it – trust, desire, intimacy, and ecstasy.

Seduction #5
Innocence and Experience

It is Saturday afternoon, and I am eating cheese on toast when Herbert decides to announce his next seduction.

He's a little nervous about this one, I can tell. It's ten days since we returned from Paris, and in fact eleven days since we last had sex. Christmas and New Year have kept us occupied. I have already had to jog his memory about arranging this seduction. We are getting behind.

'It just takes a bit of thinking through,' he said at the time. Now I can see why.

'About my next seduction,' he says. 'You might need to know about it in advance.'

'Really?' I say.

'Yes,' he says. 'To get into character.'

A bit of the aforementioned cheese on toast goes down the wrong way. 'Into character?' I splutter, tears in my eyes.

'Yes,' he says, avoiding eye contact. 'I thought we might

try a bit of role play. I've been trying to think of something that isn't too porny.'

'Does that mean you're going to come and mend my washing machine?' I smirk. 'It *is* making a bit of a funny noise.'

'No.' He's dead serious. 'You're a thirty-something woman. You're a bit spiritual and new-agey. I'm in my early twenties, and a virgin. I'm desperate for sex. Oh, and I'm a bit of a foot fetishist. We're going to meet in a café, which will be the dining room. I've tried to think of names that don't relate to anyone we know. You're called Dorothy and I'm called Lars.'

'Right,' I say, suddenly thankful that I can use the cheese on toast to disguise my rising hilarity. I cram the whole lot into my mouth at once, which stops me from asking the following questions:

How come you get the age-lift and not me?
Foot fetishist?
Will there be cake?
Am I expected to get into costume? Because I'm clean out of tasselled skirts and bangles.
Foot fetishist?!
What on earth made you choose the least sexy character imaginable for me?
FOOT FETISHIST?!

Once I have chewed and swallowed, I decide that the least crushing of these questions to voice is 'Will there be cake?'

'Cake? Oh. No. I didn't think of that. Tomorrow evening then?'

As he begins to unload the dishwasher, another

question snakes its way into my consciousness. Hang on, are we actually re-enacting Herbert's first shag? I have met the woman who inducted H into the wonderful world of penetration. She is prone to wearing tie-dye.

Come Sunday evening, I'm feeling a bit reluctant. I have absolutely no interest in divesting twenty-year-old boys of their virginity. And both of us are irritated by thirty-something women with a 'spiritual' bent. Or so I thought. I also keep having to ask Herbert to remind me of her name. Ah yes – Dorothy. That's right. Without the sexy ruby slippers.

H, though, is keen. He calls upstairs to ask if I'll be ready in an hour. 'Yes,' I say, and carry on typing. I hate acting – hated it at school, hate it now. I couldn't even bear French role play.

But there's no getting out of it. If I chicken out of just one seduction, especially so early on, it would break the spell and make us both tentative in our subsequent plans. 'Are you ready?' I yell down the stairs. 'Give me five minutes.'

I gaze into my wardrobe, looking for the right garb for a lady with esoteric interests. I am pleased to say that I don't have much to offer on that front. I find a denim smock (that usually looks rather chic) and team it with some long beads (ditto, in a better context) and my thermal Angora leggings. Before putting it on, though, I go into the bathroom and wash my feet. I have no idea what H might have in mind when he says 'foot fetishist'. I'm not taking any chances.

Downstairs, H has cleared the dining table and put a bar of chocolate on it. 'What sort of tea would you like?' he asks.

'Oh, herbal,' I say, not sure if we're in character yet. He

comes back with two teas and looks nervous. Is this Lars or him?

'Hi,' I say, 'I'm Dorothy.'

'Lars,' he almost whispers. What follows is a pretty stilted conversation. I am the sort of person who sees excessive shyness as a sort of indulgence, and so Lars would almost certainly irritate me in real life. But then, so would Dorothy. In my hands, she's rather maternal (which is what Lars seems to draw out of me) and bangs on about yoga and Druidism far too much.

I have often had cause to moan about H barely responding when I ask him anything; in character as Lars, he takes this to an absurd degree. I struggle to extract whole sentences from him, and feel like I'm dragging the conversation along all by myself. How on earth would these two people end up getting it on, I wonder? In real life, they just wouldn't. Lars is not a sexy man. I turn the conversation to tantric sex, a subject that I know nothing about.

This, thankfully, allows Lars to confess his virginity and his desire to lose it. 'Would you like a more experienced woman to show you the way?' I say.

Lars thinks that's a good idea. I invite him back to my 'flat' upstairs, leading him there by the hand.

Before we started, I had wondered what Lars would be like in bed – would he be rampant in his desperation or shy and drippy? Neither, so it turns out – slightly worshipful instead. He wants to look at Dorothy naked, and to tell her she's beautiful. I don't mind this at all, even when he takes hold of one of my feet, strokes it, and says it's lovely. Whatever you say, Lars. I personally think feet are the best evidence we have against Intelligent Design.

The only other foot-related incident comes when Lars

asks if I'll jack him off with my feet.'How did you envisage I might manage that?' I ask, trying to stay all Dorothy and spiritual. Lars reckons sideways. I try this for a few agonising seconds, but, frankly, I don't quite have the stomach muscles for it. Lars gets bored with this quicker than I do anyway.

Later, when we talk it through, H admits that the foot fetish thing was just because he wanted to make Lars a bit more interesting.

'It doesn't reflect any deep desires of yours then?' I ask him.

He looks mortified. 'No. God, no.'

Thank heavens for that. We agree that the sex between Dorothy and Lars was fine, although no better than Betty and Herbert might manage on the average night, and probably a bit less hot. I'm afraid that soppy Lars wasn't really my type; I prefer a bit more devilment in my squeezes. I suspect H found him a bit boring too. Either way, H is adamant that his scenario in no way represented him losing his virginity. He's a bit embarrassed when I point out the similarities. I let the subject drop.

What surprises me is how easy it was to get into character and stay there – I didn't feel as silly as I thought I would. It reminds me of acting out games when I was a child, when you would become totally absorbed in the character you were pretending to be. I think the trick to role play is to do it wholeheartedly – any little wink or nudge will drag self-consciousness into the equation. The other trick is to pick a scenario that arouses at least one of you.

'On reflection,' I say, 'I think I would have preferred it if you were the washing machine repairman after all.'

'Yes,' says H, 'you might be right there. I was trying to

avoid something too kitsch, but perhaps kitsch is what's needed.' He thinks for a while. 'How's your Essex house-wife accent?'

The happy day arrives: my colposcopy. Every girl's dream, right? As the leaflet they gave me after the procedure helpfully states, in most cases, colposcopies return perfectly normal results.

By the time the appointment comes round, I've got off my mental jag of 'What happens if it's cancer?' That question's by the by. I know what happens if it's cancer, in all its lurid permutations. My question is this: what happens if they don't find anything? The outcome I can face least of all is being told to take myself home and put up with the bleeding.

The nurse who collects me from the waiting room is smiling bravely. 'It's cold, isn't it?' I say, by way of conversation. She gives me a sympathetic look. 'Some of us do get cold when we're nervous, yes,' she says.

'No,' I say, 'it actually is cold. The thermometer in my car said it was two degrees on the way here.'

'Mmm,' she says. She sits me down next to a machine with a sticker saying, 'May not be Y2K compliant', and goes off to fetch me a gown. She watches me put it on. 'Don't forget to take your knicks off,' she says.

'Yes,' I say, 'I'd worked that one out.'

'It's easy to forget when you're nervous,' she says.

Do I look terrified or something? I'm pretty sure I don't. No one enjoys a visit to the gynaecologist, but I am in fact quite pleased to finally be here. I am a grown-up and my doctor is a professional. I see no reason to enter into this charade of acute embarrassment for the sake of appearances.

This, anyway, is my second colposcopy – I had my first one about ten years ago, when my coil went missing – and so I know what to expect. The first time around, I was a bit more frightened at the prospect, but I was so delighted

49

when they let me see what was happening on screen that I ended up rather enjoying it. 'I watched a documentary last week,' I said to the gynaecologist, 'that showed how your cervix sucks up sperm when you orgasm.'

A stony silence from the consultant. 'He doesn't like to be reminded that it's connected with sex,' whispered the nurse next to me.

The current gynaecologist, I'm sure, is much more sensible, but the nurse is nearly driving me out of my wits. She squeezes my arm, crumples her brow and says, 'Ohhh,' whenever the poor man gets near me. 'You're being very brave,' she says. No, I'm not. It doesn't hurt, and I'm simply treating it in exactly the same way as I would an examination of my toes.

Then I start to feel a vague tugging sensation somewhere in my vagina. 'Are you trying to get my coil out?' I ask.

'No,' says the gynaecologist, 'they've given me a blunt tool for the biopsy.'

He continues to tug. 'If you've established it's blunt,' I say, 'perhaps it's better not to use it.'

'Look,' he says to the nurse, pulling again. 'Nothing. It should just snip off. Have you got another one?'

There is a minor kerfuffle while the two nurses in the room look for a new instrument, all the time protesting that the previous one is perfectly fine. They hand him a second one, something like a long pair of tongs with a crimped end. The first pair emerges covered in blood. I hear a loud 'snip'. 'There,' he says, 'this is what they're supposed to do!'

The nurse has returned to my side. 'You're being so brave,' she says again.

'What else can I do?' I start to tell her my (in my opinion, hilarious) story about my last smear, during which, every time I opened my legs, an ice-cream van outside played its tune.

Amidst it all, the gynaecologist looks up and says, 'Is your family complete, Mrs Herbert?'

I am, for a few beats, a bit thrown-off by his curiously 1940s phrasing. 'I haven't had any,' I stammer, thinking, *Can't you tell that from there?* Then, realising that isn't enough, 'I'm not sure. We haven't decided. Not at the moment. Maybe later. We were trying. But then all this started. Now I've gone off the idea a bit.'

Too much information. He's given up making eye contact. The nurse has intensified her look of pity.

Seduction #6
Early-Morning Wake-Up Call

For most of this week, I formulate a rather cunning plan. On Tuesday morning, I will set the alarm an hour early, and will surprise Herbert with a pre-work seduction. I have read somewhere – heaven knows where – that men love to be woken up with a blow job. I'm game for that, I reckon. So long as I can remember that this is what I'm supposed to do when the alarm goes off. There's a high risk of going on to autopilot and staggering straight out of bed and into the shower.

On Monday night, I realise that this isn't going to work out. I already have lingering doubts about how well tempered Herbert will be when he finds out that it's 6 a.m. rather than 7, but my main concerns are purely circumstantial. Firstly, H showered after the gym on

Sunday evening, and so didn't bother showering again the following morning. By Monday night, he had clearly decided that he could stretch this by one more day. Did I fancy putting two-day-old penis in my mouth? Frankly, I did not. Furthermore, I cooked for dinner a pasta sauce so garlicky that I spent the evening assailed by uncontrollable and frankly startling burps. I suspected that this would lead to unpleasantness the following morning. In order to avoid the experience being grim for all concerned, I put this particular idea on ice for another day.

I decide, on balance, that it's also best to tip him off that we'll have sex the next morning.

'Oh,' he says, 'okay.'

'It sounds like a bad idea to you, doesn't it?'

'No. It sounds, um, fun.'

Herbert hates mornings. No, scrub that. He's not conscious enough in the mornings to hate them. He is pretty much a non-human being in the mornings, albeit one exuding 'fuck off and die' vibes. I couldn't exactly call myself a morning person either, but compared to Herbert I'm Julie Andrews at 7 a.m. Let's not even think about 6.

However, in my chirpy little head, I had faith that the benefits would make this all worthwhile. In actual fact, I had got rather philosophically entangled, because I decided that the main benefit would be heading off for work knowing you already had a shag under your belt.

Had I stopped to put this another way to myself, I would have realised my folly. I was expecting us both to endure a crack-of-dawn, non-spontaneous shag in order to feel smug later in the day. You can see the flaw in my reasoning – I hadn't thought about enjoying the sex; I had thought about enjoying the idea of the sex after it had happened. Convolution is not erotic (see Seduction #5).

When the alarm goes off on Wednesday morning, I come across yet another problem. I had, to be honest, not slept particularly well that night (due to repeatedly waking up thinking, *Oh God, I've got to find the enthusiasm for sex in a couple of hours*), and this means that I start the morning feeling distinctly queasy. It is immediately obvious that a blow job is out of the question. It would make me gag.

'I'll need a wee first,' says H, getting out of bed.

'Me too, actually,' I say when he returns.

I stumble back into the dark bedroom, wondering if H has gone back to sleep, and take off my pyjamas. 'Would you like a Smint?' I ask, pleased with my cunning consideration to put a pack by the bed last night.

We both eat one and snuggle up together. I have to say that this bit is rather nice, but in a 'Mmm, I could just drift back off to sleep now' kind of a way. The initiative is mine to take, I realise, and so start stroking H's body. He leans down and sucks on one of my nipples, which feels surprisingly sensitive at this time in the morning. The trick to this, I decide, will be to get it over and done with quickly, so that we can feel pleased with ourselves all the sooner. I reach down and take hold of H's penis.

However, he doesn't reciprocate. *Damn*, I think, *I'm going to need a bit more help than this.* I'm not nearly aroused. I draw closer to H and rub his penis against my clitoris, but it all feels too dry and squeaky. 'Hang on,' I say, 'I'm going to get some lube.'

H seems to dislike lube on principle. I wouldn't go so far as to say that he sees it as an affront to his sexual prowess, but he would certainly regard it as an absolute last resort. Me, I'm more pragmatic, knowing that I'm just not all that juicy at certain parts of my cycle. Also, I had bought some mint-flavoured stuff from Boots, which I thought might be a bit jollier.

I squirt some on to my fingers and rub it around a bit, and then get back into bed, climbing straight on top of H. Maybe I took too long in the bathroom (the plastic safety wrapper was a devil to get off in the dark), but he seems distinctly sleepier than when I'd left him. I slide him into me, and began to grind against him, to very little reaction. Curiously, the mint in the lube seems to be taking effect. I have the sensation of what I can only describe as a cold sort of burning. I wonder if Herbert notices. I lean down to kiss him, thinking that the Smints really aren't all that effective at disguising his morning breath – and therefore mine too. After leaping about for a few minutes with increasing vigour, I am moved to ask, 'Are you still awake?'

'Yes' comes the reply, after a suspicious pause. By now the lube is making it pretty much impossible to feel anything. Perhaps I can encourage H to come quickly, so I can go and wash it off? I suggest to H that he goes on top. He sleepily agrees. After a few minutes of this, though, I find myself fatally distracted by an internal debate about the point of lube like this. What does it mean? To what am I supposed to compare this odd sensation – am I supposed to feel tighter? Or am I being too literal?

'Herbert,' I say. 'I don't think I'll be able to come. This lube is making me feel completely numb.'

'Oh,' he says. 'Me too.'

'Right. What do we do then? Give up and make a cup of tea?'

He thinks for a while. 'I suppose so.'

'Early-morning sex was a disaster then,' I say later, over poached eggs on toast.

'Maybe we should just leave it a bit later next time. Ten o'clock instead of six.'

'Hmmm,' I say. 'Or maybe we should just never go near that lube again.'

'That too,' he says.

February

It is Friday night, and I am scrunched up on the sofa in my dressing gown. A cervical biopsy and sex in one week was probably a bit too much for me. My belly hurts.

The phone rings, an old friend from university calling to say she's pregnant. I have to confess that such conversations are ten a penny for me lately; I am at an age when all my friends are beginning to reproduce. Nevertheless, I'm delighted for her. She's been trying for quite a while, I think. We chat happily about it all for an hour, and I hang up with the vague intention to knit something. Then I text all our mutual friends to say, *Ooh, did you hear? E's pregnant!* I am met with SMS silence. Odd, I think. Perhaps I have gossiped before she's had a chance to tell everyone.

One of the mutual friends calls me the next day. 'Thank God she's finally told you,' she says. 'It was getting embarrassing.'

I'm confused. 'What?'

'She's been texting everyone saying, "How am I going to break it to Betty? She'll be so upset." We all told her to get a grip, of course.'

'Oh,' I say, feeling stupid for being so wholeheartedly pleased for her yesterday.

I don't think I've ever wailed and gnashed my teeth over a friend's pregnancy. There may have been periods of my life when I was desperate for children, but currently that desire seems to have passed. A baby in a friend's arms does not make my arms feel any emptier. I am sincerely delighted for them, and I go out of my way to be a nice auntie. I coo over babies and babysit toddlers. I even take my godchild out to the zoo, albeit sporadically.

Maybe this is my problem; maybe my helpfulness is read as desperation. God knows, I've read it in other women too. Every age has its stereotypes, and one of our most pernicious is, I think, the thirty-something woman desperate for a baby.

Ambivalence isn't allowed, is it? Well, that's the best I can offer. Reproductive ambivalence. I think babies are lovely, but hard work. I think toddlers veer between interesting and boring, often in the span of ten minutes. I think big families are wonderful, but then so are close, free couples. On the question of whether to have children, I can see a good life either way.

The world isn't set up for people like me. I'm expected to either utterly loathe children and to campaign for them to be banned from all public spaces, or to be filled with yearning envy at the sight of them. I feel neither of these things. I respect my friends' parental selves and the way that their priorities change, but I rarely come away from their houses wishing I had their lives (despite what some of them clearly assume).

There is, of course, a niggling part of me that wonders if I'm missing out on something spectacular, but by the same token there's also a niggling part of me that worries that I'd lose what I have with Herbert if a baby came along. There's also a part of me that shrinks away in horror from my friends' choices to breastfeed eternally and to give up their lives in favour of motherhood. 'What's wrong with putting them in day care and getting on with your life?' I often hear myself saying aloud, and yet I know that I'd feel guilty if I did this. Perhaps what I really want to be is a father, not a mother: a figure who's loved but detachable. The thought of a small person clinging to me makes me feel claustrophobic.

It was in this spirit that we were trying for a baby. We thought I might perhaps come off contraception and we'd see what happened. I wish I'd never told my friends now; they assumed there was much more purpose behind it. When the absence of artificial hormones brought about gynaecological Armageddon, it infuriated me that my GP's only suggestion was IVF. Suddenly, I was assumed to be a 'desperate for maternity' stereotype. Ticking clocks were evoked when I suggested that I might just want my problem treated first, thanks very much.

IVF was never supposed to become an obligation. It's a wonderful choice for those who feel that parenthood is their destiny, and I'm certainly not one of those meanies who would ban its provision on the NHS. But I want, also, the right to say it isn't for me. It's a stressful, uncertain gamble, and my choice is to make the best hash of the hand I've been dealt.

How, then, did I become the Bad Fairy of Conception in the eyes of my friends? Because I gave up wanting a baby when I found I couldn't make one easily? Or because they assume that I'm concealing a deep, traumatic yearning somewhere? Perhaps I'm unnerving because I've privileged my health above reproduction. Who knows, but what comes across too clearly is that many people assume a life without children is meaningless. Oh please. I think I'll cope.

If I feel any sadness when a friend tells me she's pregnant, it's because I know I'll lose her to that gorgeous new baby, even if it's only for a few months. It will be a long time before I can march her down to the pub on a Friday night again, or keep her up till 2 a.m. gossiping over empty plates. My sadness is not about the absence of a child; it's the feeling that, one by one, my friends are peeling away. And I must work out a life for myself in the absence of that option.

Seduction #7
Mirror, Mirror

I am getting the hang of this a bit more now. I don't even flinch when Herbert suggests that his seduction will be putting a mirror at the end of the bed while we have sex.

A few months ago, I would have said, 'Oh my GOD, NO! I am ABSOLUTELY not being subjected to watching my HIDEOUS body bounce around. Again, NO!'

I think many women will sympathise. Every time I look at myself naked – I mean, properly look at myself, not just a passing glance – I experience a minor form of trauma, flashbacks included. I mean, there are bits of me that I feel are passable, but even those aren't suitable for public display. I am definitely one of those people who look better with their clothes on.

Even that sometimes trips me up. Last week, a friend posted some photos of me on Facebook, in what I thought was my lovely new cardigan. Wrong. I had no idea that I had a spare tyre of those dimensions. In actual fact, I was continuing happily along with my life imagining I didn't have a spare tyre at all. Wrong again. I continue to shudder each time I think of it.

I am, on the other hand, not one of those women who make a habit of admitting this in public. I usually prefer to hold my own counsel when it comes to confessing my bodily anxieties. They're boring, and besides, why draw attention to them? This, in all honesty, is a form of mild gender treachery. When friends confide their physical insecurities to me, I stay quiet. Worse, I wordlessly absorb their protestations that I wouldn't understand because I'm so confident. No, I think; I suffer in silence.

Since the seductions started, though, I have noticed something of a truce being called between me and my body. For the first time in a long while, I've realised that I'm desirable in Herbert's eyes, and, although my sense of self-worth shouldn't hinge on his opinion, it's given me a huge boost.

Sex is all about the strut, isn't it? It's about throwing yourself wholeheartedly into that alter-ego that we all possess: the wicked, alive, carefree one. And beauty is nothing but sex disguised. The people we desire are beautiful. Therefore, by pulling off that sexual strut better than I have in a long time, I can feel a lot more beautiful.

That didn't stop me from taking out my contact lenses before we started. But watching our blurry movements in the mirror reminded me how much men like seeing what's happening during sex. Personally, I mostly have my eyes closed, in a world of my own, but H likes to see, literally, the ins and outs. He has pretty much seen me from every angle, so what do I think I'm hiding when I avoid this?

Do I think he doesn't know what my vulva looks like by now? It's hard for my dysmorphic brain to compute this, but watching the action-end actually improves sex for him, whether or not I can accept my body.

It also reminded me of something else. I was nineteen, and H moved me in front of the mirror while we were having sex in my room at university. I remember watching my own face arranging itself, moving between embarrassment, confusion and recognition, seeing H's olive skin against my white. 'There,' he said, 'see how beautiful you are when you're turned on?'

Despite myself, I agreed with him.

It is customary to suggest that, every now and then, life comes and bites you on the arse.

To me, this seems an unreasonable stance: I do not model 'life' as an active agent with malevolent intent. Life is a passive force that simply sits there, getting in your way, while you try to get on with things. I would rather use a different metaphor: every now and then, you bump your head against the barrier between your intentions and reality.

For this image to really work, you have to imagine (as I do) yourself sitting in the garden on a hot summer's day. *I know*, you think, *I'll go in and get a glass of water*. This is perfectly reasonable; it is not even greedy. Water is a morally and ethically neutral thing to want on a hot day. It is essential. So, you get up, stroll towards the house and then – BUMP – you bang your head against the patio door. You assumed it was open, you see, but some wag has closed it. You stand there, dazed, for a moment – perhaps you have cricked your neck, or raised a bump on your forehead; perhaps your nose is bleeding – and you think, *Damn my bastard, stinking bad luck. I don't deserve this.*

This is an extended preamble to the sticky subject of today's attempted seduction. I use the term 'sticky' literally here, but I will come to that later. Either way, I'm sure you will understand its application soon enough.

It didn't have a particularly auspicious start. Earlier in the week, Herbert called me mid-morning to say that he had crashed his car on the way to work and could I please pick him up from the hospital. This turned out to be nothing more dangerous than a bit of whiplash, but it meant that he hasn't been keen on sex all week. He finally agreed to a seduction on Friday night (my turn) and so I thought maybe I'd suggest something a bit naughty this time.

So, when he gets home on Friday night, I tell him, 'I thought I'd set us a challenge for tonight's seduction. We're going to head into town for a night out, and over the course of the evening, we have to find somewhere to have sex. In public.'

'Right,' says H, unsmiling. 'When you say "in public", how public do you mean?'

'Oh,' I say, 'not very. In the loos or something. Maybe a dark doorway. Not in the middle of the dance floor or anything.'

'I'm trying to think of where that might be,' he says, and starts to list all the bars we go to, dissecting the discreet shag possibilities in each one.

'No,' I say, 'the point is that we take an opportunity when it arises. This isn't an exercise in forward planning.'

'Right, yes, sorry. I think I'm too much of a problem-solver for this.'

'We don't have to do it if you're too tired. You've had a rough week.'

'Yes, I have. I'm thinking that maybe we could do it in the car?'

'Will that be very good for your back?'

'No.'

I give in. He clearly isn't very keen on this. On reflection, it probably is a bit ambitious for a man with whiplash.

'Let's just have sex in bed for now,' he says.

At least I won't have shaved my bikini line for nothing. I launch gamely into bed, wondering when it would be most advantageous to mention that he's the first one of us to chicken out of a seduction. I rather liked my idea; I once read an apocryphal story about Debbie Harry and Chris Stein being caught shagging in the toilets of CBGB, years into their relationship. This, therefore, is a seduction idea with provenance. I'm not willing to let it go that easily.

I light a couple of candles as H gets undressed – this is at least one gesture towards a seductive environment. Things proceed rather well. H is being fairly energetic, perhaps to make up for his lack of bottle at the prospect of my seduction, and I am feeling like a bad mama for suggesting something that he baulked at. *In your face, Herbert*, I am thinking, in a nice way. *I'm no longer the weakest link in our sex life! Oh no!*

I climb on top of him to attempt the Reverse Cowgirl, a relatively recent addition to our repertoire, and one that we both enjoy. After a short while, I become aware of a slurping, sucking noise. *Wow*, I think proudly. *What a juicy woman I am these days!*

'Sorry about the noise,' I say to H, and he doesn't seem to mind. I can feel that I'm near to orgasm, so I turn around to face him for the last few moments. We both come at the same time, and I bury my face into his neck.

'Blimey,' I say, 'I'm so wet tonight.' I put my hand down to feel the extent of it, and find something sticky, warm, thick. It is dark in the candlelight. 'Oh God,' I say, and H turns on the light.

There is blood everywhere. 'Jesus,' I say, and rush into the bathroom so that I can stand in the shower, trying not to cry. 'Not to worry,' I can hear H calling from the bedroom, 'it'll all wash out. I'll just strip the bed.'

I'm speechless with horror. I stand in the shower, wondering what on earth H must think of me. Then, I call him into the shower after me. He's unfazed, it seems. 'At least I won't have to shower tomorrow morning now,' he says merrily, while I watch the rusty water run down the plug-hole.

I am quiet over dinner that evening. There are moments that I'm afraid tears will come out unbidden. It is only after three glasses of wine and a cherry tiramisu that I feel steeled to lean over to H and whisper, 'We are NEVER doing the Reverse Cowgirl again, do you hear me?'

He laughs so hard that I have to ask whether he's crying.

Seduction #8
Tread Softly

After the unpleasant ending to our previous attempt at sex, there is a slight hiatus for a week. In fact, we don't mention it at all, and happily revert to our familiar, celibate lives. But then, for the first time, I realise the value of the seductions. We can't just forget about sex for months on end. We have to get back on the metaphorical horse.

Herbert is better at this than me. He doesn't get into a debate about it. He just pops his head around my study door one afternoon and announces that this week's seduction will be 'stair sex'.

'Stair sex?' I ask. 'As in the stairs that take you to another floor, or staring at one another?'

'The kind that take you to another floor,' he says, as if this is the most normal thing in the world. I wouldn't put it past him to go for stare sex. He is uncommonly proud that my mother once described him as having 'shifty eyes'.

'Okay,' I say. 'Can we go to the pub first?'

'After.'

'Right.'

I think I am being very tolerant here. It is, after all, Valentine's Day, and he has clearly just plucked this idea out of thin air.

'Isn't stair sex a location rather than a seduction?' I ask.

'It's a shape,' he says, 'a structure.'

'With a coir-matting runner.'

'You can keep your clothes on.'

'I might have to.'

We live in a 1930s semi, and our stairs are very narrow. It seems to me that, if I were to have sex on them, it would be because I was in a fit of passion that couldn't even wait until it got to the bedroom. To actually intend to have sex on the stairs seems to me to be wrong-headed. However, I have already conned a completely unintended Valentine's present out of H this morning (I hinted for it in front of a friend known for his tight-fistedness, thereby forcing H to cough up to prove he's the better man), so I feel duty-bound not to make too much fuss.

I gamely go upstairs and put on some long socks to protect my knees against chafing. I leave my knickers off. H is waiting for me in the hall, and he seems quite keen on the lack of knickers. I find the stairs quite fun at first too. There's a certain levity in trying to get the position right. True, due to the narrowness of the tread, we struggle to find an angle at which he can actually enter me, but eventually we manage it, doggy-style.

I have to confess, though, my good humour runs out after a while. Or not so much my good humour, but my expectation of enjoying this myself. H, you see, has free, thrusting rein, given that he's standing up with a nice banister to hold on to; I, on the other hand, can still feel the coir prickling through my socks, and I have my face pressed up against the next stair tread up. Frankly, I'd need to be a bit more drunk to enjoy this.

We turn around, this time with one of my legs over the banister and the other on H's shoulder, but the steps are so narrow that I am forced to take all my weight on my elbows so that I can tilt my pelvis upwards. We climb up the stairs a bit so that we can return to doggy, but this time with me draped over the top step on my stomach. This is a bit better, but still damned uncomfortable, and it is now accompanied by an uninterrupted view of the fluff under the bed. At this point, Bob the cat decides that she must absolutely get to the top of the stairs, even though we're in the way, so she starts trying to force herself through the banister rails behind us – and fails to be perturbed when it is clear she is too fat.

'How near are you?' says H.

'Nowhere. Go right ahead.'

It is always startling to see how a man can reach orgasm without the least bit of comfort or concentration; a few slightly-more-deliberate-than-before thrusts, and H is a happy man.

I scrabble up from my prone position on the landing, and Bob leaps over me to take her desired place on the bed. I can't help but wish I could join her.

'That was a bit rubbish, wasn't it?' says H. I want to say, 'Seemed fine for you,' but I am sensing my advantage here.

'Meh. Let's just say you owe me an orgasm.'

'It's about time we had a seduction that worked.'

'Yes,' I say. 'That might involve some forethought on your part.'

After that, we head for the pub. I've mentioned before that H is generally not keen on going to the pub alone with me – his argument is that the booze is cheaper at home, and there's a telly. I probably compound this disinclination by saving up all my Really Important Conversations for the rare moments when I have his full attention.

Tonight, though, it's different for some reason. H sips on a beer while we chat about all sorts of things. It's nice. A group of women come in, all clutching heart-shaped balloons and flowers; they have clearly decided to be their own Valentines. I, for one, am glad all that doubting and posturing is over. The first rush of passion is all very well, but it's good to be able to have failed stair sex without wondering if it is somehow pathological for your relationship.

We go home really quite tipsy, and order all the starters on the Chinese takeaway menu, as is our Valentine's tradition – mainly because we pretend we don't do Valentine's Day every year, and then succumb to it when it's too late to book a restaurant table.

This is the bit that seduces me – playing records, eating terrible food, and afterwards, curling up in bed to go to sleep.

I'm worried about Herbert. He's been quiet and irritable since his car crash. He can be taciturn at the best of times, but at the moment he's positively frosty. When he said everything was fine after the accident, I should not have taken him at his word.

On the morning it happened, he rang me from a hospital an hour away. He'd been forced to brake suddenly when turning on to a roundabout, and the driver behind him hadn't been able to stop in time. I rushed straight over to pick him up.

By the time I arrived, he was just leaving the examination room. He seemed surprised that I was there at all, like he'd forgotten he'd asked me to pick him up. We chatted for a few moments in the car park, and I tried to make him at least have a cup of coffee and a debrief, but all he wanted to do was to get to work in his battered car. I could only turn around and drive straight home again.

Life is like that with H; he would rather put his head down and ignore his worries than make a fuss. But he got home that night nervous, achy and exhausted. I tried to rub his back, and it was a mass of solid muscle. He asked me to stop; it was too painful.

His insurance company has referred him to a physiotherapist, but that doesn't seem enough somehow. His sense of adult solidity has been damaged. Whenever he tells his friends about the accident, he almost trips over himself to be fair to the driver who hit him. It wasn't his fault; H could imagine doing the same thing himself. I wonder if this doesn't make it worse: by not allowing himself to blame, Herbert just feels more exposed to the chaotic nature of driving. His stomach still flips whenever he approaches that roundabout, he admits.

While Herbert slowly absorbs the impact of his crash,

I'm awaiting my test results for cervical cancer. How am I supposed to think of my body in this dead zone? Is it a fragile thing that needs carefully protecting, or something that I should push myself to celebrate? Should I be putting everything on hold, just in case? Even though I know better, it's hard to shake the idea of contagion, the image of my body as something that's dangerous to touch, for both of us. I am tentative around myself, holding off exercise and watching out for symptoms I should be worried about.

Yet through all this, strangely, we keep up with the seductions. They are beginning to feel like a defence against our own vulnerability.

Seduction #9
A Night at the Movies

My mother has a special sound that she reserves for sex scenes on the TV. I'm not exactly sure how it would be spelt, but it is roughly the sound that a builder makes when you ask him to do, well, anything at all, or the noise you make to show you sympathise when someone else has cut their finger: a sharp sucking in of breath through pursed lips. *Fthhhh*. As in, 'Fthhhh, that'll cost yer,' or 'Fthhhh, I bet that hurt.'

I have often heard it said that her generation think they invented sex. My mother begs to differ: she thinks that she, personally, invented it, and is unwilling to share the credit with others. Her sexual conquests were legion, apparently. She is fond of pointing out that she and my father had sex every night of their marriage, even when the divorce was going through. There are some things in life you'd rather not know.

During my teenage years, she was ever-keen to ensure

that I encountered none of the sexual prudery of her upbringing. There was nothing she wouldn't talk about. Inevitably, I was horrified by this. My mother always wanted me to be the most sexually liberated girl in town. I can only speculate – though I avoid all conversation on the matter, obviously – that she's disappointed that I ended up playing the buttoned-up Saffy to her Edina.

Picture the scene: my thirteen-year-old self is sitting on the sofa watching TV, my mother in the adjoining chair. The people on the screen start kissing. There are definitely tongues involved. I experience a horrified blood-rush, and hope that she'll politely leave the room or turn it off, like other parents do. No. Mum starts fthhhh-ing. This is intended as a clear signal: 'Look, darling, something vaguely arousing is happening on TV.'

I am, of course, more than aware of this. As is customary in 80s television, the woman on the screen is taking off her clip-on earrings and heading for the bedroom. I wonder if I can get away with leaving the room. My mother is now hissing like a kettle. Fthhhh: she's unbuttoned his shirt! Fthhhh: he's unzipped her dress! Fthhhh: she's running her fingers through his copious chest hair!

At this point, the fthhhhs would get shorter, perhaps punctuated by a few oohs and even a little commentary. 'Ooh, ooh, hairy chest, fthhhh!' I can only be thankful that 80s TV would rarely linger further than this scene. The couple would fall into bed, and my mother would utter a final, tremulous fthhhh before heading off to make a cup of coffee.

I've often wondered whether she realised that she was doing this out loud, or whether she thought that she was educating me in the correct female response. If the latter was true, she needn't have bothered. My teenage hormones were doing the job quite effectively for me, thank you.

In any case, this has had a terrible long-term effect on my ability to watch anything vaguely sexy on TV. It's not that I don't feel a response to these things; it's more that I'm terrified that it will leak out of me somehow, as it did with my mother. I think I can safely trust myself not to fthhhh, but can I trust myself not to lick my lips or breathe a little more uneasily? I'm not sure.

There has only ever been one film that provoked an erotic response in Herbert and me, and that was for all the wrong reasons. After an hour of watching *Stealing Beauty*, we were so sick of its crass plotting and lingering old-man gaze that we opted to shag on the living-room floor instead. Apart from that, we don't have a long track record of sharing erotica. We went to see *Lust, Caution* together in high expectation, but both felt that its billing as a pulse-quickener was more than a little inappropriate. Is it boring of me to like my sex consensual? And – plot spoiler – not to end with one partner ordering the execution of another?

All the same, a seduction based on film seemed an obvious choice. Well, watching porn together is a more obvious choice, but the very thought of it makes me nervous. I've never really watched any, but in my mind's eye it's all exploitative and nasty. So, mainstream film it is. And after years of deliberately avoiding being turned on by film, I am utterly stumped for ideas.

Step forward the wonderful denizens of Twitter. A plaintive call for 'films that get you going without being porn' is met with an extraordinary flurry of suggestions, which range from the salty (*The Cook, The Thief, His Wife and Her Lover*) to the romantic (*The Piano*) to the slightly bizarre (*Mulholland Drive*).

The vast majority of suggestions come from women,

and their choices point to a sexuality of scenario. A lingering glance is as important here as watching people actually having sex. We seem to like the suggestion, the set-up. In many cases, we would prefer the camera to stop there, so that we can enjoy imagining the consummation for ourselves.

Repeated attempts are made to encourage men to suggest films too, but they are extremely reluctant to join in. I wonder if this is because they know that their choices will be the wrong answer as far as women are concerned? We are told over and over again that men are more visually stimulated than women and that they like to see the action-end. Perhaps, then, movies are a bit too polite for them. And perhaps, also, they know we will disapprove if they say so.

I bear this in mind when I order our DVDs; I want to ensure they've got enough fantasy to please me, and enough shagging to please Herbert. The films I choose are *9½ Weeks*, *Belle de Jour*, *Shortbus* and *Secretary*.

We decide to watch them on a Sunday afternoon. The set-up alone is an undertaking: we go for the full cinema experience, wiring up my digital projector and screen in the front room with the curtains drawn and cushions scattered over the floor. With the log burner going, this makes for quite a nice little den. I have enormous fun doing *Tales of the Unexpected*-style dances with my shadow projected on the screen. Perhaps I don't even need the films.

A friend calls just before the start of the first movie, asking if she can come round for tea. 'Erm, sorry,' I hear Herbert say, 'we're going out this afternoon.' I hope she doesn't ask him where; he's an incompetent liar and I know he'll cave. He comes back into the room with a bottle of wine. 'I feel so guilty,' he says.

We're bad at making time for ourselves like this. It's interesting just to remark on that alone: no wonder we haven't made time for sex, if we feel obliged to accept every request that comes up. Normally, we drop everything for the most casual of invitations. We are also compulsive inviters – if we're planning something fun, we ask all our friends along. We don't save enough moments for ourselves.

We watch 9½ Weeks first. H takes the armchair and I sit on the cushions, leaning against his legs. He reaches down and strokes the back of my neck. I feel rather giddy about all this: the curtains drawn against a grey afternoon, putting aside several hours to become aroused. In all honesty, I don't think we've ever done something like this before – both watching a film with the shared intention of becoming turned on.

I'm a bit worried about 9½ Weeks. H is allergic to the 80s, and I watched it once a long time ago, but didn't finish it. I have a feeling that I found it a bit creepy.

Oh. Right. It is creepy. From the moment I clock Basinger's downcast gaze and Rourke's weird, frozen-cheeked smile, my stomach starts to fizz. Not in a good way. In a 'there is absolutely no way I would even start a conversation with that man, let alone a relationship' way. He is utterly, utterly sinister, even before he starts to work Basinger like a puppet. I feel as though I am watching the Hannibal Lecter of sex. With my husband. On a Sunday afternoon. For sexual thrills.

It just doesn't work for me. I don't relate to Basinger at all. I would have walked out of that relationship when he started feeding me wine from my own glass. I just can't see why she's compelled by him. I wonder what H is thinking. I wonder, also, if it would be okay to pick up my knitting. This succession of games gets boring after a while. I have lost all sympathy for both characters. The actual sex is surprisingly polite. Most of the time we are treated to a flash of Basinger's stocking tops, and then the camera averts its gaze.

By the end of the film, I'm feeling considerably less likely to have sex than when it started.

'What did you think?' I ask Herbert.

'Awful,' he says. 'I don't want to watch someone being so horrible to a woman.'

I am relieved. We both agree we've lost all carnal feelings. We go to the kitchen and regroup, putting dinner in the oven and making coffee. It's a necessary break. Not for the first time, I wonder if being a middle-class liberal is fundamentally disruptive to sexual desire. We just disapprove of it too much; it's all too politically entangled. Sex must be a lot easier if you maintain the old 'man on top' ideology.

Thank heavens for *Secretary*. It's not hot so much as reassuring. The tale of a broken young girl who finds power via a boss who spanks her (really), it is an absolute tonic. It is un-PC, funny, wise and wonderful. If we're honest, it's only really a little bit sexy, but it's about sex between two consenting, thinking adults. The funny thing is, the subject matter of both films is the same: the man who likes to control, the woman who toys with the extent of her submission. The difference is, *Secretary* isn't interested in identifying victims.

At Herbert's suggestion, we watch *Secretary* in our underwear, which is chilly but worthwhile. H loves skin contact, and it is nice to be stroked and kissed. We are having sex before the film even finishes. As the credits roll, I get him to stand up in front of the projector's beam.

I thought he'd find it erotic to watch me take him in my mouth in silhouette on the big screen. I think, however, that the blow job may have been enough in itself.

Afterwards, I bend over the table so that H can watch his shadow go in and out of me. He has better ideas. He runs his hands over my bottom and thighs for a few moments, then there's a pause. Two stinging slaps follow, my left buttock cheek and then my right. I collapse in giggles. 'I didn't think this was going to be a re-enactment!'

He enters me and slaps again. I can't say it gives me the raging horn, but it's not unpleasant. It's appreciative, playful. The fourth slap makes me say, 'Ow!'

'Oh God, sorry,' giggles H. 'That was a bit hard, wasn't it? Did it hurt? My hand stings.'

He strokes my bottom for a while, but he's not deterred. The spanking starts again after a minute or so. I want to know what he's thinking when he does it.

'You quite enjoy smacking my bottom, don't you?' I ask.

'No,' he says, sounding flustered, 'I thought you liked it.'

Inwardly, I sigh. That liberal fear getting in the way again. *If I like smacking a woman's bottom, what am I?* If we are to get anywhere with this, one of us has to concede some ground at some point. It doesn't stop him though. He carries on smacking right until the end.

Later, apropos of nothing, he says, 'Perhaps we'll have to try smacking *my* bottom some time.'

The gynaecologist is looking at his notes when I come into his office. 'Mrs Herbert,' he says warmly, 'you'll be pleased to know that the biopsy didn't find any cancerous or pre-cancerous cells.'

I want to tell him that I'd guessed that from the fact that he forgot to share those results with either myself or my GP, and that he also forgot to book me a new appointment. I had, as his secretary said with some embarrassment, 'just dropped off his list somehow'.

'We did find some inflammation, though,' he continues, 'which may be due to repeated infection.'

Lovely. I try not to remember that this is a part of my body intimately associated with sex.

I have, apparently, a particularly wide 'transformation zone', which is the gynaecological equivalent of being told you have a fat arse and chin hair. The transformation zone is the area of your cervix where the fragile cells that line your uterus meet with the hardier ones that sit outside it. Because these cells change over time, this is the most vulnerable place for cervical cancer to develop. Mine, for some reason, is particularly wide, meaning that I have these fragile cells all over the outside of my cervix. They bleed easily, and then can't stop. My cervix is, essentially, an open wound.

'Of course,' says the gynaecologist, 'repeated collisions will make these especially likely to bleed.'

Repeated collisions? Oh, he means *sex*. I am rather amused that he can model sex as 'repeated collisions'. I resolve to use the term in the future. Presumably, my disastrous encounter with the Reverse Cowgirl counts as a pile-up.

My next step, apparently, is the cauterisation of my cervix, plus a camera inserted into my uterus to see how far the nasty cells extend. The joys don't stop there. The other symptoms (migraine, nausea, pain), it seems, are actually what my normal periods feel like when I'm not using hormonal contraception.

'It is within the range of experiences,' he says, 'and is not pathological. But it sounds pretty bad. What I don't understand is that the coil you are using should have put a stop to all that. It's rare, but it might be a faulty one. I'll change it over when I do the other things, just to make sure. You should keep taking the mini-Pill in the meantime.'

'What if we decide to have children?'

'We will cross the bridge when we come to it. You'd better get pregnant pretty quick is all I can say!'

He chuckles to himself. It must seem so simple to him.

Herbert is pleased with the outcome. He would never have dreamed of telling me this, but I think he's been very worried about what the test results might have revealed. His reaction is more than mere relief, though.

'What he's basically saying is that I've got a monster cock,' he tells me in the car on the way home. He repeats the phrase a couple more times to amuse himself, but then decides he prefers 'medically large'.

I suspect it was all he could do to stop himself from posting it on Facebook.

March

I thought, perhaps, it would be a seduction in itself to spend a night in Brighton. It's a saucy city, slightly frisky somehow, and I am dressed the part in my lovely new red wedge-heels and white stockings. One day, I will learn that such things have no effect on Herbert – they just leave me with aching feet at the end of the day. I have never attracted so many approving glances at the motorway services, though.

H is a shopping fiend, and so we head for the North Laine as soon as we can. I have a vague recollection of a lady-friendly sex shop being there, but I fail to find it today. Instead, we make the mistake of going into a new sex-and-complete-tat store nearby. The place is piled high with silly knick-knacks, which is fine if you like that sort of thing. What is not fine is being harassed nearly out of existence by their staff. As soon as we're through the door, we are approached by a pale, clammy-looking girl in her late teens, who asks if we need any help. 'No, thank you,' I say, which apparently is the universal signal for 'Please follow us around the store and point out the function of objects we've shown no interest in.' I am filled with a desperate urge to leave. Everything I look at is nasty; they are clearly trying to corner the market in wink-wink gifts to be doled out at hen nights and in secret Santas.

I am disappointed that H wants to continue on upstairs, but I follow him anyway. I suppose he thinks that it might get better once we get past the 'let's all have an embarrassed snigger' front-end of the store. He is wrong.

Upstairs, they are playing a DVD of the most rubbish type of porn (an 80s housewife with bruised thighs and a frilly garter bouncing up and down on top of what I assume to be the milkman), and this sits alongside a wall of nasty PVC underwear. A new sales assistant assails us on this floor, offering us two-for-one on all films. I assume she is talking about the price.

We scuttle out as quickly as we can. There is something about encounters such as this that make you feel as though you've failed. Do I lack a sense of fun? Am I a prude? I don't think so, but then I am also entirely resistant to talking about my choice of sex toy with a teenager who looks like she might have downed too many snakebites the night before. Does it not occur to these people that shopping for sexual props with one's partner might be part of the flirtation?

Anyway, after dinner and a few drinks, we retire back to our hotel room, clutching Coconut Mojitos from the basement bar. We have brought with us *Shortbus*, one of the films recommended for Seduction #9, and we snuggle up to watch it in the matching kimonos supplied by the hotel.

Rather pleasingly, the beginning of *Shortbus* makes Herbert gasp. 'That's about the most sexually explicit thing I've seen outside of porn,' he giggles. The extended opening sequence lingeringly portrays a man trying to film himself sucking his own cock, interspersed with shots of a woman and man going at it like the proverbial knives. The third narrative strand, a dominatrix laying out her large collection of dildos and then whipping a rather irritating man, seems positively ho-hum in comparison.

I thoroughly enjoy *Shortbus* – it is thoughtful and funny and admirably unwilling to ever turn the camera away.

However, I begin to feel anxious towards the end. I don't want it to finish. Inevitably, we will have sex afterwards, and I can't quite bear the thought of it.

I try to snap myself out of it. I'm not getting involved in this kind of thinking any more, am I? I have promised myself to be up for anything. But I'm tired. Herbert begins to stroke my knee. It feels so weird that I have to ask him not to. 'You're stroking the bit where the scar is,' I say. 'It feels wrong.' I am leaning back against his chest, resting between his legs. He starts to stroke my right breast, and that strangely hurts too. I actually flinch. 'Sorry,' I say, 'I don't know what's wrong with me tonight.'

'If you're tired, we don't have to. It's not an obligation.'

'No, no, it's a shame to have this nice room and to let it go to waste.'

I go into the bathroom and check the protesting breast. I have had abscesses there before, and they start this way, with the sudden, inexplicable pain. But tonight, nothing. I return to Herbert. 'How about we 69?' he says.

That should be fine. I find 69-ing boring, but at least it's unchallenging. Yet I can't enjoy it now. I'm totally distracted. I feel his hands stroke me, and I am dreading the moment he puts his fingers inside me. 'Don't,' I say, and then I burst into tears.

I cry for the best part of an hour – big, gasping sobs. Perhaps I've had a bit too much to drink, I don't know, but sometimes you're not even aware of what you're worrying about the most. Tonight, it is the fear of what is going on inside me: my dreadful cervix that bleeds and aches. I did a small amount of exercise the day after seeing the gynaecologist, and it hurt all week after that. I have barely even noticed it hurting, less still that I was worrying about it. Yet suddenly, my whole body is able to rise up in revolt to protect itself. I'm terrified of making it worse, especially on these lovely white sheets.

Herbert comes into his own at moments like this. He holds on to me, kisses me, and doesn't ask too many questions. He knows what's the matter without me telling him. He fetches tissues, lip balm and glasses of water, and he soothes me to sleep.

Sunday morning, and the rain runs down the gutters of Brighton in little rivers. I feel better this morning, like I've got something out of my system, but I'm tired. Crying always makes me tired.

I once went to see a counsellor for six weeks. At the end, she said, 'I think you're the only client I've ever had who didn't cry.' It felt like an accusation. Crying, to me, is too often a manipulative act, aimed at making someone else feel guilty. I usually do all my crying when H isn't there. I don't want to make him cope with it.

Today, though, I'm glad I've cried. It feels good to be allowed to be quiet and a little sad for a change. We are delivered breakfast in bed at nine, a stack of blueberry pancakes, maple syrup and bacon. We eat them watching *Friends*, saying how it's always so much funnier than we remember. H is cuddly and attentive. We take our time getting dressed, and then wander into town.

I buy us both a latte in a café that's a bit too perfectly styled. 'We need to learn how to have non-penetrative sex,' I say, and Herbert agrees. This has never been a consideration before. I know this isn't true for a lot of women, but I love to feel H inside me; no amount of clitoral contact can make up for that sensation. The orgasms I have through my clitoris alone feel shallow and fluttery compared to the deep, warm ones that emanate from penetration. I often get impatient with foreplay for that reason. I don't want to waste any time on my way to the real deal.

If we're going to continue to have sex without me worrying, though, I know that's got to change. It's not that we have to do it that way all the time; it's just that we need to have it in our repertoire. I need to be able to ask for it that way.

We head onwards to lunch in a lovely bar where we once got drunk on vodka shots, many years ago. I've warmed up by now, chattering about everything. It's all flooding out. I've been a bit depressed, I tell him. Days keep passing in which I get nothing done. I keep watching the computer screen waiting for emails to arrive. I can't shift myself into action. I worry about everything. I need a new job. I need to gain more control.

H joins in for a while, and then, suddenly, his eye contact slides away and I know I've lost his attention. I'm in the middle of telling him how I've been scanning the job pages every day, but nothing is coming up. 'I'm sure it will sort itself out,' he says, and diverts every ounce of his focus to eating his roast pork.

We fall silent. I am furious. *That was the limit of your sympathy, was it?* I think. *Just let me know when I'm getting boring.* We've rowed about this before, this ability to simply withdraw from a conversation when it gets too difficult. I stare at him for a while, but this has no effect on a man who is refusing to look at you. Eventually, I say, 'You sure know how to close down a conversation, don't you?'

He gives me one of his terrified glances, as if I'm about to throw my wine over him in public. He will do anything to avoid a scene. I take a breath and try to put it more gently. 'I find it really hard to cope when you just withdraw from a conversation like that. I need your moral support sometimes. It's not okay for you to just get bored with it.'

'Oh God,' he says, 'not here.'

'I'm not starting an argument. I just feel so stressed at the moment. I feel like I hold all the uncertainty in our relationship. It seems like I'm the one who's responsible for all the changes that have to happen. I need to talk it through sometimes.'

I don't really know what happens next, but some sort of strange shift happens, and I realise that H is fighting back tears. I must have seen him cry about ten times in our whole time together; he is not a particularly tearful man.

'Are you okay?' I say.

His voice is croaky. 'I . . . I'm just a bit down at the moment.'

I clutch at his hand across the table. 'I've been wondering,' I say. 'Everything freaks you out lately.'

'Yes.'

'Do you know what's causing it?' He shakes his head and lists stress at work, the car crash, a range of other little issues. 'But I know I don't have the right,' he says, welling up again, 'when I think about what you've been going through. I can't bear it.'

We talk for a long time after that. It's rare that I get him to really share his feelings, not in any depth. With both of us in the doldrums, we have been forgetting to take care of each other enough, I think. The world is making H feel vulnerable at the moment. His car crash, though minor, came out of nowhere and made him feel fragile. He's been arguing with colleagues at work. His wife's body is conspiring against her. His desire is feeble, and he doesn't understand why.

'Are the seductions making it worse?' I ask.

'No,' he says. 'They put me under pressure, but without

them, I think we'd have given up again. I just find it hard to feel the pull of sex like I used to. I feel like I'm faking it. Even when it's good, it's not how it used to be.'

It should be a blow, but it's great to hear him admitting that. For years, I've carried the can for our wizened sex life, but now I realise that my shrivelled desire has been masking his. He's not been brave enough to own up to it, but he's lost a big part of his sexual self too.

Since starting these seductions, I've flourished more than he has. I've changed a lot, and I don't think he's moved on yet. He's always been comfortable in the role of the long-suffering husband, deprived of his full quota by his disinterested wife, happy to settle for masturbating in the shower (which he managed to block through this very act a couple of years ago, incidentally) rather than indulging in the sulks and coercion that other men resort to. But now, with me pushing for more frequent, imaginative and passionate sex, with my new rule of saying yes to anything he asks (within reason), with my new habit of giving out blow jobs, he's floundering. He's run out of excuses. He finally has to step up to meet my sexual self. It's a 180-degree turn that he wasn't expecting.

What is funny about this is that it led to one of our most passionate seductions yet that evening. But what fascinates me more is this question: if two people agree that they don't feel much desire for each other any more, why would they make a pact to pursue that desire rather than let it die?

I don't ask that negatively or rhetorically, but in a kind of wonder. There is a yearning for each other, for a part of each other that we both still know is there, even if we can't quite find it at the moment. I find that extraordinary and miraculous.

Seduction #10
DIY

You would think, wouldn't you, that after spending the weekend in various states of tearfulness, we'd have gone on to have a thoroughly rubbish seduction. Or, indeed, that we would skip the seduction altogether in favour of a gentler pursuit – a game of cards, say, or the welcome oblivion of the TV. Oh no. We are not so easily fazed in this household. We march on.

After the lunchtime dramas, we are walking back to the car. We had planned to visit another sex shop on the way back, one I'd heard was a bit more female-friendly, but I suggest to Herbert that he might not be up for this now. He looks appalled.

'Oh no. I'd be disappointed if we didn't go. I was thinking we could get one of those remote-control vibrators, like in *Shortbus*. And I quite fancy a sex board game.'

This from a man who's worried about losing his desire. I suspect the remote-control vibrator doesn't exist in real life, but I'm delighted that he's willing to plough on, if that's not too much of a loaded phrase. 'I'd be quite interested in one of those posh vibrators,' I say. 'You know, the ones that are small and lovely to look at, that you can use in lots of different ways.'

H almost pauses in the street. 'I'd love to be able to watch you masturbate,' he says. 'You've never really let me look.'

This is only half true – I spontaneously masturbated for H when we were first together and he was offended. He thought I was doing it because he wasn't satisfying me enough. I never tried again. I am, however, too nice to point this out right now. The muscle that turns my other cheek is admittedly underused, but I manage to locate it. 'Okay, sure.'

I work from home, so the 'freelancer's lie-down' is no stranger to me. It passes the time, and keeps me from lurking on Twitter too much. It is quite the best remedy for a headache I know; it makes migraines positively erotic. I worked out how to do it when I was about five, and have continued pretty much enthusiastically ever since. In fact, when I first started having sex, I thought I couldn't orgasm for quite a while, until I realised it was the same thing I'd been doing for years. *Oh*, I thought. *That's what 'orgasm' means.*

All by myself, I developed a very specific technique, which I stick to more or less faithfully. I might sometimes make time for a more involved session, but mainly I lie on my stomach to masturbate. I was pleased to see Maggie Gyllenhaal do this in *Secretary* too. I orgasm quicker that way, and the sensations are more intense – perhaps something about the weight of my hips on my hands? Either way, masturbation, for me, largely involves touching my vulva and the top of my clitoris. I never stray into my vagina unless in need of a little moisture, because there's no point. I can reach perfectly satisfying orgasms this way, usually fully clothed.

That makes it sound really boring and mechanical, and in a way it is. The physical act of masturbation, for me, isn't the thing; it's the opportunity to fantasise that comes with it – to indulge in the very private world of my erotic imagination for a while.

Back in the present, my particular technique is problematic for putting on a show for H. I wonder if I should let him watch me masturbate in my usual way, or go for something a little more revealing. On reflection, this is a no-brainer. My way is still pretty much private and would be over very quickly; I need to go for a bit more display.

We are still tackling our list of videos from Seduction #9, so we put on *Belle de Jour* when we get home. The acting is awful, which I suggest to H might be reassuring in terms of it featuring plenty of sex. After a slow start, Belle joins a brothel in order to liberate herself from her 'frigidity' towards her husband. It's a long time since I heard the word 'frigid' used seriously. It's all pretty unenlightened stuff – it turns out that Belle just needs to be treated a bit rough to understand her own submissive desires. It's hard not to conclude that it was written by a man.

However, I do find Belle's conflict between wanting sex and fearing it quite erotic, and the uncertainty of what each new client might bring could work for me. H, I quickly realise, is bored. There's just not enough sex in it for his liking. I need to ratchet up the interest a little.

'That's like the underwear I bought last week,' I say to him, pointing at one of the on-screen prostitutes elegantly draping herself around the room. 'Shall I go and put it on?

'Okay,' he shrugs, with his usual disinterest.

This new undergarment, though, is likely to have an effect. For starters, it is deliciously retro, which is H's preferred aesthetic. Secondly, it is crotchless. It is a sort of minidress-cum-1950s-girdle, with underwired cups and suspenders, in bubblegum pink with black frills. Silly enough to be fun, but quite sexy in a burlesque way too. I run upstairs to squeeze my way into it, and attach some nice red-seamed stockings from Topshop. I saunter down-stairs.

'What do you think?'

He looks up, smirks. 'Nice.'

I lie against the opposite end of the sofa to him, and open my legs. He shifts round to give me his full atten-tion. It's quite hard to get started, actually. I feel like I've forgotten how to do it. I'm self-conscious, but only because I'm suddenly aware that I'm giving a lesson here. I need to lead by example, but it doesn't quite feel right. Irritat-ingly, Herbert's attention is drifting between me and the TV.

I make a decision. I need to actually masturbate, rather than do it for Herbert's entertainment. This is all about me. I take off my glasses and close my eyes. I let my legs straighten and my stomach muscles tense. I lick my lips, breathe a little heavier. When I next open my eyes, H has forgotten about what's happening on the telly. He's watching me intently, his face drawn close to me. I ignore him again, fall back into my own little world. It's trickier doing this lying on my back, but I'm getting there slowly. It takes a little more concentration than usual. H begins to stroke my thighs and then to kiss them, and this fills me with desire, the sight of him holding back from touching me when he's clearly desperate to. Eventually, I can bear it no more, and I push his face down towards me, an offer he gratefully accepts.

I have one of the best orgasms I've had in ages – a real screamer – and I immediately get up and return the favour, letting him come in my mouth, which, believe me, is a rare favour even in the new world order. He is bigger and harder than I've seen him in a long time.

Even after this, I still have unspent desire. I pull him on top of me so that I can rub his penis between my legs until it's erect again, and then we have the penetrative sex that I couldn't bear the thought of yesterday, but which I'm now desperate for. He whispers in my ear, 'Carry on touching yourself,' so I sit on top of him so that he can get a better view. I have another surging orgasm before he's even gathered his thoughts.

'Good,' he says. 'My turn. I'll masturbate while you lick my nipples.'

As ever, I'm happy to oblige.

I have a difficult history with blow jobs. I used to hate them, and avoided them at all costs. I would estimate that, for our first decade together, I probably gave Herbert less than one a year.

What can I say in my defence? I'm not sure. Perhaps that I just never got into the habit. I wouldn't have admitted it at the time, but when I first met Herbert, I had never given a blow job. I knew I ought to, but felt utterly incompetent. I wanted to seem like such a grown-up to him (at eighteen, we are prone to thinking we can pull off this act) that I couldn't admit that I didn't know how to do it. He was too polite to ask at first, but later on he did, and for some reason I thought it appropriate to make a meal of my response and tell him that I found them politically unacceptable.

Maybe I even thought that was true at the time – who knows? I was a bit of a firebrand at that age, and was studying a paper at university that contained an awful lot of feminist theory. I fear that I fell under the influence of Andrea Dworkin rather than Germaine Greer. I was a bit worried that male sexuality might be oppressing me, perhaps in a way that I hadn't noticed. Frankly, I thought it best not to go down on my knees before any man.

The years went on, and it became quite a joke. H mentioned to a friend one night that he was hoping for a Christmas blow job, and it became something of a catch-phrase within our circle of acquaintances. Several people still ask me, every year, whether H has had his Christmas blow job. I grin and bear it.

Herbert, bless him, has never withheld the equivalent favour. He can spend hours down there, licking and suck-ing away. Sometimes I have to ask him to stop because I'm getting bored. Other times, he coaxes me into spec-tacular, juddering orgasms.

And, Lord, has he tried hard to encourage me. He's never whined or wheedled (or, like a friend of ours, offered new shoes in return). He has occasionally positioned himself so that his penis hovers near my face, hopeful that I'll latch on like some reluctant infant. No dice. Years ago, after I'd blamed my avoidance on my advanced sense of smell (my nose is as sensitive as a cat's), he started to wash his penis in the sink every time he peed. He still does it to this day – years of quiet optimism which has, finally, paid off.

I came to the realisation many years ago that I actually had no objection to giving blow jobs at all. My friends all seemed to be giving them quite merrily, and I didn't want to be left behind. By then, though, I felt that I couldn't just backflip like that. I couldn't just say, 'Okay, I've had a change of heart.' As much as anything, I still felt utterly incompetent. I was afraid of getting it wrong, of being a bit disappointing. Still the same misplaced pride. I just couldn't let go.

What changed? I'm not sure. I think at first I might have just been a bit more co-operative when he waved it in the vicinity of my face. We fell into the habit of 69-ing for a while, although I was still reluctant to go solo. I blush to confess that it was only on the day that we conceived of the seductions that I really got into the swing of it.

We were sharing a Jacuzzi in our upgraded Honeymoon Suite, which we were offered for an extra £30 because the hotel was having a quiet week. H was lying in the water, and I was crouching by his head on the little corner seat. The room was dark, lit only from under the door. It made our skin glow. At this point, we hadn't had sex since the Great Vagina Row, as I affectionately like to call it.

H has always been more courageous than me. He began to stroke me, just gently at first, but then more and more insistently. I had been withholding for so long that I didn't know how to get started again. I let the hot water and darkness carry me along. He raised himself up to sit on the side, and I knelt in the water and took his penis in my mouth. I suspect he was quite surprised, but I loved the way he tasted of clean water. With the effect of the Jacuzzi jets, I came before he did. I felt like I had given him something: a signal that I cared about his pleasure.

In the weeks that followed, I did a bit of research, but I also practised (on him, of course). It was lovely to hear him being so appreciative – I'm sure he was deliberately instructing me on how to do it, and I was grateful for the moral support.

I've learned a few tricks – varying my strokes, but not changing them too frequently. Like me, he likes to feel the intensity build. He loves it when I run my tongue hard down his whole length, and when I gently tickle his head with the tip of my tongue. But the one that always makes him moan is when I let his head rest on the roof of my mouth as I suck, whilst making my tongue protrude slightly over my bottom lip. I imagine it must feel very luxurious. It makes me dribble a bit, but I don't think that matters.

The point is – and I haven't told him this yet – that I've started to really enjoy giving blow jobs. It makes me feel sort of whizzy. I love how pleased it makes him – although we are now suffering from what I term 'blow job inflation'. The least little droop in his erection and he says, 'I think I might need a blow job.'

Yesterday, when I was walking down the street, I was suddenly overwhelmed by a sensory memory of the smell and taste of him – that salty, soapy smell that hangs around his pubic hair. It was quite, quite startling. *I have finally learned to love his body*, I thought, *after all these years*.

Seduction #11
The Silent Treatment

I am on my way upstairs to bed when Herbert catches me on the stairs. I have just returned from the pub, where I have spent an evening being led astray (in terms of alcohol consumption) by my lovely friend P.

'You said you were going to tell me what the seduction is for tomorrow,' says H. 'You told me to remind you.'

'Oh,' I say, and pause to straighten my face. 'We're not allowed to talk to each other tomorrow. Night-night.'

'Can I text you?'

'No.'

'Email?'

'NO!'

'What if it's an emergency?'

'For fuck's sake! If it's an emergency, then you can talk to me. There's unlikely to be an emergency. I need to go to sleep.'

If I had been a little more sober, I would have probably

thought to explain my reasoning. I've chosen a day of silence because I want to make us both think a bit harder about communication. Silence comes easily to Herbert; it doesn't take much for him to fall into his thoughts. Many's the time I've received no reply to a question I've asked, only to find that he's answered it in his head and is surprised he didn't say anything out loud. I often get embarrassed when we're in restaurants, because he sees no reason to keep the conversation afloat.

On the other hand, I acknowledge that my desire to fill the space between us with words often drives him mad. I needle into his every thought and action, often pointlessly. I am a communicator. I want to talk my way through life. That night, I even wake myself up talking in my sleep. I am also drunkenly sitting up in bed and stroking H's face, but that's another matter entirely. Luckily he sleeps through it.

So, a day without words, because both of us need to think about communicating without talking. H is up before me the next morning, and I lie there for a while, wondering whether I'm hungover. It appears, mainly, that I am not, although a couple of aspirin have a steadying influence. H brings me a cup of tea in bed and kisses me on the head instead of his usual 'Time to get up'. This, I think, is a highly positive innovation in my morning routine.

I shower, dress, and go downstairs. H is just cleaning up after breakfast. I am unnerved to hear him talking to the cat, but, with only mime at my disposal, I realise that I am unable to snap at him about following the spirit of the rules and not the letter. He strokes my arm and kisses me as he passes on the way to the door. Then, as an afterthought, he returns to blow a raspberry on my stomach. I reflect that a vow of silence each morning could save all manner of foul-tempered exchanges.

After he's gone, I realise that I feel very strange about this start to the day. I am due at a meeting in an hour's time, and I am struggling to shake the impression that I'm not allowed to speak at all, to anyone. I also feel as though we've had a row. It's all a bit confusing somehow, and I keep having to remind myself what's happening. I exercise my vocal cords by chatting to Bob the cat while I make my breakfast.

I realise that I am relieved by the idea of a day without emails pinging between H and I to process a range of household chores. My satnav breaks, and I can't tell him. This is strangely comforting – it's less of a big deal somehow. Similarly, I order the shopping without telling him about it. There's no need. I feel as though I have just removed a load of chores from my day.

H clearly struggles with this concept a bit more than I do. At midday, he emails to ask me for a serial number from the cooker hood. I am not sure why this counts as urgent – the bulb blew a month ago. *Ignoring you,* I email back, and then kick myself for replying at all.

It feels good, too, not to be able to moan at him for his email when he gets in that evening. Being silent means that it's hard to be negative. We are limited to positive questions and friendly gestures ('Shall we cook or get a takeaway?' is asked by waving a saucepan and a curry-house menu and assuming a quizzical expression). It's hard to get on each other's nerves in silence. H makes much more eye contact than usual, and we spend ten minutes snogging on the sofa before he collects the inevitable takeaway, leaving me dizzy with desire.

Somehow, though, it's hard to sustain. H puts some records on, and we cuddle up on the sofa listening to them, both of us humming along. I'm beginning to feel lethargic, so I root around the cupboards and find Jenga. H smiles, but before we start to play, he leaves the room and comes back rolling a joint.

This irritates me: I have had a cough all week, and the last thing I want him to do is fill the room with smoke. More than that, I've noticed that he's beginning to use weed like Viagra. We've both commented that he's much more amorous when he's a bit stoned, and a few times I've remarked that I rather like him that way, unable to put me down. However, I'm less keen on the idea of him using it to conjure up desire for me. That just feels insulting, particularly in the midst of a seduction.

I have to let it pass. I wait until he's lost the first round, and then indicate that this is strip Jenga. He takes off a sock. This is a bad move on my part – I'm rubbish at Jenga. I end up sitting naked on the sofa, while he's fully clothed. Meanwhile, that joint he's smoked seems to have removed all the wonderful non-verbal communication that was going on between us. He's fixated on the game, while I am cold and meaninglessly naked.

I wonder if I can't resurrect this. I stalk to the bedroom, and whistle from the top step for him to join me. I had envisaged the silent evening leading to long, slow love-making, letting our whole bodies communicate with each other. H, though, seems to be on autopilot. He steams into the same old routine that we've been doing for ages, first of all trying to position me into an uncomfortable 69, and then repeatedly prodding my clitoris painfully with his tongue until I am forced to cover it up with both my hands, my more subtle messages having failed. I draw him back up towards me, and begin to stroke his body all over, trying to convey the message that I want to slow down, to be a bit more intimate. 'This is supposed to be about communication!' I want to shout, but I can't. I wonder if he understands the point of this seduction at all. I feel guilty that I'm angry with him without having explained it properly.

And then, suddenly, he grasps his neck and grimaces. I look at him for a while, trying to judge what's going on, and then I say, 'You okay?'

'Neck hurts,' he says.

'Your whiplash?'

'Think so.'

'Lie down and let's go to sleep then,' I say, relieved.

The next morning, when he's in the bath, I crouch down next to him and explain how I was disappointed last night. 'I don't want you to get into the habit of smoking a joint every time we have sex,' I say. 'It's not the answer.'

I am surprised by the way that he takes it all in. A few months ago, I think we would both have thrown ourselves into histrionics over a conversation like this. Now, we can talk about it calmly and cleanly. 'Okay,' he says, 'I didn't realise. Maybe we can start the silence again tomorrow night, and do it clear-headed this time?'

And that's that. It is that simple. We do not argue or get upset. We just talk about it. Clearly the sex still isn't perfect; clearly our broken desire isn't quite mended. But there has been a change in the air, and I think it comes from this: Herbert no longer doubts that I want to have sex with him. There is no way he can, after all the effort I've put in. He no longer suspects that I'm trying to worm my way out of sex, trying to cast around for excuses.

And for my part, I'm relieved too, because I wasn't even sure why I was making those excuses.

'**Y**our turn to think up a seduction. I mean, I'm not nagging. Just mentioning it. We need to keep up! Or keep IT up! Ha ha.'

Damn. My attempt at a light tone completely failed there. I hate to have to nag, but sometimes I feel forced into it. When it's Herbert's turn to run a seduction, I've noticed that there's always a very long wait.

Herbert sighs. 'It's just such hard work. I can't think of anything new.'

'It's hard for me too. But I do some research. Otherwise I'd never have any ideas.'

'That's easier for you than for me. You work from home. I can't read that stuff in the office.'

This is slightly disingenuous; even if H wasn't in an office, he still wouldn't be doing the research. It's just not his style. I refrain from mentioning that he sleeps at least two hours less than me each night, leaving him with some nice, quiet time after I go to bed. Sometimes I am the very model of restraint.

'So what are you saying? Do you want to give up?'

'No, not give up,' he says. 'But can't we just agree on the seductions rather than taking it in turns? It's too much pressure.'

I am not keen on this. One of the things I have loved about the seductions so far is the sense that H is putting some forethought into our romantic life, rather than passively waiting for erotic moments to happen. It's been good to feel like I'm in his thoughts when I'm out of sight.

'I don't know, Herbert. That feels to me like you're saying, "I want you to arrange all the seductions."'

'That's not fair! I've put loads of effort in so far!'

'Yes, and now you've run out of oomph. We've only done a few, and you're bored already.'

'I'm not bored. I just want to make sure I'm pitching it right.'

'And I want to be seduced for once in my life, rather than constantly doing all the hard work!'

'You will be seduced, just not every bloody time! Sometimes we might want to work things out together! And sometimes we might have two ideas in a row and don't want to wait our turn!'

'Well, fine then!' This is said, if I am honest, in a slightly stroppy tone. 'As long as you're going to still make an effort, I don't care!'

'Fine!'

'Fine!'

I have a feeling I lost that one.

Seduction #12
Witchery

Sunday morning, and I am ambling about the bedroom in my bra and knickers, trying to decide what to wear. This can take anything upwards of half an hour on a weekend, and I confess that I have fallen into something of a trance.

I am gazing stupidly into my T-shirt drawer when Herbert storms into the bedroom, pushes me backwards on to the bed, removes my knickers and enters me, just like that.

Goodness, I think, *this never happens.* 'I'm just suddenly so turned on,' he whispers into my ear. Bloody hell. So am I, now.

Half an hour later, when we are both getting dressed, he says, 'By the way, I reckon that counts as my seduction. Not my only seduction today, by the way. But it definitely counts.'

And who am I to argue? I can't resist such enthusiasm. However, I have one objection.

'Actually,' I say, 'I seduced you.'

'Oh yeah? How?'

'I snuck some oil into your bath. It always drives you crazy.'

He thinks for a moment. 'Really?' he says. 'Have you done that before?'

'Yup.'

'How often?'

'A few times.'

'That's practically witchcraft,' he says. 'We'll call it a joint effort then.'

Seduction #13
A Little Shopping

Herbert has rather gamely offered to buy me some new lingerie. When I say 'offered', I really mean 'responded to an ultimatum', because I have just realised that all the expenses incurred through these seductions so far (DVDs, underwear, books, a remote-control vibrator that is so loud that we will have to wait for a riot to kick off before we can use it) have come from my pocket.

'You have a choice,' I say. 'You can pay me half of every-thing I've bought so far, or you can buy me something nice and I'll call it quits.'

I'm pleased to say he opts for the latter, because I have something in mind. I strayed into Ann Summers on Friday while I was supposed to be buying birthday cards, and surprised myself by falling for a rather nice underwear set with a boned half-cup bra and a deep, retro suspender belt, all in delicate pink lace with leopard trim.

I locate this on their website, and sit him down in front of it. 'Nice, isn't it?' I say. He agrees, and so I discreetly withdraw, hoping to give him some privacy in which to play with his credit card. When I return, I am disappointed to see that Herbert has used his initiative and is gazing adoringly at a fishnet body-stocking. 'How about this?' he says.

I attempt levity. 'You'd have to take the whole thing off to do anything,' I say weakly. 'Pointless.'

'Nope,' he says. 'Crotchless.'

I should have known better than to expect to get something I actually want out of this. There's no point in making him pay for underwear he doesn't find remotely erotic, though. 'Maybe we should visit the actual shop,' I say.

You will have already gathered that I'm not a fan of Ann Summers. I'm an aesthetic snob, and the whole place reeks of hen party. I lead H over to the stand where my preferred underwear hangs, and he says, 'Oh yes, that's nice,' and then charges off enthusiastically to look at the nurse outfits.

'If I'm going to dress up as a nurse,' I say, 'I want a proper dress. Not some kitsch imitation.' Fortunately, he agrees, but does seem unfathomably drawn to the Beer Wench costume instead. Then he's distracted by the pink furry handcuffs, which he insists I try on, in the shop. Once again, I bring my sense of taste to bear on the matter. 'I'll consent to a plain pair,' I say, 'but I couldn't get the horn in fun fur.'

H picks up an alternative set. 'Ooh,' he says, 'these come with a blindfold too. Excellent.' He tucks it under his arm, along with the body-stocking (which I was hoping he'd forgotten about), and, inexplicably, a cat costume. I wonder if I should lock up Bob when I get home.

I try to interest myself in the penis picnic set (with realistic veins – ugh!), and I have become really quite engrossed when I hear him yell – across the whole shop – 'Is it 36C?'

He is waving my lingerie set in the air. Bless him.

When we get home, he carries his goodies up to the bedroom and says, 'Right, which one are you going to wear first?'

I'm feeling good-natured, so I take the infernal body-stocking into the bathroom and put it on. I'm surprised to find that it looks quite good. In the same way that fishnet stockings can add wonderful contours to your legs, this thing makes me look like I was born to wear a catsuit. It is actually, I reason, quite a female-friendly garment, skimming over all manner of unsightly lumps and bumps, and making nudity a bit more, well, covered-up. Warmer than naked too. I am surprised to admit this even now, but I admire myself in the mirror, and then stalk into the bedroom.

H has decided to contribute to proceedings by poking his erection out of the front of his pants. 'Look,' he says, 'mine are crotchless too.'

Well, sex is rather marvellous in the body-stocking. My boobs keep popping out, but I'm guessing that's the point. Every now and then I try to anchor it over my nipples, but to no avail. Clearly, the visual element is great for H. He asks me to get on all fours, and I slide myself on and off his penis while he stays still, which we've discovered is a much more pleasurable way of working doggy-style for both of us. I can tell he's really enjoying watching, and I suddenly remember a purchase I made last week, just for this eventuality.

'Hang on,' I say, and run off downstairs, returning with

a wooden hand mirror I bought at a boot fair. 'Belle de Jour says she always carries one in her handbag.' H has fun angling the mirror to get a better view, watching himself move in and out of me.

All this excitement means, unfortunately, that his concentration slips and he comes just when I'm nearing the home straight, but this doesn't bother me too much. As discussed in Seduction #10, I'm more than capable of rectifying that myself, and I'd trade an orgasm for a man who loses control at the sight of me any day.

Now that we are a quarter of the way through the seductions, I'm suddenly puzzled at how we got started in the first place.

I feel as though I have climbed a hill and am now gazing back at my starting point. It seems impossibly far away. From here, it's already easy to see why the seductions are necessary, and why sex is important to us. But how did I know, back then, that this would be the case? What made us turn to sex again when it had clearly been such a contentious presence in our lives?

Maybe it was nostalgia for what we once had, the memory of being irresistible to each other. I have never forgotten the days when sex was compulsive, electric, addictive. It is hard to concede that I'll never feel that again, the sensation of your whole body animating itself in the expectation of one touch. By starting the seductions again, I was quietly hoping that I'd drag this physical mania out of the attic and dust it down for another go.

That hasn't happened yet, and I'm not sure I even believe it will. From all I've read, that feeling is the result of a very distinct cocktail of chemicals whirring through your bloodstream, and won't be repeated. In any case, that giddiness always trades on uncertainty. You spend your hours apart wondering if your partner still loves you back, and then, when you find that this is true, you celebrate, bodily, together. I don't think I could face that see-saw of churning anxiety and unbridled relief again.

But I think that I was pulled back to sex by more than this anyway. What I wanted most of all was intimacy. We already had a form of intimacy, of course, but a hard-edged sort, the kind that exists between two busy people who know everything about each other and have formed a small, practical team. It is love that has set like a jelly, that is no longer mouldable, mutable; it is love in which all the parameters have been decided. I was bored of this kind of love, with its blunt, arrogant certainties. I wanted something a little softer around the edges.

The idea of the seductions may have felt like it sprang out of nowhere for me, but it is probably no coincidence that I had taken H on a weekend away when they started. I remember secretly thinking that if only I could extract him from the structure of our everyday lives, we had a chance of becoming lovers again. It is so often the case that every ounce of our spare time is booked up a month in advance. I was beginning to feel that we were a double-act rather than a couple. I wanted to make contact again.

Since the seductions started, I've noticed that my instinct was right: even though we have always shared our feelings and talked through our problems, there is something about sex that adds a different quality to our communications. There is a greater sense of ease between us, a greater attunement, and less suspicion that the other partner wants what we cannot give. We are, quite simply, more satisfied.

Seduction #14
The Daily Grind

Day One

Before we start, I should point out that we've tried shagging every day once before. It was, I think, 1998 and we had just moved into our first flat together. By sheer coincidence, we had sex three days in a row, and this led Herbert to joke, 'Same time tomorrow then?' I'm a sucker for a challenge. The fourth day was fun; the fifth merely dutiful. On the sixth day, we both agreed we couldn't be bothered, and crawled into bed feeling slightly ashamed of ourselves.

It is a commonly held myth amongst women that their menfolk would have sex every day given the chance. We women often see ourselves as the gatekeepers of sex, carefully limiting our partners' worst excesses. It took me years to work out that this isn't the case for me and Herbert. He got bored with the daily sex quicker than I did.

However, with my usual blithe optimism, I'm hoping

we've picked up a few more tools of the trade in the last few months, and so I'm willing to try again. If nothing else, I want to prove that we can fit sex into those awkward weekdays when we're both tired and overstretched. Whether H will be very keen on sacrificing the latest episode of *Lost*, or *Survivors*, or whatever other nonsense he follows, remains to be seen.

Starting is easy enough anyway. I suggest sex while he's milling about in the kitchen, and he immediately says yes, glances out the window (to see if anyone's in the garden, maybe? That would be a disturbing first if so), and then undoes my jeans. I bend over the work surface and rub his penis between my thighs for a while, and then we spend an entertaining and giggly half-hour trying out a range of positions, first on the kitchen units and then on the sofa.

Job done, very pleasurably. A good start.

Day Two

We have friends over for Sunday lunch, which means a morning spent cooking and clearing up the house, and then an afternoon spent eating and drinking. By the time they leave, at 7 p.m., we are both bloated, exhausted, and encountering the arse-end of lunchtime drinking.

We flop in front of the TV to watch a film and then I become deeply engrossed in a programme about French pastry chefs. By the time we go up to bed, it's nearly midnight.

I undress while Herbert is in the bathroom, and notice a sore lump just above my clitoris. On closer inspection, I can see that this is a boil. The irony is not lost on me that this happens at the beginning of a week of daily sex. It has, after all, never once happened before. Maybe it's due to general wear and tear. Before I realise what I'm doing, I am attempting to burst it with a sterilised (well, I licked it first) pin. Ouch.

I do not wish to speculate on whether or not this is a good idea (although I will confess to spending ten minutes the next morning trying to work out how to stick a plaster to my vulva), but by the time H makes it into the bedroom, it is my sad duty to inform him that he is not getting within ten yards of my lady garden, not for no one.

We lie contemplatively in bed for a while, ashamed that our intention to have sex every day has ended so soon. But then, suddenly, my competitive spirit kicks in and I sit up. 'Shall I give you a hand job instead?' I say. 'I'm sure that counts as sex.'

H couldn't look more delighted, and I am soon merrily giving myself arm-ache in the name of seduction. He gets a little fed-up of me making light conversation throughout ('To think men pay for this!'), but in all fairness, it does feel a little odd to be masturbating one's husband, fully clothed, with no prospect of a return trip. In many ways, it reminds me of being fifteen again. The old Betty wouldn't have done this; in fact, I would have told him that he was perfectly capable of doing it himself. The new Betty, however, is game for anything. I might say this out loud. Poor H; he is probably trying to concentrate.

I expect he's grateful when he finally comes.

Day Three

We planned to go to see a film tonight; Herbert even took the precaution of emailing me a timetable for the evening so that we could fit it all in (with a mere thirty minutes set aside for shagging). However, last night's late shenanigans have taken their toll, and I find myself yawning through my afternoon meeting. Under normal circumstances, I would not even contemplate sex tonight. The film's definitely off.

Herbert comes home from the gym to find me soaking in a very off-timetable bath. This is, in part, an attempt to remove the plaster that I stuck on yesterday's boil, which remains likely to get in the way of my sexual pleasure tonight. Actually, a throbbing boil just above my clitoris seems unlikely to enhance sexual response in either of us. This all feels like a bit of a bad idea.

I cook dinner and we eat it in front of *The Wire* (we're limping through season four), and then H washes up. It's time to head to the bedroom. I try to stall by becoming engrossed in *Masterchef*, but it is to no avail. H likes a challenge.

In the bedroom, we negotiate around the boil. H thinks that maybe we should stick to doggy-style. I argue that we shouldn't over-think it in advance –'I'll yelp if it hurts,' I say. H hopes that this is not some weird ploy of mine to burst it. I wish I'd thought of that before.

There are a few moments when I think it won't happen, that we'll both decide that it's a stupid idea and will turn on the bedside lamps and read a book. However, H gamely dips between my legs and begins to lap at me with small, delicate strokes. It's divine. There's no way in hell I'd put my mouth near that thing (the boil, I mean, not my fanny), but I am once again grateful for his comparative lack of yuck-reflex. I sink back into the pillows and let him patiently bring me to an orgasm that makes my whole body convulse. After that, I climb on top of him.

Day Four

I wake up this morning and find that I'm bleeding again. Of course. It amazes me that I manage to forget that this will inevitably happen. Also, the boil has burst, which I am somewhat delighted about.

When we head to the bedroom at 10 p.m., we are confronted by an utter indifference to sex. I have eaten too much; Herbert is exhausted. We would both welcome unconsciousness right now.

'Maybe we can toss a coin,' I say, 'and the winner gets to sleep through the whole thing.'

'Unfair,' says H, who is only too aware that I have the luck of the devil.

'Okay, what's the lowest-energy position?'

'Spoons.'

'That's what we'll do then.'

I lay a towel underneath us both, and reverse up to H, imagining that we can begin sex by an act of will. This is optimistic. Poor H is struggling to muster an erection, and I'm not doing much better. How on earth do some people do this every night of their lives?

'We're going to need lube,' I say. As I've mentioned before, H usually sees the use of lube as a personal affront, but tonight he is docile. He potters out to the bathroom and comes back with a tube. I smear some on me and some on him; then, in an uncharacteristic act of imagination, I swivel round from the classic spoons position (which I've never liked much – it feels like an uncomfortable angle to me) to the 'T' shape, in which he's on his side and I am on my back at a right angle to his groin, my legs draped over his hip.

We've never used this position much, and I'm not sure why because it strikes me immediately how lovely it is. It's comfortable and unencumbered; it also rubs up against unusual places somehow. H, I think, is averse to positions like this because they feel a bit distant and impersonal, but it's perfect tonight because we are really both longing for our own personal space.

However, as we jiggle along quite merrily, I begin to feel distinctly sick. It is my own fault. I ate a chocolate pudding that I didn't need, and now it's taking revenge. I wonder if I'll make it to the end.

'Feel free to come if you want to,' I say. 'Don't hold back on my account.'

'Same goes for you,' he chuckles. Yes, ha ha, Herbert. Mock the delicate and effortful balance of the female orgasm at your peril.

He speeds up a bit, and I make a few encouraging noises. It's not unpleasant, actually. The great benefit of daily sex, as far as I can tell, is the feeling of accomplishment that you gain from it. It's a bit like cleaning out the fridge – the knowledge that you've done it is enough.

H comes, slumps on to his back, and says, 'Thank God we're over the hump.' Then, hurriedly, 'I mean, that was very nice . . .'

'It's okay, I know what you mean,' I say, and then retire to the bathroom to decide whether, on balance, it's best to retain the contents of my stomach.

Mental note: conduct tomorrow's seduction before dinner.

Day Five

What strikes me the most about this daily sex malarkey is just how much time it takes up. I'm sad to report that I don't usually spend my evenings lounging around wondering what to do. There is just no obvious sex-shaped gap in my schedule.

Tonight is a good example. We've booked dinner at eight in a restaurant a few towns away, and before then

H has arranged to drop in on a friend. I've been out for a meeting all afternoon, and we both arrive home at six-thirty. That leaves roughly thirty minutes for sex. H declares that he needs a shower beforehand. I wonder aloud if we ought to wait until after dinner in that case.

'No,' he says, 'come and join me in the shower instead.' It's a sweet gesture, given that we both hate shower sex. We are both tall, and therefore don't cope well in confined spaces; I think it's slippery and there-fore borderline dangerous; one of you is always under the warm stream of water, and one of you is always outside it and therefore cold; and, worst of all, it's squeaky. I assume the water washes away your natural lubrication, but for whatever reason, I hate the sensa-tion of sex when both of us are underwater. It's like biting into polystyrene.

I can, however, see that this may be our only chance of a shag, so I gamely undress and hop in with him. Not before I've taken a bottle of baby oil out of the cupboard, though.

I love baby oil – the way it smells and the way it feels on your skin. Does anyone actually use it on babies, or is it solely purchased for sex and cleaning stainless steel cookers?

I press my body against Herbert's and drizzle the oil between us. It instantly feels good to move together, letting it slide against our chests. I lean down and rub some over his penis, and then take him between my thighs. Poor H, he's quite spent after a week of daily seduc-tions. It's pretty hard to bring some life into his cock, and even when we manage to, it's a fairly deflated erection.

Conscious of time, I bend over the shelf at the end of the bath, and we guide him in. H pours more baby oil on to my back, so that it dribbles down between my buttock cheeks, cold and shocking. Then I feel a stinging slap on my bottom, followed by another one.

'Ow,' I say. 'What are you doing that with?'

'I dunno,' says H. 'This thing.'

I turn to see that he's waving my foot rasper at me.

'Ew, don't use that! I use it to take the hard skin off my feet.'

He drops it quickly back into the mug from whence it came.

I confess that I'm surprised we both manage to orgasm, but only once we've moved out of the shower and into bed. After we've both come round a bit, I look at the clock and see that we ought to have left for the restaurant five minutes ago. There is no chance of making it to our friend's house. While we dress, we try to concoct good reasons for not turning up.

Day Six

This may possibly be cheating, but I turned Day Six into Seduction #15. So sue me.

Day Seven

Well, to paraphrase Bill Clinton, I did not have relations with Herbert on Day Seven of our week of having sex. Except the difference is that I actually mean it. We didn't even do anything saucy with a cigar that everyone would construe as a sex act except President Clinton himself.

The reason: a mixture of exhaustion and disinterest. I was bleeding again, which meant that I'd ruled my lady parts a no-go area. H, bless him, was suffering from a protesting penis. Despite this, he offered me a list of imaginative ways to have sex without either of us having working genitals, the best of which was: 'I could try to have a wank while you blow on my balls.'

It is eleven o'clock on a Friday night. I have just eaten quite a lot of pizza and drunk quite a lot of wine. 'No,' I say. 'Bollocks. I'm not doing it.'

Sometimes you have to know when you're beat. Six days in a row ain't bad. A seventh would have felt like prostitution.

Seduction #15
Sundae Girl

Have you ever invented a password so magnificently clever that you want to tell everyone what it is? Not only does Google declare it 'very strong', but it is also somehow witty, fiendishly difficult to guess, and wonderfully easy to remember. The very nature of this sort of password makes you want to share it with everyone, which would defeat the object entirely.

Well, that roughly describes my feelings after drawing a bikini on myself in whipped cream. Accessorised with raspberries. Goddamn, it looked good – so good, in fact, that I nearly reached for my iPhone so that I could post a picture of it on Twitter. But then I realised that I was naked and covered in squirty cream. That split-second urge to share too much is surely one of the major perils of the internet age.

Now, I am what you might call 'ideologically opposed' to squirty cream. It is, in my opinion, the bane of modern eating, a disgusting non-food that actively detracts from whatever it adorns. It jumps out at you from the most astonishing of places – perfectly good coffee shops seemingly can't resist a quick whoosh of it on the side of your home-made cake – and I have been known to interrogate waiters about the meaning of 'cream' on their menu.

This is the reason I have never covered myself in whipped cream for Herbert before. I just couldn't bear for that cream to be UHT and out of a can. I have, in the past few months, wondered extensively whether there is a way around this. A piping bag? Or just a bowl and a spoon? I considered briefly whether it's possible to get hold of those contraptions they use in Starbucks to pipe unwanted whipped cream on to your hot chocolate. But even I could see that this was too elaborate. I may make my own mayonnaise, but I acknowledge that squirty cream has a place in the bedroom.

Herbert, anyhow, actively loves squirty cream, largely because it comes in a handy dispenser that drastically cuts the time it takes to get it into his mouth. Therefore, at lunchtime on Thursday, I find myself in Sainsbury's buying the infernal UHT canister, a packet of raspberries (woefully out of season, but you can't achieve such things with spring greens), a jar of chocolate sauce and a bottle of Cava. And don't think I didn't consider making the chocolate sauce myself either.

That evening, I wait until H has got into his post-gym shower, and then I swiftly arrange myself. I cover the bed, first with the oilcloth that sits on the kitchen table, and then in two duvet covers. Then, I lie back and pipe the cream bikini on myself, garnishing it elegantly with raspberries. I decide to leave the garnishing with chocolate sauce to H, mainly because I will ruin my creation if I move too much. So I lie back and wait. He's taking ages in the shower. The cream feels cold, and it's beginning to slide off in places. I wish I'd poured myself a glass of the Cava to pass the time.

Eventually, he comes into the bedroom, and I say, 'Surprise!' He squints at me for a while. 'I'm covered in whipped cream,' I say.

'Oh,' he says. 'I wondered. I've not got my glasses on.'

He dives in enthusiastically with the bottle of chocolate sauce. Combined with the cream, it makes us both taste like a profiterole. The raspberries are less popular, being a fruit and therefore non-kosher for H, but he willingly consents to a game of 'hide the raspberry'. The best bit, though, is the way that the chocolate sauce clings to our skin, making us lick more insistently than usual.

We also, at my suggestion, try dipping parts of us in the Cava, an idea I got from Nancy Friday's *My Secret Garden*. This is a surprisingly bad idea. We try it first with H's penis. The bubbles fizz madly, and then gather themselves around him like a tank of piranhas. 'Ow,' he yelps, 'that hurts!' Disbelievingly, I dip a nipple into the glass, only to find the same effect – the bubbles feel like hundreds of little needles, which is pleasant for the first few seconds, but then builds into something much more painful. Not to be recommended. It also leaves your Cava tasting of penis.

After half an hour, we are both smeared head to toe in cream, chocolate sauce and crushed raspberries. For a while, this makes for deliciously slimy body contact, but there's a distinct point at which both of us are ready to get in the shower. While we're standing there, supervising the removal of chocolate sauce from each other's hair, H looks at me with what can only be described as admiration.

'I can't believe you let yourself get that dirty,' he says.

'I can't believe I bought UHT cream,' I reply.

April

After the week of daily sex, we retreat to Barcelona for a few days to recover.

It's a city we first visited when I was still at university, and we've been in love with it ever since. Back then, we stayed in a grim hostel with a shower that drained into the floor by the bed. This time, we house-swap, and spend our week looking after a psychotic cat named, ironically, Paz (peace), who hates our presence so much that she launches an attack on Herbert's ankles whenever he tries to walk across the room.

Most of our days are spent walking though the city, barrio by barrio, occasionally stopping for a coffee or a tart glass of wine. Herbert is a lover of old vinyl, so I pass most of my afternoons reading in bars, so as to avoid having to trail around after him through racks of records. He is a little more considerate about this than he used to be. For a start, the internet now means that he can find pretty much what he wants, whenever he wants it, but there was also a watershed moment in Athens a few years ago, when he spent three hours in one shop while I paced the streets outside. We will not mention the incident in Delhi, when he disappeared off in a tuk-tuk to an out-of-town warehouse for a whole afternoon, leaving me wondering at what point I should start to worry. He has since learned to be a bit more self-limiting.

Holidays are always my thinking time; I rarely emerge from them without wanting to make some change or other. In Barcelona, I start to crave the bigness of the life there, the way that cities lay such a huge array of experiences at your feet. Herbert and I have always lived in small towns, and have made a huge point of considering this to be enough. I am beginning to wonder if we're right about this, or if we actually just settled down to the same life as our parents without questioning it much.

We are eating lunch somewhere in the Raval, when I say to Herbert, 'What if we lived here? What would life be like?'

I mean nothing by it, mostly, but I suppose I don't want to exclude any possibilities. We are youngish, solvent, child-free; I see no reason why we couldn't live somewhere unusual if we both fancied it. Such things make H nervous. For every 'what if', he suspects a change is coming. H believes – and I think he's probably right in the long term – that the route to happiness lies in choosing your life and sticking with it, and not wasting time on chasing all those other possibilities. For me, it's the possibilities that get me out of bed in the morning.

The conversation gets more intense, veering towards that awful territory that long-term couples stray into: arguing about the way you argue.

'Why do you always do this?' I say. 'Why can't you just let me enjoy imagining things? You hate change.'

H rolls his eyes. 'Don't start this again.'

'I'm not starting! I just want to be able to have a conversation about my dreams. I don't want to assume that there's only one way of living our life.'

'You always make out I'm completely stuck where I am. It's not true. I'm not as boring as you make me sound.'

'I never said you were boring!'

'I think you use me as an excuse. I think you know that

you can blame me for not wanting to do all these things, but you'd never do them yourself either.'

'No,' I say, adjusting the tone of my voice in the hope that, for a non-English speaker, this might sound like a heated debate rather than an argument, 'I think the truth is that you don't trust me to stay in love with you through those changes.'

It's a truth so blatant and simple that I feel my breath catch on it. Hearing it out loud seems to calm us both. This black dog has followed us around for years, and now it's out in the fresh air, gazing, dazed, at both of us.

Fear has always been the dark side of love. It is only when our lovers are precious enough that we begin to wonder if they won't, one day, leave us behind.

I remember seeing that fear in Herbert's eyes for the first time when we had been together for a year. I met him during my last year at school, and we conducted a happy little love affair for a few months while I finished my A Levels. I had a place at a good university that I had no intention of turning down, and to be honest, I assumed it would all fizzle out once I started living in a new city with new friends. I was too afraid to ask what he thought.

But Herbert was braver than me. 'I'll be up every weekend,' he announced one evening, and he stuck to his word for the whole three years. That moment was like a floodgate for me, a moment when I finally allowed myself to believe that my instincts were true: I was in love. It was not just a childish fantasy.

One weekend, a few months into my time at college, I decided that I would visit H for a change. I was diabolically homesick for his company, and was gradually learning that I hated the petty intricacies of academic life. I caught the train back, and he met me at the station.

I remember that it was dark and rainy. I got into the car, buoyed up by being home, and as I turned to him, he flinched. It was the most heartbreaking thing I ever saw, a sort of animal cowering that I didn't understand until we pulled up outside our flat and he burst into tears and let out a tight breath. 'You're going to leave me, aren't you?' he said.

I can't describe how painful it is, even now, to conjure up that scene in my imagination. Fortunately, he was easily reassured: he had read far too much into several innocent comments and gestures, and we were both more than happy to set the record straight. But it stayed with me, that moment. I suddenly understood the hideous power that comes with love.

I can honestly say that I've never questioned that I'll love Herbert always. After that day, I realised that there was another dimension to it too: I owed it to him to never give him cause to doubt. I have never indulged in so much as a flirtation with another man, have never lied to him about anything. I can do this willingly because he's never sought to control me. I have been free to choose, and I have chosen him, over and over again.

I understand, of course, why he sees love as a slippery thing. He wasn't brought up to trust it. Herbert's father left his mother for her best friend when he was eight. That much is more or less normal now; my father left too. But the difference between us is that, even though I felt rejected by my dad, there were other people around me who kept loving me, and whom I knew would never leave.

This wasn't true for H. His mother remarried a man whose presence in the house made him miserable. Eventually, H felt forced to move out. He was fourteen. He spent some time living with his father and his new wife, but he didn't feel welcome there either, and, later, some time living with his elder sister. He eventually found himself living alone at seventeen.

You will have to imagine how self-sufficient I found this man when I met him at twenty-four, but how isolated too. He had no faith that there was such a thing as love in the first instance, and then, as soon as he admitted to himself that he loved me, he became afraid that I would leave.

This all sounds very sad, but really it isn't: it's a triumph, because this poor little boy has grown up to be one of the most loving, affectionate, considerate and downright sexy men I know. That fear that he used to feel is quite far buried now, and if I can spot it sometimes, it's because I know him so well.

When I see myself through his eyes, I often think what a risk I am to him, this woman he could have lost any number of ways but who, vitally, chooses to be with him. And that isn't any flimsy commitment; it's a 'forever, what-ever happens'. I find it hard to commit to a weekly yoga class because it seems like too much of a burden, but I willingly say 'forever' to Herbert because I know when I'm on to a good thing.

Seduction #16
X-Rated, Part 1

Because of an unshiftable chest infection (sex with a hacking cough, anyone? Thought not . . .), this seduction is long overdue.

In all honesty, H and I have fallen back into our pattern of happy celibacy over the last couple of weeks. I, for one, am not subject to any libidinous demands from my sex-deprived body. To the best of my knowledge, neither is Herbert. It's disappointing to realise that, outside the structure of the seductions, little has changed. We still tick along quite happily without sex. We are not surfing on waves of uncontrollable desire just yet.

Moreover, I've had time to worry about this seduction. It was H's suggestion, made a week ago. Porn. The watching together thereof. Because the Hollywood movies were a bit lame for his tastes.

I have a difficult relationship with porn. I can't turn off

my feminist brain long enough to cope with it. I studied a paper on it as part of my degree, and then, as now, I found its politics impossible to unpick. Do we have a right to call the women who act in it victims, even when they feel they are not? Is it fair to condemn porn for its shoddy gender roles when we often resort to the same stereotypes when the bedroom door is closed? Does porn change the way men behave towards women, or is it the stuff of fantasy only? Is non-sexist porn possible – and if so, would it be sexy?

H pretty much agrees with all my concerns about porn, but says it doesn't change the fact that it turns him on to watch men and women have sex. 'There's porn, and there's *porn*,' he says, somewhat cryptically. I take that to mean that he doesn't like watching bottle blondes with over-inflated lips and tits any more than I do.

He really wanted me to help him choose a film, and I declined; it seemed to me that this should be an exercise in him showing me the way. 'Just rent what you'd choose for yourself,' I say.

'Oh no, I'm not doing that,' he replies, looking horrified.

'Why would that be a problem?'

'I'm not ready for that yet.'

'Are you trying to tell me you've got some arcane taste that I'd be shocked by?'

'No. *No!* I actually don't know what I'd buy for myself. It's been a long time. I'd prefer to make sure you won't be offended.'

He then dithers over what to hire for the rest of the week. He's more worried about this than I am. Eventually, after a lot of umm-ing and ahh-ing – and several more requests for me to help him choose – he announces that he's gone for a 'classic', *The Devil in Miss Jones*, which I have never heard of, and he's never seen. 'It's supposed to actually have a plot,' he tells me, 'and it's made in the 70s, so the people are a bit more normal-looking. Hopefully.'

Great; it's going to be some sort of soft nonsense that panders to an imagined 'couples' audience. I am disabused of this impression the second it starts. At first, I can't make out the slightly pixelated image, but then I realise that it is a close-up of the star's vagina as she thrusts her fingers in and out of it.

'What a sight!' I say, entirely involuntarily, then realise I sound exactly like my mother. No, scrub that: my grandmother. 'Sorry,' I say, and resolve to be a little more open-minded. I pour myself a glass of wine.

The Devil in Miss Jones, if anything, suffers from a little too much plot. After the brief opening scene, we have to sit through ten minutes of explanation (and a suicide) before any sex occurs at all. Even I know that this isn't the point. 'If I was watching this on my own, I'd have done a lot of fast-forwarding,' says H. The attempt at plot soon dissolves away, though, and we get pretty much the scenes I expected. The loss of Miss Jones's virginity, quite a few enthusiastic blow jobs, vaginal sex, anal sex, lesbian sex, two women and one man, two men and one woman . . . oh, and a couple of bizarre filler scenes involving a snake and a fruit bowl, which mainly seem to be there to kill time.

What I will say is that it is refreshing to see relatively normal women with small breasts having sex. The partner in Miss Jones's lesbian encounter even has shockingly hairy thighs. And, as Herbert is keen to point out, Miss Jones is not exploited or humiliated; she is a willing and enthusiastic participant who quickly takes the lead in her sexual adventures.

Does this make it a non-sexist movie? No, not particularly. It's a representation of a woman being excessively keen on the kind of things men love – she gives worshipful blow jobs (all the while talking to the penis about how wonderful it is), requires no foreplay to have delirious orgasms and does a nice line in selfless 'Oh, it hurts so much, but don't stop' commentary which becomes quite annoying after a while. Overall, *The Devil in Miss Jones* is about how sex feels to men, rather than to women – a lot of in and out and display.

As I remark to H halfway through, I don't find it remotely arousing to look at other women's vaginas, or, in fact, at the sturdy erections of strangers. Sex really is about sensation to me, rather than visual stimulus, and I'm still a bit surprised whenever I see female genitals from a man's eye view – that's not how I encounter mine at all.

As an aside, I went to see a comedian recently, who told us that his friend, for whatever reason, has only just seen his first vagina at the age of thirty-six. 'What did you think?' asked the comedian. His friend shrugged. 'It just looked kind of sore,' he replied. Watching Miss Jones's vagina in close-up, I couldn't help but agree. It's as if the sight of one doesn't quite match the experience of owning one.

The thing about watching porn is that it's moderately arousing, but only on a mechanical level – that lizard part of your brain that recognises sex, and says, *Oh yes, I can do that too*. But for me, it didn't really transcend that. I couldn't turn my late-twentieth-century brain off long enough to stop analysing it. I wonder if porn made by a woman would have a different quality?

However, one thing I do enjoy is H reaching across and

gently massaging my clitoris while the film is on. Slow and steady, it builds up to a wonderful level of sensitivity for me when we have sex afterwards. H thinks that this means that the film had more effect on me than I'm admitting.

I disagree, but I'm willing to put my theory to the test. The next evening, we try the same thing while watching the televised Leadership Debate for the general election.

Exactly the same effect. With the added bonus that we were both seeking a way of relieving the boredom.

It is Sunday afternoon, and I am making a salad in the kitchen.

Herbert comes downstairs fresh from a shower, and I bury my nose in his neck and breathe in deeply. I love that smell behind his ear, like damp forests and buttered toast. I feel the signal from that scent in the base of my pelvis, a small but definite explosion.

Then I turn away and get on with my cooking. It is only when I hear Herbert leaving the room that I realise what has happened. It wasn't that I hadn't thought of sex; it was that I'd pushed it away before the thought became conscious. Not, 'We can't have sex now,' but, 'We don't have sex now.' It's just not what we do. It's not the done thing.

I should drop everything and chase him up the damned stairs. But I don't. Not the done thing either, I suppose. Even after all these months of seduction, it would still be a shock for us both if I expressed desire like that.

But it's a progress of sorts to have noticed that little thought, to have caught it in a net. I am still resisting my own desires. I am still resisting the idea of myself as a person who has desires.

It makes me wonder about our seduction this week, watching porn together. Would I ever have allowed myself to like it, under any circumstances? I think not. I think it would signify a lack of power to me, a sense that my sexual responses are subject to forces outside my control. I don't like that idea much, somehow. I prize being clever and cynical over surrender.

Seduction #16
X-Rated, Part 2

I am lying on my back on the sofa, as Herbert stands above me. I slowly run my tongue up and down his penis, and he hops from foot to foot gasping, 'Ahh! It's too good! I can't take it! Everything feels too sensitive!'

The difference, as H archly suggests later, is that he let me choose the porn this time. Setting aside the implication that I like getting my own way (well, I do), he's not wrong. It was easy for me to decide in advance that I wasn't going to respond to the film H chose, even if that was subconscious. When it came to making my own selection, I had to seek out something that turned me on.

Mind you, I found plenty that didn't. I put in hours of research, mostly with a knot in my stomach that told me I wouldn't ever find anything I was comfortable with. I found the bigger download sites utterly baffling with their highly specific categories that I just didn't have the expertise to interpret. I thought that 'camel toe' and 'bubble gum' were two encounters that might make a Saturday afternoon on the high street unpleasant; apparently, they constitute genres in porn.

What I eventually came to realise was that I had to form a taste just as specific as this in order to find the porn I wanted. And when I thought about it, this was easy. My specification ran thus:

- It should feature people I might actually fancy, rather than the kind of idiots I would cross the road to avoid.
- It should consider the woman's pleasure as well as the man's.
- I'm not at all interested in women being described as sluts, whores or bitches, or seeing them being humiliated or degraded. I want them to be treated as I would expect to be treated.
- Reasonable production values would be appreciated.
- I still want it to be explicit. I'm not convinced by the idea that women like their porn to avert its gaze below the waistline.
- This is a non-aesthetic consideration, but I need to be able to download it.

Of course, the great joy of the internet is that you can always find like-minded people, providing you can work out the right search term. After a great deal of Googling, I timidly type in 'feminist porn', expecting my laptop to flash 'oxymoron alert' at me and to promptly explode. But it doesn't. Hell, there's even an award ceremony for it.

Eventually, I choose *Five Hot Stories for Her* from Lust

Films. It isn't perfect – the second short film about a foot-baller's wife indulging in a decidedly rubbish threesome makes me want to crawl up the walls, particularly seeing as one of the 'studs' seems to be a compulsive masturbator whose approach to cunnilingus involves nothing more than swinging his head from side to side in the general direction. The man in the domination short also seems to struggle to maintain a meaningful erection. However, the two lesbians in the first story are delightful to watch, and there is no sense that they are performing for a male gaze.

I couldn't tell you about the last two stories, sorry. We were a bit too distracted.

May

I sit down in my consultant's office and watch him read through my notes. Then he asks me, 'Has anything changed down below?'

'No,' I say, 'exactly the same.' I really wish we didn't need to resort to baby language in these situations. Your cervix is as legitimate a part of your body as, say, your arm or your ear. Let's not pretend we're embarrassed to know it exists. Particularly seeing as you, sir, make your living out of these peculiar little doughnuts of flesh.

'Okay,' he says, and makes some notes. 'I think we'll go ahead with a cautery, then. Are you okay with that?'

'Yes,' I say. 'Absolutely.'

'And how soon would you like it done? Shall I mark it urgent?'

'Erm, yes.' I say. 'I thought you were going to do it today.'

He chuckles in the manner of Dr Hibbert from *The Simpsons*. 'Oh no, we can't do it today. We need to do it under general anaesthetic, which means you'll need another assessment appointment before then. Take this form out to the nurses. See you soon.'

I wander out to the next room, where there's one of those gynaecological chairs all set up with a tray of instruments next to it. There are two nurses sitting in wait.

'Oh,' says one of them, reading my piece of paper. 'Don't you want it done today then? We were all ready.'

'So was I,' I say, restraining myself from adding, *I even shaved my bikini line.*

'Well, we can do it now if you like.'

'The doctor says I've got to wait for a general anaesthetic.'

'Really?' says the nurse in utter disbelief. She rolls her eyes at her companion. 'You don't have to, you know. It's your choice. Has he even discussed your choices with you? You weren't in there for long.'

'Erm . . .' I'm really not sure what to say. I don't tend to hold opinions about whether or not I need a general anaesthetic for any given procedure. It's pretty much outside my area of expertise. 'If he thinks I need a general, I guess I do,' I offer, weakly.

'Hah!' says the nurse in a manner which I take to imply, *What does he know?* 'I bet you've been waiting for ages for this, haven't you, love?'

'Two years, give or take.'

'Don't worry. We'll get you in quickly.' She winks, glances over my medical forms, and then spends the next ten minutes gossiping about what a moron my GP is.

I emerge into the waiting room, reeling from the Kafkaesque workings of the NHS, and unnerved by the sense that those two nurses had managed to empathetically absorb all my worry and indignation, leaving me, strangely, with none.

Seduction #17
The Power of Now

I am still wondering about my feeble desire, how to nurture it back into life. It seems to me that it has become detached from its moorings somehow, and is now floating adrift in the vast sea of my consciousness. I know it's there, and sometimes I can even detect its presence on my radar. But it is stray, elusive. I can't seem to make it stand still for long enough to understand it.

Part of the problem is that I find it hard to admit to myself when I'm turned on. I'm just not used to seeing myself in that way any more. And even when I do register it, a bizarre self-consciousness kicks in when I even think of telling Herbert. I say 'bizarre' because, after all, it would benefit both of us to know what turns me on. I need to find a way of helping myself over the hump of my own embarrassment.

The idea I come up with is simple: we will text the word 'now' to each other whenever we think about sex.

We don't have to say any more than that, or to act on the signal. We just have to acknowledge our own, ongoing sexuality.

I hope that this might help us to simmer with latent arousal throughout our days spent apart, leading to fireworks in the bedroom when we get home. When I suggest it, I imagine we'll be 'now'-ing maybe four or five times a day in each direction. True to form, however, this level of spontaneous desire is a little bit beyond us.

In fact, no 'nows' occur at all on the first day, or indeed the second. For my part, I keep mentally scanning my genitalia for any minute electric signal that might denote a turn-on. Nothing. If anything, it makes me feel more like a dried-up old twig than ever, rather than a sexually vibrant woman tuning into her desires while she waits for her lover to come home. I consider faking a 'now' at the end of day two, but that just seems dishonest.

Herbert, I think, must surely be having more 'now' moments than me. Aren't men supposed to think about sex every seven seconds or something? Perhaps he hasn't read my email properly. Or perhaps, as usual, his mobile phone is languishing at the bottom of his man-bag with empty batteries.

No. When I ask him, he shrugs and giggles, and says, 'I know! I had no idea how little I think about sex.'

By day three, I am concluding that this one has died on its arse, and I will have to go back to the drawing board. But then – lo! – H sends me an email, which is mainly about transfers of money between our bank accounts, but which ends with the sentence: *Oh, and 'now' by the way.*

Just reading it makes me have a little 'now' moment, too, and I email back to this effect. He sends me an ASCII wink.

We don't have sex that night, though. We've forgotten about it by the time we get home. We don't even see each other the next night until bedtime, when we're ready for nothing but sleep. But the following day is a Saturday, and we have more time together. Mid-afternoon, H creeps up behind me, wraps his arms around me, and says, 'Now.' We have some of the best sex we've had for weeks. And on Sunday too.

Seduction #18
Lady Boy

At eight-thirty on Sunday night, Herbert puts down his dinner tray and says, 'Right, I'm going upstairs to shave off my beard.'

Bloody hell, I think, *he's actually serious.*

He's been threatening a seduction in drag for about a month now. I'm not entirely sure whether he's playing out a fantasy or just investigating a morbid curiosity. I suspect the latter; Herbert is not a particularly feminine man. In any case, as nothing had actually emerged up to now, I thought the whole idea had died a death. Not so. He's been mulling it over, that's all.

'Bring me some underwear,' he says between strokes of the razor.

'Just knickers?' I ask.

'Bra too. And suspenders.'

'There's no way you'll fit into any of my bras.'

'I reckon I can fill it. I've got decent moobs.'

'No, I mean I haven't got one that will stretch around

your chest.' H, it should be explained, has a 48-inch chest. My 36C doesn't stand a chance. But he looks terribly dejected at the prospect of being denied his hour in a bra, so I pick out a pair of black lace French knickers (which offer the best chance of fitting), and grab the bra to match. I hesitate over offering him my Agent Provocateur suspender belt, but then I'm not sure whether hold-ups will work on hairy thighs.

H is drying his face and applying a huge quantity of my best moisturiser in a slapping motion that he must have learned from the Brut adverts in the 80s. I loosen the bra straps to their fullest extent, hook them over his arms, and then use a silk scarf to tie them together around his back. When he stands up, it's an approximation of a bra, even if it does keep riding up. 'Ooh,' he says, 'I've got underboob,' and he cups one in his hand lasciviously.

'Are you doing this for you or for me?' I ask, not sure if I really want to know the answer.

'Don't get any ideas,' he says. 'I'm only doing it because it's funny. And because I don't see why you should have all the fun with the make-up and the underwear. Can I have the stockings now?'

The suspender belt just about stretches around his hips, but I can't see it ever being the same again. He has no idea how to attach the (mulberry lace) stockings, and so I have to do it for him. He pulls the knickers on over the top, and we quickly realise that they flash either testicle or buttock crack, depending on how they're positioned.

H is not deterred. He announces that it would be 'probably dangerous' to apply his own make-up, and sits down obediently for me to give him the full works: concealer, base, blusher, eyeshadow, eyeliner and lipstick. He elects to apply the mascara himself, having already grown

153

suspicious that I'm trying to blind him during the eyeshadow stage.

I sit and watch him. Herbert has a lazy eye, and so when he focuses on things close-up, he can only see out of one eye at a time. This means he doesn't have the best depth perception. First, he somehow covers his hands in mascara. Then he jabs the wand into the side of his head, leaving a thick, black smear. Finally, he manages to blink his lashes on to the wand, and immediately opens his eyes wide so that his lids are striped black.

His make-up complete, he stands back to admire himself in the mirror, making those pouty mouth gestures that trampy women make in bad films. 'What do you think?' he asks.

'Erm,' I say, 'I'm not sure if you're my type of girl.' He tuts and fluffs up his hair, and goes into the bedroom to choose a string of beads from my dressing table. I squirt perfume behind his ears.

It's odd to see him like this. His skin looks dead underneath the weight of the foundation, and the underwear seems like a parody of female sexuality. But it's my make-up and my underwear that he's wearing. I wonder if I fall into the same trap, of putting on the accoutrements of desire in the hope of short-cutting to the real thing. I wonder if I, too, look less than I really am in all this get-up.

It doesn't help that he's decided to put on a soft voice, and is ignoring the squalls of laughter this provokes in me. I stroke the bare sections of thigh above his stockings, and lick his nipples, which are poking out from under his bra.

'Is there any particular way that you imagined doing this?' I ask, and he says, 'I dunno. Maybe you get between my legs this time.'

We try this and it doesn't work; we can't get the right

angle, and his penis keeps popping out of me. 'Doggy-style?' he suggests, and I say, 'Just to be clear, what do you expect that to entail?'

'Well, I'm not aware of you owning a strap-on, so I was just hoping for a reach-around.'

'Right,' I say, 'just checking.' I bang along behind H for a while, until he says, 'Okay, I feel silly now,' and I am grateful to give up.

We go on to have the sex we would have had without H dressed as a woman. It's good, although it takes me a while to feel truly turned on.

Afterwards, when I have rescued my used stockings from the bin (they're not disposable, Herbert!) and demonstrated the use of Eve Lom cleanser (H: 'Do you actually have to do this every day?'), I ask him, 'So, did you enjoy that?'

He shrugs. 'It was okay. Can't say I'd bother to do it again.'

And I must say I am relieved.

Fifteen years into a relationship, I find it almost impossible to imagine how anyone has sex with a new partner. I just can't visualise the mechanics of getting from the first moment of eye contact to showing someone my fanny. This far down the line, it seems like an unutterably bizarre thing to do.

And yet, strangely, sex seemed easier back then. I didn't feel quite so awkward about wanting it, or trying something new. I felt as though there was a sort of privacy in which I could express my desire. I knew I was a mystery to Herbert, and he was a mystery to me. Anything I offered into the sexual arena was mine, and mine alone. He didn't know me well enough to declare on whether I'd done it before, or if it was out of character. It was liberating to be able to make myself anew in his eyes.

When I compare myself to the girl who met Herbert, I am ever so slightly amazed at how self-conscious I've become. Shouldn't all this security have freed me to express my inner desires? Shouldn't I feel comfortable and secure enough to experiment, in the full knowledge that my lover is kind and trustworthy? Shouldn't I have had many years to explore and progress, leaving me with some kind of expertise?

The truth is the opposite. Over the course of our relationship, I have got progressively less experimental, and progressively more ashamed of my own desires. I have allowed myself to be put off things because they have failed once; and we have both fallen into dull sexual routines that arouse neither of us.

I am pretty sure that, if I took a new lover, I would revert to my liberated self again. And yet, to Herbert, I am his practical, sensible wife, the household organiser and the allocator of chores. Somewhere down the line, I must have chosen to be this instead of his wild lover. I obviously couldn't countenance being both.

It seems like an odd choice to make, in retrospect. These days, I would choose the role of the wild lover any day. But I can remember a time in my twenties, when my heart's desire was to be domestic, to be certain and settled. Up to that point, life had seemed so wobbly to me. I wanted to be sure about my world, and I wanted to create some stability for Herbert. So I painted walls and ran up curtains on the sewing machine I inherited from my grandma, and I learned to cook, and petitioned H for children. In my mind's eye, I was making a sensible future for us. Looking back, I can see that I was even boring myself.

I feel as though I am living my life backwards. The older I get, and the more my friends settle down, the more I want to push against it. I don't want my life to be structured around mortgage payments and Saturday evening TV. There's a whole world out there, waiting for me.

And sex is part of that. I want to rekindle the wildness of my own lust before it disappears altogether. That means that, somehow, I have to lay aside the formality that has grown up in me, and fight against this odd self-consciousness. Easier said than done. I see it in Herbert too. For years he has eked out a semblance of wild sexuality for himself, subsisting on hints and insinuations that he's secretly kinkier than I know. Now, with the songbook of modern sexuality laid open before him, he's floundering. When thwarted, his desire felt like something dark and unacceptable to him, something that was too much for me. Now it's like a ghost that vanishes in the light of day. He finds it hard to want anything in particular, and he resorts to experiments rather than seductions, things that he thinks up logically rather than being led there by desire.

The question is, how do we banish this self-consciousness? Because, at the moment, it feels almost impossible to defeat.

Seduction #19
Remote Control

'Nothing's happening.'
'Perhaps the batteries are flat.'
'Didn't you charge them?'

We are hissing this conversation across the table of a remarkably quiet restaurant. I say 'remarkably' because we had chosen it specifically for being the noisiest place in town, with the furthest-apart tables. Thursday night, it seems, is not its night. Aside from us, there is one other couple in the room, and they aren't saying much.

Herbert begins to fumble about in his pocket again, withdrawing it sharply when he realises the waitress is standing behind him.

'Um, would you like to order any drinks?'

We both shift uncomfortably – well, possibly me more than Herbert. I am, you see, rigged up to a remote-control bullet vibrator, and it is beginning to fall out.

'A large glass of red wine for me,' I say. 'And a rare steak.'

The waitress smiles, closes her notebook and turns to leave; and at that exact moment, Herbert must finally lean on the right button, because the vibrator suddenly kicks into life, making me emit an involuntary yelp. I attempt to turn this into a coughing fit as the waitress glances back at me. H is giggling like a lunatic.

'I'm going to have to go to the loos and sort this thing out,' I say. 'Can you turn it off for a moment?'

H pushes the button again, and the vibration changes from an intense, smooth buzz to a regular pulse.

'Oh,' I say, 'that's much nicer, we'll bear that in mind. Try again.'

This time, it becomes a low rumble, like an engine ticking over. 'Nope,' I say, 'it's still going.'

The silent couple are leaning in to talk to each other, and occasionally looking over towards us. 'I think we're going to need a codeword.'

'How about "dormouse"?' suggests H.

'Right, because that's going to be really discreet, isn't it? It's the kind of word that comes up in conversation all the time.'

H chuckles away to himself and pushes the button again. 'Ah, okay, dormouse,' I say.

I limp over to the bathroom, where I have to untangle the long wire between the vibe and its battery pack before I can get my jeans down. I am wearing a smock tonight, because it is the only thing I own that disguises the mauve box clipped to my jeans, with its pulsing red light and protruding wires. In my first choice of outfit, I looked like a particularly incompetent suicide bomber. But I'll admit it was a slightly sexier get-up than this.

The jeans, too, are significant: they act as a silencer. My vagina, it appears, is not insulating enough to prevent the insidious buzzing sound from leaking out, a noise reminiscent of sharing your bedroom with a ravenous mosquito. H suggested I wear a sanitary towel as a muffler. Not an appealing option.

I return to the table and see that our food has arrived. H lets me take a couple of mouthfuls, and then I see his hand stray into his pocket again.

'Nothing?' he says.

'No,' I reply. He takes another mouthful of his chicken, and clicks the button again.

'Oh! Badger! Hedgehog! DORMOUSE!' I trill, and H attempts to nonchalantly sip his Coke.

So, I am sitting in the Day Surgery waiting room on Monday afternoon. I have seen a nurse, an anaesthetist and a registrar, and I have been asked four times if there's any chance I might be pregnant. I have also taken a pregnancy test, so I am even less sure than usual why this question is relevant to me.

But I am rather content. Everyone has been kind to me today; everything has been carefully discussed. The nurse who checks me in even explains, unbidden, why I've been asked to remove my toenail polish. This mostly means that she has clocked the heinous condition of my nails *sans* polish, but I am trying not to dwell on this fact.

Glancing around the waiting room, I observe that everyone else looks a lot more nervous than me. The woman to my left is clutching her husband's hand and biting her bottom lip. 'You should tell them you're this worried,' he whispers to her. 'They can give you something to help.'

'Shh,' she says. 'Be quiet now.'

Herbert is not waiting with me. I have sent him home. There are times when you have to cope with things alone, and given how jittery he looked this morning, I don't think it would help to have him with me. Better, I think, to bury my head in a book and let the time pass that way. Alone, I am really quite calm.

This is partly, I suppose, because I have been looking forward to this for a long time. In fact, I've fought to get here. The idea that there might be a treatment that makes everything better is pretty wonderful.

But it is also because I could live without it. Over the last few months, Herbert and I have gradually negotiated our way around my insubordinate body. I've stopped mentally modelling it as an erotic dead-zone, a broken piece of equipment. Together, we've found ways around its flaws. Even when the worst happened, we coped. We carried on having sex regardless, and enjoyed it. Herbert is a lot less deterred by blood than I am, so it turns out.

And so, even if this operation doesn't work out, it's okay. Nothing hinges on this, except, perhaps, the Reverse Cowgirl.

'Betty, would you like to put your gown on now?' I get changed in a clean little examination room, and send a final text to H (*Ooh, it's my turn!*) before handing my bag over to the nurse and padding down the corridor after another nurse in surgical garb, who chats to me about her son starting pre-school.

I lie down. The anaesthetist I met earlier fits a cannula into my hand, and the nurse takes my glasses away, assuring me I won't be far from them. 'Okay,' says the anaesthetist, 'I'm going to give you some oxygen, and in twenty seconds you'll be asleep.'

I nod, and the mask goes on. Then I blink and notice my eyes are blurry. A second, blurrier blink, and then the next thing I hear is someone saying, 'Betty, Betty, time to wake up now.'

Seduction #20
In and Out the Dusty Bluebells

I have spent most of the last week wondering when it's alright to do things: driving, exercise, alcohol, and, of course, dear old sex. I don't want to undo my gynaecologist's good work, nor make myself keel over, and I absolutely want to avoid either of these things while driving. In any case, I have learned that general anaesthetics make you feel very odd indeed for quite some time, and it is hard to even contemplate doing anything much for at least a working week.

However, by Sunday I begin to feel like a normal human being again. Actually, I am quite rabidly desperate to leave the house. We head out to the location of Seduction #19 for their splendid roast lunch, and then H suggests we drive out to the woods for a walk through the bluebells.

Bluebells rank amongst some of my favourite things

(alongside the sea, swallows, snow, and lots of other non-natural phenomena such as Stevie Wonder, gin Martinis and salted almonds, preferably served together). Today, I wonder if they will have wilted in the heat, but we can see them from the car park: an almost supernatural blue crowding the spaces between the trees.

It is shady in the woods, but the air is still surprisingly warm and full of the heady bluebell smell, like honey and hyacinths. As we stroll along, we barely see another soul. There are a few squirrels and the odd pigeon, but humanity appears, quite ungratefully, to be staying away from the woods on a sunny day.

I'm not really sure who has the idea first. Maybe it's simultaneous. I find myself stroking H's back as we walk along. He stops and kisses me. Then we come to a gate, and as I pause to open it, H presses himself up against me and nuzzles into the back of my neck. We cross an open field and reach another section of woodland, this one even quieter than before. I stop to kiss H, and he reaches into the front of my blouse and kisses my breast. I shriek with laughter. He unzips my skirt.

'We can't do this standing in the middle of the path,' I say.

'We'd see anyone coming.'

'Only once they'd seen us first!'

I carry on down the path, and then head off between the trees. There's not much cover here either, but at least it would take a while to spot us. I lean against a tree and H catches up with me. 'I thought you were turning me down altogether,' he says. He kisses me.

He's not wasting any time. He undoes his jeans and hitches up my skirt. Am I allowed to have sex yet? I'm not sure. Perhaps I should say something . . . Ah, but no;

165

H has already thought of that. He carefully puts his penis between my thighs, and we proceed like that. Actually, this is a much better way to have sex standing up – so much easier than the constant angling and balance-shifting that's usually required.

And, from my point of view, it's really quite lovely. I keep forgetting to stay on the lookout, although I do conscientiously appoint myself to the role of not letting H's trousers fall down altogether. Even so, every now and then I come to my senses and scan the horizon for other human beings. No one comes. Except both of us.

Sorry, cheap joke.

Seduction #21
Call Me

Herbert and I spent three years living apart when I went to university. We were in the first sexual flush of our relationship for at least some of that time. Not once did we even contemplate having phone sex.

That should give you an idea of how unkeen I am on the idea. I hate talking dirty; I just don't have the language for it. I'm pretty quiet in the bedroom, aside from the occasional 'That feels good,' and even that's something I have to remind myself to do. The thought of coming over all 'Ooh baby' on the phone is enough to bring me out in hives.

But Herbert is off on a rare business trip to Germany, and announced several weeks ago that he would be taking this opportunity to engage in a bit of phone sex. There's really no avoiding it. I gather it's a standard part of the repertoire these days.

All the same, I am quite tempted to sabotage the whole thing by heading for the pub. It doesn't help that H can't get any time alone until late in the evening, and by then I have been wondering what on earth I'll say all night. I have also drunk three glasses of wine, just for the moral support. This may or may not be a good thing.

I try to get in the mood by undressing and getting into bed with a copy of *My Secret Garden*, but every page I open seems to be about some bizarre sexual practice that makes me want to retract my vagina.

Eventually, H texts. *Shall we use Skype?*

No, I reply, *I can stay in bed if we use my mobile.*

Right. But unless you're very quick, I'm going to have one hell of a phone bill to claim on expenses.

Oh, okay, I text back, hoping to convey a suitable level of bad will. I go downstairs and log on, putting on the ridiculously large headset that H owns. This is not a good look.

It takes me about five minutes to adjust everything so that I can hear him, during which time I have threatened to downgrade this seduction to text sex instead. However, I eventually hear H's voice faintly, and then louder as I adjust the volume control.

'Erm, how do you feel?' he says.

'Nervous,' I say, knowing this isn't the right answer.

Silence on the other end of the line. I sigh. 'Describe where you are then.'

'I'm in my hotel room,' he says. 'I've got my cock in my hand. It's hard.'

'Really?' I squeal. 'Are you making that up?'

'No,' he says patiently. 'I'm stroking my left nipple.'

'Well, I'm glad you're being so specific. I'd hate to be left wondering which nipple you're stroking.'

'It's all part of building up a picture. What about you?'

'Oh,' I say. 'Right. Um, I'm naked, sitting at my desk. I'm stroking myself.'

'Which particular part of yourself would that be?'

'My vulva,' I say, gulping on the ugliness of the word. 'I'm running my fingers down between my lips and dipping them in my cunt.'

'You have to actually do it, Betty.'

'I am!'

I hurriedly start.

'How does it feel?'

'It feels good. I've got my feet up on the desk. If I turned the webcam on, you'd have such a good view.'

'Turn it on!'

I sit up and click around Skype, hoping a picture will appear, but nothing happens.

'Okay,' says H, 'don't worry. You're getting distracted.'

And then, on impulse, I do something I've never done before: I grab my phone, take a photo of my hand on my naked fanny, and text it to Herbert. For a few seconds I am stung with a hideous anxiety that I might have accidentally sent it to the wrong person, but then I hear a reassuring beep at the other end of the line.

'What's that supposed to be?' says H.

'Well, it's dark in here.'

I hear him chuckle, and a message pings on to my phone, a close-up of his penis with his feet far away in the distance. He still has his shoes on.

'Okay, I accept your lighting is better,' I concede, and I try to take another photo, but this just looks like a random twist of flesh. I put the phone down. Something about the idea of texting photos of our genitals to each other feels, well, intimate in a good way.

Betty Herbert

'Hey, H,' I say, 'guess what I'm doing? There's a nail-varnish bottle on my desk. I'm running it up and down my lips. Mmm, it feels lovely and cold. I've pushed it into my vagina now.'

This is the first time I've ever done anything remotely saucy with a nail-varnish bottle, but I have to admit it feels genuinely good. H has gone quiet, so I take another photo, this time angling myself towards the light, and send it over to him.

'Oh, that's a nice one,' he says, and sends back another picture of his penis but from the opposite direction, with himself smiling proudly in the background. I dissolve into giggles, and we stop talking after that. I can hear him breathing at the other end of the line, and I change positions so that I can lean over the armchair in my study, burying my face into the cushion. The headset slips sideways off my head so I can only hear H very faintly, but I make sure the microphone stays near my mouth, so that he can hear my breath become more and more ragged.

I manage to transmit what I think is a pretty good-sounding orgasm, and just about then H sends another picture to me, what I think is known in the trade as a money shot.

'Simultaneous orgasms, even this far apart,' I say, and get no reply. 'Herbert?' I say, 'Herbert? Can you hear me?'

It turns out that H missed my rather splendid orgasm because I had accidentally unplugged my microphone feed. 'Bloody typical,' I say.

'Never mind. Some other time!'

'That was good though. Not half so bad as I expected.'

'No. And I got to text you photos of my knob!'

'Yes, you did. You'd best delete those before work tomorrow, eh?'

'Yes, best had.'

There is a slightly awkward silence for a beat, and then H takes a breath and says, 'So, I got stuck in two hours of traffic on the way over here today. And the coffee machine doesn't work in my room . . .'

I'm left a little shocked at how quickly we flit back to reality.

June

ometimes, I'm a bit embarrassed to admit I'm married. It's hardly the radical choice. Faced with the multitude of ways that human beings can live their lives these days, we chose the same institution as our grandparents. Worse than that, it's an institution that carries a slight taint of oppression, of amassing property and nailing people down.

But then, Herbert and I got married because we didn't believe in marriage.

We got married because we didn't believe it was the moral or ethical thing to do. We didn't believe it would validate or sanctify our relationship in any way. We didn't believe it would stick us together for longer.

We got married because our parents couldn't make it work. We got married because we grew up thinking that marriage was an absurd, oppressive institution that inevitably went nuclear. We got married because we thought the very idea of marriage hinged on a skewed notion of the nature of men and women.

Not everyone will understand this, but in the face of these beliefs, getting married was the most wildly romantic gesture we could think of, an act of blind faith in the two of us and our ability to stay the distance. We didn't think that the institution could bind us together; we thought that we could.

It is fashionable to say that monogamy can't possibly work. The good old adulterer's excuse that men can't help but sow their seed has now been enshrined in the new evolutionary discourse of which we are all suddenly so fond. On the other side of the fence, we find the religious right curiously agreeing, arguing that men require the structure and discipline of God to keep them on the straight and narrow path.

And who would want tired old monogamy anyway, when there are so many more juicy options out there?

Well, I do, but not because I think it's any better than any other choice. Quite the contrary: particularly before the seductions started, I would often feel a stab of envy at the polyamorous exploits of single friends.

I've recently been devouring the literature on keeping long-term relationships alive, and so many of them open with a variation on the line 'Monogamy is best.' I find this attitude infuriating and small-minded. There is no best way, even for any one individual. We must all make our own compact with our partner, if we want to have a partner at all. So long as both parties agree, anything goes. It's, frankly, none of my business.

And in all choices there are benefits and drawbacks. The compact of monogamy requires a huge effort on both sides to keep it alive and well, especially over the scale of an adult lifetime. Everyone interprets it differently, but for us it has always meant a commitment to staying above reproach, and not even indulging in minor flirtations that might give others cause to suspect our fidelity. Clearly, it also means missing out on pursuing the attractions that arise from time to time; monogamy doesn't make you immune from them. We old marrieds still yearn for the head-rush of risk and romance, the thrill of the chase, and to some extent we have to accept that we're done with all that.

And the benefits? Well, there's the growing sense of

trust and certainty, and the privilege of having someone all to yourself. But most of all, there's a kind of freedom in having made that choice. Perhaps this is the freedom of submission; but perhaps it is also the freedom of choosing not to continually wonder if your partner is good enough, if you are good enough. So long as you've picked someone pretty good in the first place, you can keep working towards that elusive state of perfection.

Monogamy isn't just one, dead choice. It is a daily, hourly choice that should be made in full acceptance of the other choices available. It should be a conscious choice made by two people, rather than a bland acceptance of 'the done thing'. If we fall into monogamy by default and never question it again, it will die. The compact can be broken by secret infidelities, but it can equally be broken by withdrawing love and affection.

Taken in this way, monogamy is a radical choice among many rather than a bland following of convention. It is not for everyone, and no one should imply otherwise. But for me, it's just right.

Seduction #22
Razzle-Jazzle 'Em

'You'd be surprised how many customers have it all waxed off like this. I bet they don't tell anyone.'

Blimey, I think, *where's the benefit in that?* At least I can get good copy out of a Hollywood.

I was looking for a place that offered vajazzling (the American practice of having a good ol' wax and then decorating your bald pubic area with jewels), but it appears that the salons of genteel Kent don't currently sense a demand for such a service. Instead, I have had to settle for the Hollywood (everything off), and then some quality time later, applying the vajazzles myself.

Arriving at the salon, I am handed what the technician optimistically terms 'a pair of paper knickers', but which is actually a thin strip of black tissue with elastic loops. One size fits all apparently, which means that I have no hope of hiding much behind them. It turns out that this matters very little: the knickers are merely a symbolic gesture towards my dignity. The technician's first act is to push them to one side so that she can wax around my labia.

We will not speak of the pain. However, I will say this: even in the course of the seductions, I have never yet found myself laying face down on a table, holding apart my own buttock cheeks, while a young girl waxes my anus.

It is unseemly to admire one's own hairless fanny whilst still at the salon, so I follow convention and have a good look when I get home. It's a bit red and angry-looking, but – and I'm pained to admit this, because it commits me to years of expensive brutality at the hands of the beautician – it's quite resplendently lovely. It feels smooth and new, but there's nothing 'little girl' about it at all; in fact, it's distinctly adult, distinctly knowing.

It is also quite fascinatingly sensitive. I keep compulsively reaching down into my knickers to check it's still there, and it's oddly like touching someone else's vagina. Not only does it feel completely unfamiliar under my fingers, but the sensations are different on the receiving end too. I am like a child with a new toy.

When Herbert gets home, I refuse to let him see it (I want the redness to go down first; I don't want his first response to be 'Ooh, ouch!'), but at bedtime, I do let him reach down my pyjamas and touch it. He seems a bit tentative, and quickly withdraws his hand. I'm not sure it could take too much stroking anyway.

The next day it's looking a lot calmer, and I remain enchanted by this new body part I've uncovered. At about six, I prop myself up on some pillows and then set about vajazzling myself. After a great deal of fruitless websearching (and a brief flirtation with Coco de Mer's butterfly merkin, before I realised it cost £100), I had finally found some children's crystal tattoos and some violet body crystals for £1.99 apiece on eBay. I'd had no idea that either of these fashion items existed before last week, but, as I have often had cause to comment in the course of these seductions, every day's a school day.

The art of the vajazzle, according to my online reading, is to keep the decoration high up, lest one accidentally gets a crystal wedged in a delicate area. I am more than happy to follow this rule. I have an advanced sense of kitsch at the best of times, but tonight it really comes into its own. Across my bald pudenda, I create what I like to think of as a Deco-inspired display, with touches of Vegas thrown in. Oh, and I also manage to write 'B 4 H' in purple crystals, just so you can picture it in your mind.

At seven, H texts to say he's leaving work. I hastily take a picture of my vajazzled fanny, with the demure addition of a fig leaf from the garden, and text it straight back. *Glittertastic*, comes the response, and then, a few seconds later, *Now*.

I should bloody hope so after all that effort! I reply.

I'll admit to some concerns that H wouldn't be keen on the vajazzles. He's quite invested in his self-image as a hippy boy, and even as I was applying the jewels, I was wondering whether a Hollywood wax really needs any embellishment.

Judging from his response, I had nothing to worry about. Although given how much the crystals have moved around during our congress, I wish I'd counted how many I stuck on there in the first place.

Afterwards, though, I feel the familiar pains in my abdomen. I try to write them off and don't even mention them to Herbert. There's bound to be a bit of discomfort. It's early days since my operation.

The next day, I ask H what he'd like to do with his afternoon, and his rather flattering reply is, 'I'd like to spend some more time with your bald fanny, please.' Which is all very lovely. Except that, after a few minutes, I start making some odd squelchy noises.

'Oh God, I'm sorry about the fanny farts,' I say.

'They happen,' says H. 'I like to think of them as appreciative.'

'I fanny-farted all through our first shag, so you can't say you weren't warned.'

'I remember it well,' he says, and laughs, and then looks down. 'Oh God, blood!'

It looks like the operation has made no difference at all.

ometimes I feel like I have the spines of a hedgehog. They are a spiky barrier I just can't retract.

I thought I'd managed to lower them a little over the last few months, or at least to thin them out. But then, this week, there they were again: abrupt, prickly, impenetrable.

I've had a weird, frustrated, angry week. Nothing in particular has happened, but it's hot, I'm insanely busy at work and not everyone's being co-operative. But more than that, I feel as though my body's drawn in on itself. Everything feels and smells wrong. Quite often, just the sound of the radio has been too much for me. If Herbert has tried to talk to me at the same time that it's on, I've barked at him. I can't bear to be touched. I feel like my skin is too thin.

Twice this week I've rushed out of bed in the middle of the night, convinced I've felt a glut of blood surge out over my legs. Twice I've realised I was only dreaming. The mind is slow to catch up with the body. Mine, it seems, is fearfully protective of it.

I'm a meditator, and I know that these phases are necessary. Meditation is like the slow action of water on rock. Gradually, it wears through layers and layers of sediment, and every now and then something unknown is exposed to the light, a deposit of ancient bones. These too are eased away in time, but they must be revealed to be soothed away. Over the years, I've learned how my body holds an imprint of my fears, a physical defence against them that over the years becomes an immovable ache.

This morning, for example, I went to yoga class, only the second one since my gynaecological problems made me give up. Once, I could fold myself in half like a deckchair, not because of my yogi prowess, but because I had double-jointed hips. Today, I was shocked to discover that I couldn't bend at all, that my pelvic girdle had tightened itself into a rigid knot. Once I'd got over the flush of humiliation (a seventy-year-old woman was performing a perfect forward bend next to me), I saw just how much I've been imagining my body as a fragile thing in need of protection. I have been curled inwards like that hedgehog, and even the parts of my body that I can't command have joined in.

But even realising this, what do I do with the information? It is one thing to understand that my body has rolled up to protect itself, but how can I make it unfurl?

Seduction #23
Game On.

I am, by nature, a competitive soul. It took me years to work this out, largely because I'm rubbish at sport. However, after I left school, I realised that you can be competitive without running around, and since then I have become frankly terrifying in the face of any given challenge. I can squeeze a win out of most situations. You should see me at the width restriction at the bottom of our road.

This is relevant because Herbert's seduction this week is a sex board game. We bought this months ago, during our trip to Brighton, and it has been languishing in our wardrobe for a long time, mainly because I have been avoiding it like the proverbial plague. Don't ask me why; I couldn't articulate a reason. It just feels a bit 'spicing it up' to me.

Herbert, however, is keen, and did not get where he is today without a fair amount of low cunning. His masterstroke is to give me a choice of two seductions I don't much fancy: 'The board game or the cat costume.' This is the kind of non-choice I have seen particularly canny parents offer to recalcitrant toddlers ('You eat the spinach or you go and sit in the pushchair'). I choose the board game.

The particular item in question is called Lust. It requires that we move our counter along a series of coloured footprints, leading us to pick up a card that suggests something romantic or erotic to do as foreplay. If we do these things to our partner's satisfaction, we are rewarded with lovemaking cards that build into a 'love-making experience' (i.e. a shag) at the end of the game.

Me: 'So, we see who makes the best love-making experience, and that person wins.'

H: 'No. We co-operate to decide on one love-making experience.'

'What's the point in that?'

'It's nice. You're working together.'

'They can't really call it a game, though, can they?'

Herbert ignores me, and manfully proceeds to lay out the pieces. He has come to expect this behaviour.

My first foreplay card tells me to serenade H with a romantic song. For some reason, I find this utterly impossible. I am crippled with fear and embarrassment. 'I just can't think of anything appropriate,' I say.

'Sing anything, it doesn't matter.'

'But I've got "Fight the Power" going round and round in my head.'

'You're right. That's not appropriate.'

My main concern about Lust is that it will pull its punches and refrain from telling you to actually have sex. I am wrong. The first love-making card I pull out of the pack is 'The Turtle' (kind of like the missionary position, but with my legs hooked over his arms); the second is 'Light S&M'. Suddenly, I am faced with the proposition that Lust may not be quite lame enough for me. I am, in truth, still bleeding slightly from last week's seduction, and I am also recovering from a bout of cystitis. I was rather invested in penetrative sex not being on the cards.

I do not say this to Herbert; there is, after all, a win at stake here. I quite like Lust, despite myself. The erotic challenges it suggests are genuine ones – at one point, I have to get into character as a nurse and give H a bed-bath – and it seems to be aimed at couples like us who have been together for a while, with its emphasis on reminiscing together. H actively loves it. He is immune to the more soppy challenges (he wholeheartedly acts out Romeo being reunited with Juliet after a long separation, while I giggle and cringe in horror). I actually find it really touching that he so readily carries out each task with such sincerity, but then he always is a stickler for the rules. H secretly likes doing as he's told. Me, I'll resist authority even if it's in my best interests. 'Fight the Power' could probably be my anthem.

There are a couple of minor skirmishes along the way. The first comes when I let Bob the cat in the room (I cannot lick the backs of Herbert's knees as requested if I am distracted by meowing), which inevitably means that Bob jumps straight on to the bed, picks up the die in her mouth and runs away with it. I try to convince H that (a) this is hilarious and (b) at least we now know where all our dice go, but he's not happy. It is apparently My Fault and I am Not Concentrating. I retrieve the die, run it under the tap and we continue.

The second skirmish arises when I am requested to

look deeply into H's eyes and kiss him. I still maintain that this isn't a commandment to keep my eyes open during the kiss. Open-eyed snogging is weird and should probably be officially discouraged in *Debrett's*. H tries to deny me a love-making card because of this infraction. I possibly become ill-tempered; I couldn't possibly say. But the love-making card is awarded.

Overall, we have fun, and I become slightly less grumpy as the evening progresses. My highlight: H positioning himself over my knee for a spanking (we couldn't think of anything else to do with that 'Light S&M' card) and squealing, 'I can't bear it! It's the anticipation!' with his hands clasped over his head.

Before that, though, there is a moment that makes my heart wrench. I draw a card that asks me to tell H the ways in which he's become more beautiful since we met. Before I can even open my mouth, he says, 'Oh, well, you won't have anything to say there then,' and almost physically retreats.

'Herbert,' I say, 'you are far more beautiful to me than when we met because you've grown into your own skin. You're comfortable and assured. You know who you are. I love the way you smell. And your face is like home to me.'

Seduction #24
Sure Likes to Ball

Not for the first time, I am wondering what the neighbours must think. It is a muggy Sunday morning, all the windows are open, and I am emitting a noise that's a mixture of screaming and hysterical laughter. It's not the sort of noise that you would make, for example, if you were watching something funny on TV, or if your partner had cracked a joke. It is roughly the sort of noise a four-year-old might make when dangled upside down by the legs. Or, in my case, the sound a thirty-three-year-old woman might make when her partner is performing cunnilingus on her while she attempts to balance face down on a Fitball.

I am not good at surrendering control. A few minutes earlier, H was showing me how it was done by resting serenely back against the ball while I licked his penis. Nice, comfortable, calm. Now I am gurgling and flailing and occasionally kicking my legs, between bouts of maniacal laughter.

'Are you okay?' says H, keeping hold of my thighs so I don't topple over altogether. 'I mean, you are actually enjoying this, aren't you?'

My response could be accurately summarised as: 'Gaaah, prrrt, argh – yes! Waaah, squeeee – I'm gonna fall off! Eeeee!'

'It's perfectly safe,' says H. 'I won't let you go.' This is all very well for him to say; I am having to endure the disconcerting sight of the floor rolling back and forth as he adjusts the ball to get a better angle. Meanwhile, so much blood has rushed to my head that I feel like my cheeks might explode. The nearest I have ever come to this before was when I was fourteen and my friends and I decided to spend a happy summer afternoon sniffing a bottle of amyl nitrate in the allotments behind my school. Then, I was sick. Now –

'Eurgggh, seasick!'

Herbert places my feet down on the floor, and I roll on to my knees. He's not taking any chances. I managed to be sick after taking the bus home last week. I have a very tenuous sense of equilibrium.

'God, you're ever so red in the face,' says H.

The room is spinning. 'Dizzy!' I giggle. I am quite out of breath, and I can feel my non-existent stomach muscles smarting after a rare bout of engagement.

'Your turn,' I say.

Herbert sits on the Fitball, and I climb on top of him. This is rather like having sex on a Space Hopper, although far bouncier, and without anything to hold on to. The challenge is that each bounce is bigger than the last one, which means that I bounce off H entirely after every sixth thrust. He's beginning to look nervous.

'What happens if this thing bursts?' he says, steadying himself on the wall.

'It's burst-proof,' I say, clutching on to his shoulders for purchase. 'It'll deflate slowly.'

We bounce along for a few seconds more. Kissing is impossible, as there's a distinct risk of knocking each other's teeth out. This is more like an aerobic workout than an act of intimacy.

'I think it's getting flatter!'

We stand up and check; it's still fully pumped up. 'Nope,' I say, 'it's fine. You're just paranoid.'

However, at this point it emerges that H cannot get an erection and sit on the Fitball at the same time. I am initially inclined to suggest that this is due to the male incapacity to multitask, but, on reflection, I think it might be an inability to get an erection whilst doing something dangerous.

Bravo, evolution: another entirely sensible adaptation. We retire to bed, and finish our seduction in a more traditional (and safe) manner.

July

Herbert and I go to see *Hair* in the West End. Watching the holy cows of 60s youth rebellion – free love, nudity, marijuana, dropping out – arrayed before me, I can't help but smile to myself. Far from the challenging text of forty years ago, *Hair* now seems like a period piece, its values naive and newly formed, its tenets of rebellion now mostly taken for granted.

Yet as the finale comes around and the audience are invited to dance on the stage, I feel myself freeze in my seat. H is straight up there; I have photos of him waving his arms in the air as he merges with the crowd. But for me, no way. It sets me off on a spiral of thoughts: I couldn't get up on stage and dance because I'd be too self-conscious; and I certainly couldn't have stripped naked, as the cast had earlier, low lighting or no.

It makes me think about a summer holiday I took with my mother when I was six, when she, newly divorced, spent the entire fortnight in nothing but a pair of turquoise knickers, turning herself a deep brown. Going topless is perhaps out of fashion now, but I've never ventured out in so much as a bikini. I even ensure my swimsuits have little hotpant legs.

What makes me so inhibited? My mother and her generation had to fight to shake off the bodily shame that was instilled in them, and yet here am I, appalled at the sight of my own flesh, without the excuse of an oppressive parent or a disapproving society. The same goes for sex:

why do I feel like I have to fight to understand my own erotic motivations, when I have never lacked the permission from those around me?

I say this to Herbert afterwards, as we sit in a bar behind Carnaby Street drinking Mojitos. 'I feel like I've hit a wall. We've got so far with the seductions, and the sex is vastly improved, but I'm plateauing. I'm looking for safe things to do rather than challenging myself. There's a wall of inhibition there that's almost tangible.'

H smirks. 'So you're enjoying it. It's fine then, isn't it? Who says it has to be challenging?'

'It's not that it has to be challenging. I can just feel this barrier there. I don't even know what's on the other side of it. It's not like there's something I want to do, but I can't bring myself to do it. It's just that I'm not abandoning myself to it, quite. I'm still over-thinking everything.'

He's sympathetic, but I can tell he doesn't really get it. H doesn't have inhibitions; he's pretty much game to try anything. But for me, there's a protection-impulse that's always there, an urge to roll into that safe hedgehog-ball rather than expose myself to anything new. This applies to dancing as much as it applies to sex; I was always the kid who wouldn't ride rollercoasters or go down the highest slide. It's a heady mixture of physical fear and projected shame. More than that, it's completely inscrutable. I don't know what I'm afraid of, but I do know that there's this looming presence of inhibition there, which I bounce off whenever I try to let go.

I change tack. 'Okay, let's put it this way,' I say. 'We're nearly halfway through the seductions. When they're all over, and there's no structure that we're working to, what do you think will happen then? Will we keep having sex, and will we keep doing interesting things?'

He thinks for a while. 'I don't know,' he says. 'I mean, I've enjoyed the seductions, but I still don't feel like I'm quite there. I couldn't honestly say that I'll be hounding you for sex once they're over.'

There. Exactly. My inhibition and Herbert's lack of desire: they're cut from the same cloth. They are, for both of us, unquestionably there. They are an edifice to us, a mystifying force field that we can't quite cross. Yet we know instinctively that there's something on the other side – for me, the ability to access abandon; for H, a sense of desire that pulls him forwards without the need for conscious reasoning.

There is still something in both of us that is exercising restraint against our will. And I can't seem to decide that I don't want it any more. I feel like I need someone to help me through.

A few days later, Herbert suggests a tantric sex seduction. I am not against this on principle, but neither of us really knows what it is, let alone how we might go about it. I dawdle through a few websites looking for a decent workshop, but everything I come across makes me cringe. There is an alarming amount of pseudo-spiritual jargon, and an even more worrying number of references to dancing. I do not dance. Worse, a couple of the sites I find make it clear that this is for heterosexual couples only. I may be one half of a straight couple, but I have no desire to work with organisations that see this as the only valid configuration.

Thinking that I can maybe work out something for myself, I turn to Amazon, where I come across Barbara Carrellas' book *Urban Tantra*. Hallelujah! This isn't just what I want from tantra: it's what I want from sex itself. A kind of boundless, comfortable joy oozes from every page the woman writes. I recognise immediately that this is the state I am longing for. Hunting through her website, I'm initially disappointed to see that she's based in New York. But I email her, tell her our story, and ask if she'll consider coaching me over Skype for a while.

She agrees, but says she can't start until she's back from Berlin, where she's teaching at a sex festival called Xplore. And for some reason that I can't quite account for, I find myself buying tickets for me and Herbert and booking us both on to a plane to Berlin.

Ha! I spit at myself. *You may be inhibited, but no one can say you're not spontaneous.*

Seduction #25
Going Digital

On Saturday night, I am in the pub with some friends. We are sitting around a table drinking wine and generally casting aspersions on mutual acquaintances. Unusually, I am not giving this my full attention. I am instead wondering how to turn the conversation to anuses. It is probably for the best that I am not quite drunk enough to start this particular discussion. But it is also a shame, because I could do with a bit of moral support.

There is a seduction looming, you see, and I'm already worrying about it. Tomorrow afternoon, I have promised – and there's no romantic way of putting this – to stick my finger up Herbert's bottom. I suspect, really, that this sort of thing is not to be discussed and over-thought; it is just to be done in a fit of passion, and thereafter to be allowed to either fall into one's erotic repertoire or not, depending on the response. But, you see, having got fifteen years into our relationship without crossing this particular boundary (although he's done it to me), it feels like it merits a bit more fanfare.

I have already mooted it with H and he's sunnily agreed. Curses! I was rather hoping he'd refuse. But no. Herbert has heard that lots of gentlemen rather like a spot of prostate play, and so it remains for me to battle past my own gag reflex in order to carry this out.

In acknowledgement that not everyone is quite like me, I should perhaps explain here that I suffer from an obsession with hygiene which, depending on your perspective, is either cripplingly oppressive (Herbert) or perfectly rational (me). I just don't like dirty things, and the inside of someone's rectum must surely merit a place on this list (other things include camping, feet and dogs). I am a bit of a handwasher. I also have a hauntingly sharp sense of smell, which I fear to activate. These things make prostate play (who ever thought this was an appealing term?) a distinctly horrifying idea.

Come the appointed hour, H is sensing my discomfort. 'You can use the rubber gloves if it would make you feel better,' he helpfully suggests.

'I don't think I could bear to watch the cleaner put them on after that,' I say. 'And besides, that seems like a different seduction entirely.' No, I must be grown-up about this. I pour myself a glass of wine, despite it only being five o'clock.

We undress and lie on the bed. 'I just need a few minutes to get in the mindset,' I say.

'It's *my* bum!' says H. 'I'm the one who should be worried.'

I gulp my wine.

'Anyway,' he says, 'I've made sure it's extra clean for you.'

I don't ask what this entails. 'How shall we manage this

then?' I ask. 'Shall I just go in there, or would you like a blow job at the same time?'

H, predictably, opts for the simultaneous blow job. At least this gives me a starting point. It also means I don't actually have to look. I lube up a finger, and slide on in.

Now, I've been reading up about this. Apparently, I'm supposed to seek out his prostate gland, which is about a (convenient) finger's length inside his rectum, and is slightly raised. I'm damned if I can feel anything. I hunt around carefully, but I can sense no variation, just a lot of yielding flesh. It's not nearly as unpleasant as I'd feared. I realise, though, that I'm probably supposed to move my finger in and out a bit more, rather than simply seeking the elusive prostate.

'Um,' I hear H say from above me, 'would you mind just keeping still for a while so I can get used to it?'

'Oh, sorry,' I say. I'd sort of forgotten to check if he was enjoying it. 'What do you think?'

'Well, it feels a bit medical at the moment.' He's nothing if not sharp, my H. He's accurately discerned that I'm examining him. 'The outside feels nice, but the inside just feels a bit . . .' he tails off.

'Oh,' I say again, and withdraw my finger.

'I'm not *not* enjoying it,' he says. 'I mean, I've still got an erection.'

'I was half expecting it to shrivel as soon as I started, so I'm quite impressed.'

'Yes,' says H, 'me too, actually. It will shrivel if you keep talking about it, though.'

Right. I keep forgetting that talking about Herbert's penis makes it go limp. 'How about I stick to the outside?' I suggest, and begin to rub my finger gently around the pucker of his anus.

'Mmm, that's nicer,' he says. I return to the blow job. But I notice, after a while, that he seems to be enjoying it less than normal; he's watching me quietly, without making any of the little sighs of pleasure that he usually emits at such times.

'I'm not convinced this is really doing it for you,' I say. 'It's okay.'

'Well, if it's only okay, can I please go and wash my hands?'

Nice clean hands. I feel much better when I return to bed. H is deep in thought. 'I read somewhere that men don't like it when you talk to them about that sort of thing. They like it but don't want to admit it.'

'No, Herbert,' I say, 'you didn't read that. You saw it happen in *Sex and the City*.'

He smirks. 'That's where I get all my best information.'

'But, in general, I don't think you've got a particularly sensitive prostate.' I manage to omit the 'thank God' from the end of this sentence.

'Maybe not, no. But I tell you what: I quite like the idea of you rimming me.'

I stare at him in horror. 'Okay,' he says, 'not to worry. That might be a step too far for you.'

I stutter for a few moments, trying to think of a scenario in which I would merrily lick someone's anus. 'No way,' I say. 'I mean, I'm trying to be more open-minded these days, but: no.'

At that thought, I wonder if I might be able to sneak out and wash my hands again.

A year ago, Herbert and I had our second wedding. Not that we got divorced in the middle or anything. Rather, the first wedding was so piffling that we needed to redress the balance.

The first one was a highly secretive affair. We just didn't feel like we could trust our families not to ruin it for us. The very thought of all four of our parents in a room together, with their new partners in tow, filled us with trepidation. The only way we could have profited from it would have been to organise a sweepstake on who would fight first. Not an appealing option.

Of course, once you've decided to exclude your parents from the wedding plans, it's hard to justify inviting anyone else. We told only my best friend and her partner, and then, in a last-minute guilty spasm, my cousin. It took eight weeks from start to finish to arrange, the earliest date we could get. In my desperation to unburden myself of all the fizzing thoughts that a wedding brought, I took to confiding in hairdressers and beauty-counter assistants, anyone who would stand still long enough to listen.

In the event, it was uneventful. I felt silly reading out my vows to a nearly empty room, my two female guests dutifully snuffling behind me. I said 'I do' instead of 'I will' and giggled every time H spoke. I cracked an inappropriate joke about Princess Diana while I was signing the register. I also spent the day wondering why my stockings were falling down, only to discover at bedtime that they were not the hold-up variety.

After that, we slunk off on honeymoon to Devon, and informed everyone of our news by postcard. Some took it better than others. Most people, I think, were delighted for us. For my father, it was the last straw. We haven't spoken since.

As our tenth anniversary drew nearer, all that uncertainty seemed very far away. Perhaps, if I'm honest, we felt as though we'd earned our stripes. We got married a week after I left university, and both of us knew that it was a grand gesture and that life would change in ways we didn't yet understand. Our small wedding reflected the fact that we felt small too, and more than a little anxious about whether we could stick together into adulthood. In truth, there were times in our first decade when being married kept us from drifting apart. It was a reminder that we'd made a happy commitment in easier times. It forced us to find ways through problems.

With ten years under our belts, I wanted an opportunity to celebrate. I had always regretted missing my chance to pull all our friends into one room and eat, drink and dance. I never wanted the white dress or to be a princess for a day; I just wanted a knees-up, a chance to gather my world around me. As we began to plan a party, we realised that it wasn't a renewal of our vows so much as the wedding we should always have had, slightly delayed.

The invitations said Delayed Wedding, which baffled some and tickled others. We booked out a restaurant on the beach where we live, and I even had a frock made, a kind of 50s prom dress in an African print. We began our day with a cream tea and a short ceremony in the loft of the restaurant. One friend decorated the place with yards of newspaper birds and balloons; others read poems and gave speeches. After that, there was champagne and paddling in the sea.

As the evening came, more guests arrived. We laid out a wonderful Moroccan buffet cooked by a friend who is usually an archaeologist. She spent the evening fielding enquiries about catering future events and politely pointing out that she had a perfectly good job at the British Museum. We'd booked a band who arrived dressed as characters from *Joe 90*; later, Herbert DJ-ed. Everybody danced, even me. There was an outbreak of spontaneous skinny-dipping. At midnight, we let off sky lanterns and watched them slowly drift along the coast.

Even taking into account the monster hangover I acquired (I'd been so over-excited that I'd entirely forgotten to eat any of that marvellous food), it was a perfect, perfect day. But the best of it was this: after everyone had gone home, and long after we should have been in bed, Herbert and I walked down to the beach. We were wired and exhausted. There was not a soul in sight. Down by the water's edge, it was dark and silent. We stripped off our clothes and waded in naked. Well, I did; H only got ankle-deep before calling me back to him. We kissed standing in the water with the sound of a nightclub further up the coast pulsing around us. Then we made love on the darkest part of the beach. We forgot to consummate our marriage the first time around; this time, we made it memorable.

Seduction #26
Love Buzz

Well. After the last seduction, we are both distinctly in need of something that might actually be enjoyable. Fortunately, I am ready for this eventuality. I have, nestling happily in my knicker drawer, a brand-new Lelo vibrator.

I have an unpromising history with vibrators. The first one I came across was my mother's, when I was seven. We were living with my grandparents at the time, post-divorce, and she was clearly concerned that my grandma would find it. For reasons best known to herself, she decided to wrap it in tinfoil and stash it in the glove compartment of the car. You can only imagine my surprise: I thought I'd found a baguette. Mum hurriedly wrapped it back up and we spoke no more of it.

The second was in Herbert's house when I first met him. It actually came in a dusty briefcase, with a range of attachments arrayed for you to choose. All of them looked grim. One of them was called Anal Intruder. I made him get rid of it, particularly seeing as he couldn't remember how he'd acquired it in the first place. See Seduction #25 for notes on my hygiene concerns.

Later in our relationship, I bought myself a Rampant Rabbit from Ann Summers, as was the fashion at the time. It was candy-pink and wobbly, smelled strongly of chemicals and had a dangling battery pack that the sales assistant assured me was a vast improvement on the old plug-in kind. I doubt this was true; the Rabbit was prone to cutting out at key moments. What I hated the most about it was the way it sought to dominate your whole experience, with those silly whiffling ears that never quite met my clitoris, and the perpetually churning balls which felt as though someone was rummaging around inside me. I probably used it twice, and then threw it out. It struck me as a more inconvenient form of masturbation.

So what on earth possessed me to buy a new one? Well, I hadn't really planned to. But I came face to face with this one in a shop last week, and something about it spoke to me. It looked solid, refined and elegant, with its clean lines and iPod styling. It didn't smell funny (yes, I did sniff it). More than that, the shape looked really appealing somehow: not too big, but curvy and intriguing. In all frankness, I just quite fancied the idea of using it. Which, given the above history, is saying something.

We try it first on Herbert, letting it vibrate on his nipples, penis, balls, perineum . . . He begins to look alarmed. Nice enough, is his conclusion, but not something he'd bother to use on his own. We try it on me. I confess that I like the sensation of the bulbous end going in and out of me, but I am generally left a little bit unmoved. It's okay, but nothing special.

But then H makes a suggestion. 'Let's see if it makes doggy-style any better for you.' Doggy-style is something that H is very enthusiastic about, and I don't entirely mind it, but it really does require me to abandon all hope of having an orgasm. Also, we always seem to position ourselves in such a way that my head repeatedly bangs against something. I realise that this isn't native to the position itself, but rather it is native to our general incompetence. Even so, it wouldn't be my first choice.

However, today I kneel at the end of the bed, set the Lelo to pulse and clutch it against my clitoris. 'Ooh,' says H, 'I can feel the vibrations running through you.' It's quite pleasant. I turn it up a bit higher and put it on to a more consistent buzz. Better still. Then, by accident, my hand slips slightly and I find myself holding it lower down, where it rests against Herbert's penis. H groans and I – well, I blush to say this, but I start making entirely involuntary squeaking sounds, such as I have never heard emerging from my mouth before. I keep trying to stop making them, but I can't. The sensation is extraordinarily intense, and I feel slightly out of control. I want it to stop, but I don't want it to ever stop. I bury my face in the duvet, hoping that the neighbours can't hear me.

Oddly, I don't have an orgasm to speak of (although this may be an issue of timing – H not unreasonably interprets my weird squealing as a climax, and so opens the floodgates himself), but the whole thing feels orgasmic, and just a little bit – whisper it – uninhibited.

It is only afterwards that I do the maths and realise that this is Seduction #26, the halfway mark.

'Not bad,' I say.

'Oh God,' H replies, 'you mean we've still got to think of another twenty-six?'

ow many people does it take to make a marriage? Well, you can vary your answer according to the time or society you live in, but that's not what I'm getting at. Here and now, in the western world, the answer is legally two. Ideologically, though, it's a different story. Often, we're striving for one.

The propaganda of the modern marriage is absolute. We're no longer two people choosing to spend a life together. We are instead supposed to become each other. This is the beautiful, blissful ideal, a sign that we're fully compatible. We want to be so similar that we blend into each other, like a fuzzy still life done with pastels.

This was what I always strove for too. This was what I have been proud of all my marriage. Suddenly, though, I see it as something I must rage against.

On the evening of our eleventh wedding anniversary, Herbert and I sit in a restaurant together. I chat about this and that, how quickly the wine goes lukewarm in this weather, how good the chips are. 'Eleven years,' I keep saying. Eleven years! There is an increasing desperation in my voice. I realise I am holding up the conversation on my own. Herbert's eyes are darting all over the room; he has sunk into a private reverie. This is often the case with H, but tonight it is infuriating.

'For fuck's sake,' I say. 'You could at least pay attention. Tonight, of all nights, I think communicating with me is on the agenda.'

'Sorry,' says H. 'You're right. Sometimes I forget you're a separate person.'

This is a shortened version of a somewhat longer and more heated discussion, but you get the picture. It's not even that he's complacent. It's just that our boundaries are so blurred that there's not enough to say.

Maybe this is the natural fate of the childless couple. Without the addition of small people, we run out of things to talk about. Perhaps this merger is necessary for parenting, structuring a bond of sympathy between you that can weather the inevitable neglect of each other's needs. But when there's two of you alone, that bond feels almost deathly sometimes. It feels like a status quo that has been attained, which can therefore be left to coast.

It is this extreme closeness that makes sex difficult. How can a merged couple offer each other new mysteries? Or, to put it another way, how can we bear to admit new passions and desires to the person who is supposed to know our soul inside out? It would feel like a betrayal. In our bid for togetherness, we smother newness.

When I think of it, this muddling together has made me put up barriers. Perhaps consciously, perhaps not, I have gradually identified all the things that I believe make me acceptable to Herbert and drawn them to the surface. Meanwhile, the wilder, less predictable part of me has refused to go away. She's still there, but I've grown a skin around her, a hard pelt that I can no longer get through. It reminds me of the scar on my elbow where a stone got trapped when I was nine years old. It's still there, vaguely black under the skin, but picking it out now would be agonising.

That's exactly what I've been doing this year, picking at the stone in my elbow and wondering why it's so difficult to get it out. I used to think that love was an either/ or: either nurturing and supportive, or passionate, risky and chaotic. I sensibly opted for the former. Now I think I can have the best of both worlds. I can have a husband who is my lover, who excites and surprises me, but whom I can also trust to take care of me if the need arises. I can trust him with both of those things because I can trust myself with them too.

So, the most romantic gesture I can make to Herbert now is to separate myself from him, just a little bit. I must learn that some things are none of my business. Many nights I find myself checking that he's brushed his teeth. I must stop trying to bring him up like a fussy mother hen. I must learn to be alone a little more, to stop trying to impose a consensus on what we do.

Because then, when we are together, we will be able to enjoy the newness of each other's company.

Seduction #27
Potty Mouth

Herbert has cooked dinner, washed up and is now folding washing around me while I stand, dazed, in the kitchen. I am not entirely sure from whence this burst of domestic enthusiasm came, but I like it. Not enough to join in, you understand, but it makes a very good spectator sport.

The laundry basket neatly loaded, he says, 'You'd better pour yourself a G&T for tonight's seduction,' and then skips upstairs to take a shower.

I am nothing if not obedient, particularly where Bombay Sapphire is concerned. I gulp at my gin, and wonder what on earth he's got planned.

He comes downstairs smelling freshly of mint shampoo and takes my glass. 'Not finished yet? You're going to need more than one.'

I sigh. 'Come on. What is it then?'

'Dirty talk.'

'Oh God, Herbert,' I say, 'that's my worst nightmare.'

'You just need enough gin.'

'I already did phone sex. What's the difference?'

He looks at me as if I'm a child worrying about going to school. 'You didn't really do much dirty talking then, did you?'

'No,' I say, 'you're quite right. I skipped to the heavy breathing as fast as I could.'

'And before that you took photos.'

'Yes.'

'Anyway, this time you have to look me in the eye.'

'Oh God.'

Up in the bedroom, he's wasting no time. As soon as I take my knickers off, he attaches his mouth to my groin in a manner that I believe is supposed to signify enthusiasm. It's as if he thinks he can surprise me into spontaneously talking dirty. Unlikely.

'How does that feel?' he asks, muffled.

'Lovely,' I say quite honestly. I lie back and close my eyes for a few seconds, and then realise I'm not really allowed to just enjoy this. 'I suppose "lovely" wasn't what you were looking for?'

'Nope.'

What am I supposed to do, offer a commentary? 'But I don't want to talk about it; I just want to feel it. I use words all day. This is different. It's nice to communicate in a different way.'

A pause from H. 'So you're basically going to boycott this then?'

Boycott is such a strong word. 'No,' I say, 'I suppose not.' I try to think of something – anything – to say, but I don't seem to have any words at all. 'Can't you start?'

It is at these moments that I most admire H. He steps

right up to the podium. He really has no shame. 'Okay,' he says brightly. 'I love the feeling of your smooth, wet pussy on my tongue.'

'Ew,' I say, 'I hate the word pussy. It makes me think of my mum. Don't know why.'

He ignores me. 'I've got such a great view from here. I'm fantasising about slipping my cock inside you.'

'Okay, go on then,' I say. He rolls his eyes. This would become his special superpower if he were ever struck by a radioactive ray.

'I can feel your clit getting harder under my tongue.'

'Where do you get this stuff from?'

'I love being down here when you come. I can see your cunt and your arsehole twitch. It's gorgeous.'

'I'm not sure I wanted to know that. Do they really do that?'

'Your turn. Come on.'

'Um . . .'

'What are you thinking?'

'Your hair looks big and bouffy from this angle.'

'Your fanny lips look big and bouffy.'

'In girl-world, H, that's not considered a compliment.'

He grins. He really is the most extraordinarily patient man. I am hurling every bit of resistance I have at him, and he's batting it away like smoke. 'What do you want to do next?' he asks.

Is that a trick question? I want to be allowed to have an orgasm in peace. 'I want to suck your cock,' I say, reluctantly.

He happily flips on to his back.

'Ooh,' he says in a somewhat camp tone, 'lovely. I love how intense it feels. I can't even describe how good it is.'

'I love feeling you get harder and harder,' I say, warming

to my theme. 'And I love looking up at your face and seeing you all blissed out with your eyes closed.'

'Do you know what I love?' Someone stop this man talking. 'I love it when we're fucking, and we're both completely absorbed in it, like we've forgotten who we are.'

I can't help but smile. 'Yes, I love that too.'

'Sometimes I almost wake up in the middle of it and realise I've lost myself for a while.'

'We've managed to turn our brains off,' I say between mouthfuls.

'Yes, we've stopped over-thinking and we've both fallen silent.'

'See?' I say. 'Silent. Silent is good.'

The assembled ladies in the waiting room are considering an uprising. We have just been told that the colposcopy clinic is running forty-five minutes behind schedule. I, for one, know that this is an understatement. I have been waiting for forty minutes already, and there is someone else ahead of me in the queue. She is so cross that she is emitting little squeaks that I think are supposed to signify her dissatisfaction.

'It's like this every time,' she says, alternately catching my eye and the nurse's. We both try to make sympathetic expressions, but, yes, it is like this every time. The miracle is that she expected it to be any different, and that she didn't think to bring a book. In my recent experience, it seems to be NHS policy to have you sitting around waiting for a consultant to grace you with their regal presence. Your time is there to be sacrificed. If you make too much fuss, they have the ultimate disciplinary sanction at their disposal: the next appointment they can offer you is in six weeks.

'It's alright at the Wednesday clinic,' says the nurse with impressive calmness, 'because that starts at eleven. Monday's starts at nine, and he—' she flicks her head resentfully towards the consultant's office '—doesn't see fit to arrive until nine-thirty.' We all tut. 'Also,' she adds, gaining resentful momentum, 'he books all his appointments in fifteen-minute slots, regardless of what needs doing. Some mornings, we get more and more behind, and others, everyone's in and out so quick we're sitting around.'

'Well, I'll be bloody quick, you watch me,' says the cross woman. She is not. She is, by my count, in there for twenty minutes. I have finished my book and am chatting to the receptionist about her birthday party by the time it's my turn.

The gynaecologist starts our conversation as is his

custom – vague, paternal chuckling, through which no actual words are discernible until he reaches his destination: 'How are things down there?'

'I'm not convinced they're much different,' I say. 'I'm still getting spotting after sex, sometimes heavy bleeding. And I'm still in pain afterwards.'

He is busy gazing over my notes, within which I can see lurid pink photographs of what I take to be my cervix. 'But generally better though?'

'No, I don't think so.'

He looks up, a slightly disgruntled expression on his face. 'Have you had any histology results back?'

'No,' I say, 'have you?'

He goes rifling through the file again, finds nothing, and then turns to his computer and enters my name into a database. 'There,' he says, 'all clear.'

'Well, that's good.'

He shrugs. 'When was your last period?'

'Ages ago. Um, last November. When I went on the Pill.'

'The Pill? But you've got a coil in. Why are you using both?'

'Because you told me to.'

He looks a little startled. 'I don't have your case nurse with me today,' he says. 'You'll need to explain.'

'The coil didn't stop the awful menstrual symptoms I was having, so we tried the Pill as well,' I say, thinking: *I don't have a case nurse.*

He sighs. 'Well, we need to consider whether you're suffering from a mixture of hormonal and physical conditions.'

'I am. We already agreed that. Months ago.'

More rifling through the file. 'Perhaps you need to stop taking the Pill.'

'No,' I say, 'I'd rather have the coil taken out. It's the Pill that seems to work.'

He ignores me. 'We'd better have a look then.'

On the ceiling of the colposcopy suite, they have plastered a poster of humorous movie quotes so that you can pretend you aren't there. They also lay on a charming nurse to distract you from the alarming moment when a close-up of your vulva appears on the screen beside you, before they insert the speculum. Fame at last.

My cervix looks like it's made of the same pink flesh as the inside of my mouth. The hole in the middle isn't a perfect circle, but rather a crescent shape. It looks like it's smiling at me drunkenly. I say this to the doctor and he replies, with great discomfort, 'All completely normal, I assure you.'

Below the smile and a little to the left is a darker-red patch of flesh. I watch as the gynaecologist prods it with a cotton bud; a bubble of blood immediately gathers itself from no discernible wound and dribbles across the rosy flesh.

'Do you mind if I take another biopsy?' he says.

As I'm getting dressed, the nurse hands me a pantyliner with 'aloe and avocado' written on the peel-off strip. 'Blimey,' I say, 'these are a bit posh for the NHS, aren't they? It's usually one of those big mattresses.'

'Yup,' she says, 'I've started buying them myself in Lidl. Much nicer.'

'That is really, really thoughtful of you,' I say, strangely moved by this little gesture of humanity. 'Thanks.'

Herbert gets home that evening just as I'm getting in the shower. He puts his head round the door briefly to say hello, and then re-emerges a minute later with no clothes on.

'Oh no,' I say, 'you're out of luck. I've got silver nitrate on my cervix, and unless you fancy a cauterised knob-end, you can make alternative arrangements.'

'Actually,' he says, 'I was just planning to get in after you.'

We chat for a while about my appointment. 'Why do they keep taking biopsies?' says H.

'I dunno. They can't seem to think of anything else.'

'Do they think they missed a bit with the cauterisation? Or that it just didn't work on that particular bit?'

'I don't know,' I say. 'I run out of the will to ask questions after a while.'

'That's your third biopsy, isn't it?'

'Yes. I don't know what makes them think they'll find something this time.'

'It reminds me of my dad,' says H, 'the way they kept taking biopsies and when they finally found something he was nearly dead anyway.'

'Thanks.'

'I don't mean it's the same for you. I just mean that they keep taking them because a negative result doesn't always mean anything.'

'Again, thanks.'

'How long do you have to wait for the result?'

'Six to eight weeks.'

'Jesus.'

That evening, we carry on as normal. We have dinner together, walk down to the seafront to see the sun setting, and then head home. H goes into the study to tinker with his computer for a while, and I read in bed until I fall asleep.

I feel cross with him for leaving me alone, but what else is he supposed to do? On nights like this, no amount of his company would be enough. I want to talk things over until they're smooth and worn; H doesn't have the stomach for it. More than this, I want to absorb him into me somehow, as if he's a lotion, an after-sun for the soul. I know that this is wanting the impossible. A partner can comfort you, but they can only delay the inevitable moment when you will be on your own with all your fears, anxieties and frustrations. Ultimately, you still have to cope with things alone.

I don't know how long I have been asleep when I hear H come into the room. 'You didn't say goodnight,' he says, and curls his body into mine.

I arrive in Berlin with my heart in my throat. Herbert is no better; he has retreated entirely into silence. I would be lying if I didn't admit to having serious reservations about coming here. What seemed like an amusing act of spontaneity a couple of weeks ago now feels deeply intimidating. I am out of my depth. What on earth do people do at sex festivals anyway?

To make it worse, the city itself is charming, full of the sort of bars that make you want to pass an afternoon in their depths and broad pavements that are a pleasure to walk. The food is cheap and the people are friendly. There are a lot of very reasonable arguments for just making this weekend into a holiday.

However, we find ourselves navigating to a warehouse space in the former East and checking in at the front desk. Everyone else looks deeply comfortable to be there; I can hardly persuade my lungs to draw in breath. Smiling young Germans are milling around, greeting old friends and clearly wondering when they can get down to business. Like most of the British nation, I have always assumed that Germans possess a much healthier attitude towards sex than we do; now I know this for sure. My hedgehog spines are standing on end.

We skulk around at the sides of the room, drinking tea, and then make our way to Barbara Carrellas's first workshop. I introduce myself, and she's reassuringly friendly. I think I may cope with this after all. I am, however, worried how Herbert will manage. He finds yoga a bit hippy-dippy for his tastes, so heaven only knows what he'll make of this.

The room is filling up. We sit on the floor and watch people file in. Barbara is playing rhythmic music while we wait, and one couple get up and dance to it, their bodies twisting and writhing together. I catch Herbert's gaze, and he widens his eyes at me as if to say, 'For fuck's sake!' I laugh and stroke his knee, hoping he won't walk out or have a nervous breakdown in the middle of this.

It turns out that the first workshop is easy: we are only required to breathe and maybe do a few pelvic-floor contractions. Herbert throws himself into the exercises with great gusto, and I am once again in deep awe of his ability to try new things without reserve. The overall effect is calming and energising, even though it seems that Germans take the invitation to add sexual noises to their breathing very seriously. There are moments when they groan so loudly that my fight or flight response is activated.

We probably don't engage with the wider festival as much as we should, but then we're not entirely sure where to put ourselves between workshops. In the main space, most of the other guests are quite merrily indulging in their preferred predilections right before our eyes. Frankly, I have never watched anyone else have sex before. There is nothing remotely sleazy about it because there is a total absence of shame or embarrassment in the room, and a total absence of judgement. Given that we are the squarest people at the festival, I am unutterably grateful for this atmosphere of tolerance. We nevertheless slip out for lunch because we don't feel like we're exactly contributing to the atmosphere.

I am worried about Barbara's second workshop of the day. For a start, it's called Kinky Twisted Tantra. Throughout the previous twenty-seven seductions, I think we've all established that I'm neither kinky nor twisted. For seconds, it requires me to bring along a twelve-foot length of rope. If Heathrow airport security have an issue with me carrying an average-sized bottle of shampoo in my hand-luggage, just imagine what they'd make of a rope. Also, where do you buy such things? B&Q?

'I just don't think I have the expertise,' I say to H during lunch. 'I already feel like the lame nerd at the back of the classroom. This can only make it worse.'

'We've come all the way to Berlin,' says H, not unrea-sonably. 'I think we should give it a go.'

'Can't. No rope.'

'We'll sit that bit out if we need to.'

I stare H down for a few moments. 'Why are you so keen to go? You were more worried than me this morning.'

'I've settled down into it. It's fine.'

'You actually fancy this, don't you?'

'No, I'm just being open-minded.'

'If you think it might be your thing, just say so.'

'Nope. That's not it at all.'

'Are you sure?'

'YES.'

Let's cut forward two hours, and you can make your own decision.

We have been working on power exchange in tantra, first of all creating a sense of balance by breathing and rocking together. Then we take it in turns to be in charge of that rocking, whilst our partners cede control of their bodies. I quite enjoy H rocking me back and forth on his lap (once I've got over a fit of giggles caused by the demonic look in his eye), but H hates it in return. He's much heavier than me, and completely rigid. 'Just go floppy,' I tell him, but he can't. In the end, I get him to lie on his back, which is a bad idea in a packed room full of gyrating couples. The woman next to us lands squarely on H's head, and doesn't notice. He looks tense.

Barbara brings the room back to order. 'Next,' she says, 'we're going to play with a little intense sensation.' A pause. 'That's pain, by the way.' A relieved laugh from the Germans. She goes on to describe how the 'receptive' partner can guide what the 'active' partner does, using a traffic-lights system and the words 'more', 'less', 'harder' and 'softer'. The tantric part is that the receptive partner gets time to breathe in the sensation afterwards, to allow the sensations to become more delightful. 'You don't have to be too hardcore about it,' she says. 'For example, if your partner chooses biting, start with something that doesn't leave marks.'

I turn to H. 'Okay, you first. What do you want?'

'Biting,' he says, somewhat predictably. The people around us are removing clothes.

'Okay, give me your arm.'

He obeys, and I give him the merest bite on the forearm. He breathes. 'More,' he says, 'harder.'

I bite again, this time leaving little indents where my teeth have been. 'More, slower, harder.'

I administer a third bite, this one more deliberate. It

feels a bit obscene to be biting into human flesh like this. It's completely unyielding and almost crunchy, like cotton wool. H closes his eyes, breathes, and says, 'That's surprisingly nice. Do you fancy doing it to my nipple?'

I look at him for a few beats. *Fine*, I think. *Fine*. 'Okay, but if you start calling me "Mistress" or anything, I'll fucking kill you.'

He grins and unbuttons his shirt. I am biting someone's nipple in public. If we are doing this, I dread to think what everyone else in the room is up to.

Strangely, it feels less obscene to bite a nipple than to bite an arm. A nipple, after all, is something that's designed to withstand the odd tooth. Even so, it feels horribly fragile between my teeth. 'Harder,' says H.

'Are you sure?'

'Mmm,' he says. I bite harder. He breathes. 'Try pulling it upwards as you do it.' I obey. It seems as though he's really the one in charge. I'm grateful for this. He tips his head back in delight and groans, just as Barbara tells us our time's up.

As she's talking, he buttons up his shirt, leans over, and whispers in my ear, 'I've got the most enormous erection.'

Seduction #28
Baby Tantrikas

Herbert and I are sitting on the bed, attempting to get into the basic tantric sex position of yab-yum. In theory, he should be sitting with his legs outstretched, with me on his lap with my legs around him. We are failing miserably at this first hurdle.

H: 'My back hurts. . . can I just . . . nope, that's still not right . . . ow . . . can you move off a second?'

We pile up cushions behind him and assume the position again. Still not right. He's practically lying down now, but if he makes himself any more upright, I've got nowhere to put my feet.

'Shall we try being cross-legged instead?' I suggest. Nope. H doesn't really do cross-legged. There's no part of him that really bends, to be honest. I suspect I will spend my twilight years picking things up off the floor on his behalf.

'Chairs?'

'But then our chakras won't be lined up.'

'Herbert, you don't believe in chakras.'

'I'm just getting into the spirit of the thing.'

'Let's just start the breathing and see if we stop noticing the discomfort.'

We get back into yab-yum and begin to gaze into each other's eyes. I challenge anyone to do this without giggling, particularly with H, who, I learn, doesn't actually blink.

It feels almost painfully intimate to stare at someone for that long; there's something startling about it that eventually knocks you into seriousness. We synchronise our breaths, dropping into the heart-breathing that we learned at Xplore, sucking in air through our mouths and letting it release with a sigh. Then, once that's in place, we place our left hands on each other's hearts, and our right hands over our partner's. We breathe some more, and then begin to gently rock. At this moment, I must relax another notch, because I let out the most cacophonous fart.

We collapse from yab-yum in hysterics. 'I think this is going to take a bit more practice,' I say. H complains that his feet were going dead anyway.

I try another tack. *Urban Tantra* talks about 'the resilient edge of resistance', meaning that when you touch your partner, you should do so with such consciousness that you can feel the moment your touch is too much for them – too soft or too hard. By aiming to touch on this edge of pleasure and overwhelmedness, rather than comfortably within it, you are enlivening the experience for both of you. I explain this to H, who says, 'A bit like the way you learn to stroke a cat,' and I think that's the perfect analogy.

I try it on him first. 'Talk to me,' I say. 'Tell me what you feel.' I run my hand along his arms first, trying to make my palms and fingers feel alive. 'Too hard,' he says. I go lighter, and lighter still, until I am running the backs of my fingers over him, down his chest and across his stomach. He whimpers. 'Lovely.' I slowly learn how lightly he likes to be touched, and how pleasurable it is to do the touching. We swap, and I find that I like different touches in different places, light over my back, but firm over my thighs so that it's not ticklish. For the first time, I realise that touching is different to massage, aiming to stimulate the skin rather than the muscles.

'Shall we try something a bit harder?' I ask. H smiles. He's been looking forward to this part. I start with the nipple-biting we did in the workshop. Same response; his face falls into blissful calm. When I've finished, I kiss him, and he says, 'Let me try that on you.'

It's surprising how hard he has to bite before I feel anything at all.

'It just feels like a delicate prickle,' I say.

'But I'm worried I'm going to bite the thing off in a minute!'

'I suppose female nipples get bitten a lot.'

'There's me thinking you were just hard-as.'

I'm quite happy to stick with hard-as. But then he suggests spanking me instead. I am not hard-as, it turns out. I can't help but squeal, sincerely, 'Ow!' every time he does it, and I am even more agonised by the wait in-between. 'Are you actually enjoying this?' asks H.

'Um,' I say, 'not sure.'

Seduction #29
Sob Story

I have already mentioned that I've seen Herbert cry about ten times in the whole fifteen years I've known him. He refuses to do it, not through any macho intent, but because he would do anything to avoid being vulnerable. 'Don't take this personally,' he said to me once, 'but I just don't trust anyone else with my emotions like that, including you.'

The rare times I've seen him crying, it's felt so catastrophic – for both of us – that it's immediately shaken us out of whatever row we were locked in at the time. When H cries, it's like watching a building fall down. I can't bear it, and neither can he.

When I'm alone, I often find big, stupid tears running down my face at the merest provocation, be it sad or heart-warming. The newspaper induces tears most mornings, as does the evening news. But when Herbert is around, I censor myself. No newspaper tears for me, nor movie grizzles. I take it as a matter of personal pride to remain dry-eyed in his company. Even in the face of an unbearably sad film, the most either of us will do is a few extra blinks or a sniff, but never enough to require a tissue.

Despite this, H is under the impression that I'm as tearful as a newborn. I suppose it's because I cry when we argue, or when I'm upset. This seems perfectly normal to me, but in relation to him, it's positively lachrymose. I dread to think what he'd make of me if I cried all the other times I wanted to.

Recently, though, H came home and said, 'I had to pull the car over on my way to work this morning, I was crying so much.' He'd been listening to *The Book Thief* on audiobook. This surprised me, not so much that he cried at all, but that he was willing to admit it. Suddenly, it seemed ridiculous to me that we were depriving each other of this act of intimacy. We agreed to abandon sex for the next seduction, and just learn to cry in each other's presence instead.

As a means to achieve this, we choose *Where the Wild Things Are*, Spike Jonze's transformative take on the famous children's book. It's a pristinely sad film, capturing the dislocation and loneliness of being a child. I feel my throat tighten in the first five minutes, when Max's igloo gets kicked down by his sister's friends, and I catch, immediately, the impulse to hold back the tears, even in the darkness. H is lying against me, and I can't help but suppress the reflex for my stomach to jolt. Too much, too soon. 'This is sad already,' I say, and H replies, 'I'm trying not to over-think it.'

Fair enough. He's got more to lose than me. I let him sink quietly into me, and we watch the rest of the film in silence. It makes my mind do funny things, all those allusions to mothers and fathers, and how they can't help but show you their flaws. Max's little robot dance, performed for his mother while she takes a difficult work call, reminds me of being four years old and waiting while my mum talked to my dad on the phone during their divorce, ready to sing every song I knew to make her smile again. When the huge monster Carol smashes up his fort in frustration, I am pulled back to the afternoon when my dad put his face in my lap and sobbed, after wasting one of our rare days together by arguing with his new wife.

By the end of the film, I am convulsed with tears, full of the sense of what it was like to be that lonely, bewildered child again. The adult in me is crying too, feeling a strange, bodily connection between those times and these, that martyred mother and my own childlessness.

H watches me, quiet and serious. 'Did you cry?' I ask.

'No,' he says, 'it just didn't happen. I was very sad though.'

After that, I go into the bathroom and cry some more, this time for the little boy who learned not to cry at sad things.

August

I've had my second Hollywood wax. I didn't really expect that to happen. It's just that I liked the first one so much that nothing seemed quite as good afterwards.

I would once have disapproved slightly of women who have all their pubic hair removed. I would have been too polite to say so, but I would have felt they were betraying the sisterhood somehow, making too many concessions to the male gaze. It never occurred to me that it might be fun. After my first Hollywood, I noted that it felt distinctly adult rather than infantilising; but now I'd also add that it gives me a sense of control over a sometimes unruly body. Checkmate. I can make this body sexy.

Herbert, too, has fought his own battle with liking my waxed pudenda. Bless him, he wanted with all his heart not to find it attractive. But he couldn't stop looking at it, and couldn't stop his body responding to it. When I was wondering aloud whether to go for a second Hollywood, he stoically said, 'I like it either way, I don't have a preference,' but, eventually, he admitted that he really, really liked my fanny bald.

He added – guiltily – 'I could have mine waxed too, if you like?'

'Why would you do that?'

'So that it's not just you. So that it's equal.'

'Do you fancy having it done? Would it turn you on?'

'No, not really.'

'So don't do it.'

It seems like we've invented a ridiculous set of rules around women's bodies. We're only trying to get it right, and we're concerned about the way women can lose their power in some relationships (and some whole societies). We're disgusted by the extent of domestic violence, and by the way women's bodies are seen as magnets for rape and abuse. We are sick to the teeth of the parade of objectified female forms, devoid of any personality or preference.

The problem is, those bodies are not my body. And if I create a set of personal rules in response to these horrors, I don't protect those women, and I degrade my conscious relationship with my own flesh. I don't want women in general to be treated as children, but whether or not I wax off my pubic hair makes not one scrap of difference to that. And if I de-sexualise my body entirely, I don't give one in the eye to patriarchy; I just restrict my own choices and get further away from understanding the truth about my own sexuality. That isn't liberation.

People talk about post-feminism: the idea that, with feminism's battles won, women can begin to take their pick from the spectrum of identities out there, even if some of them look pretty similar to the traditional roles we thought we'd abolished. But to me, this isn't really about feminism at all. I'm concerned about human rights in general. I don't want anyone to hurt anyone else. Misogyny makes me as angry as the next woman (with all her pubes intact), but then so does the opposing female attitude that men are vile and worthless.

If I've learned anything this year, it's that we need to take the 'should' out of sex. There is no particular way I 'should' wear my pubic hair. There is no particular way I 'should' want to have sex. It is my business, and my business alone. What I negotiate with my partner is down to me.

I know that some people will say, 'Ah, but you're lucky to have a choice.' Absolutely, I am. I see no conflict between waxing my pubic hair and defending women against forced circumcision. The two attitudes are perfectly compatible. I have the wonderful choice to figure out what makes my body sing, and to pursue it. What's the point of developing new tyrannies in the absence of the old ones?

Seduction #30
Erotic Awakening

If anyone walked into the room right now, they would think that Herbert was whispering to my clitoris.

It's not deliberate. It's just that he's pressed his face up close, and I keep telling him to touch gentler, gentler, gentler; with each adjustment, his voice softens a notch. 'Am I actually touching it at all?' he asks eventually.

'Yes,' I say, 'I think so. That's just about right.'

It is customary for me to observe at this juncture that you'd expect him to know this after fifteen years together, but if we've learned anything throughout these seductions, it's that all bets are off. We are practising the strokes involved in the Erotic Awakening Massage from *Urban Tantra*, and it's an object lesson in how little we know about each other's genitalia. Actually, it's also an object lesson in how little we know about our own.

During Herbert's massage, I am variously required to stretch, rotate, twist, pinch and squeeze his penis; I have to pay careful attention to his scrotum, urethral meatus (that's pee-hole to me), frenulum and perineum. Every now and then, he says, 'I'm going to have to not look to decide whether I like that,' and he closes his eyes and generally finds that he does.

All of this is enormous fun. It makes me realise how limited my repertoire has been thus far. Penises, it seems, will tolerate all manner of contortions and still come out the other end looking pleased with themselves. H certainly says 'harder' more times than he says 'softer', and only says 'ouch' once. The fact that he says anything at all is the best bit; it makes me realise that I learned to handle a penis in the complete absence of feedback. How on earth are we supposed to work out what to do with such an alien creature all by ourselves? It's no wonder I settled for the one-handed shuffle years ago and stuck with it. It seemed to produce results.

The Erotic Awakening Massage is gloriously method-ical. You work your way around your partner's privates until you feel as though you've mapped every inch of them. When it's my turn to receive, I find that I am unex-pectedly keen on having my uterus massaged, and the small, delicate touches that H makes around my clitoris and vulva are often delicious. He tends to default to performing oral sex as foreplay, so I'm pleased to see him gazing into the book in great puzzlement, trying to work out which bit is which.

I think I'd rather he never attempted direct contact with my clitoris ever again, but then I suppose that's good to know. As he holds back the little hood that covers it, he says, 'I keep losing it,' and I am moved to hiss, 'Yes, that's because you keep bloody well prodding it and it's hiding.' I have always maintained that a little knowledge is a dangerous thing when it comes to men and clitorises, and this particular stroke bears me out.

It surprises him how gently I like to be touched, and how precise the sensations are. Moving his fingers a few millimetres makes the difference between heaven and utter indifference.

You notice things much more when you're only receiving and not trying to reciprocate. My hands keep wandering over to his body because I'm not sure what to do. I find it hard to stay in the moment, to just focus on the sensations he's giving me. More than that, I find it hard to quite trust him, particularly when he's distracted by reading the book. A couple of times, I have to say to him, 'Listen!' when I'm giving feedback, because he's not quite paying attention. This makes me increasingly tense.

What I notice most of all is how my mood shifts when we move to the part of the massage that's inside my vagina. I'm flooded with obsessive thoughts about whether he might start off the bleeding again. I suppose I feel out of control; I keep asking, 'What are you doing now?' and he has to read out the description from the book so that I feel comfortable again. I try to focus on the sensations, but my brain isn't turned on enough to really enjoy them. My body is pulling up its drawbridge.

Then H turns a page and says, 'Oh.'

'What?'

'I've come to the section on the cervix.'

'Okay, that's enough for me then.'

'We can backtrack a bit, go back to the things you were enjoying?'

'No,' I say, 'I think we'll leave it for tonight.'

Herbert is upstairs in bed. He's still feeling dizzy and can't stay awake.

It's clearly just a little virus. As we all know, they're untreatable and need to be rested off and waited out. But I tend to think that these things only hit us when we let them in – the little, niggling illnesses too often signal that we're run down, stressed or anxious.

The seductions are hanging heavily around Herbert's neck at the moment. With nineteen to go, he's concerned he'll run out of ideas. When we're in bed together, he loses concentration easily and worries about technique. I've noticed that he's grown a few grey pubic hairs; their symbolism isn't lost on me. At what point did we switch from being willing students of seduction to worrying whether we are expert enough?

A case in point: last week, he announced he'd seen something on Channel 5 late at night about how to give cunnilingus. 'I've been doing it wrong all these years,' he said. It didn't feel so wrong to me, but I let him try out the new way anyway. Apparently, the 'right way' is to approach from the side (like playing a harmonica), with one hand on the perineum and one on the lower belly, stretching the two points apart. Then you lick only the clitoris. We tried it for a while, and it was very nice (in the way that all oral sex is nice), but mechanical and unvaried. Why miss out all those other wonderfully sensitive parts just for the sake of having a technique that's easy to summarise?

'You were much better off doing it your way,' I told him. 'You worked it out for yourself.'

If I have learned anything about sex in the thirty seductions we've done so far, it's that technique is the death of lust. By all means be a knowledgeable lover, but never forget that what really makes desire fly is contact. Good sex is no more or less than the free flow of communication. When we listen, when we really tune into our lover's body and mind, it's like making an electrical connection. We get no closer to that moment of flow by slavishly following the guide-book.

When I started my coaching sessions with Barbara Carrellas, she asked me what issues I wanted to focus on. 'My inhibition,' I said, 'my inability to find abandon.' This week, she laughed and said to me, 'You are NOT inhibited. British maybe. But you're just not interested in going through the motions. You've got no patience for things that aren't sincere. You're a sex geek. You're one of us.'

It's odd, because after that I felt like a curtain had been raised. I've been changed by this. There's no going back. I'm not the most sexually charged being in the world, but I do have desire, and it knocks on my door with increasing regularity. I'm no longer worried that everyone else is having better sex than me. Some people are having more, but I've seen enough to know that it isn't comparable. My sex is my sex, and their sex is theirs.

I feel as though I've shed a skin. Or maybe I can just lower those hedgehog spines. And, like Herbert, I'm terrified, exhausted and tight-throated because there's no going back now. Change is always painful. Just standing on this earth as it turns is enough to make me feel dizzy sometimes. But I'm finally convinced that we're changing for the better.

Seduction #31
Firebreath

Herbert is still stricken with his mysterious virus. He's exhausted, has a headache and his shoulders ache. I was initially tempted to think that this was a hysterical illness brought on by my new-found enthusiasm for tantric sex, but I have since conceded that perhaps his symptoms are genuine. He has spent most of the week watching *Stargate Atlantis* in bed, a sure-fire way of repelling me from the room.

This is unfortunate, because my Hollywood wax is working its magic. Without harping on about this too much, the Hollywood makes me feel like a new woman – one whose vulva is no longer cushioned by pubic hair, and so is now rubbing against a range of new and interesting surfaces. I am – and let's face it, this is rare – Good to Go. H is definitely not. On Thursday night, he makes the weary suggestion, 'I'm happy to watch you masturbate,' but this is the most he's willing to give.

Well, I think, *I suppose I'll have to seduce myself.* He goes to work on Friday, and I am left home alone. And now I come to think of it, there *is* something I've fancied trying for a while, which really doesn't benefit from being in a pair: the tantric Firebreath Orgasm.

There's something of a mystique around the Firebreath, which is a combination of breathing, visualisation and pelvic-floor clenches. When I mention that I'm going to try it on Twitter, someone immediately tweets back to warn me that she's heard it can send you mad. I take this with a pinch of salt, because I can't quite see how that could happen. It's just a bit of breathing, isn't it?

The Firebreath is supposed to help you to access an ecstatic state, feeling a surge of energy throughout your whole body, rather than just limited to your genitals. By repute, it can also dredge up very strong emotions, be they happy or sad. You don't get to choose. But like the risk of madness, I struggle to believe that I could be affected this strongly. I am undeterred. In any case, I have already been through the basic technique during my workshop at Xplore. No limbs were lost, although several people were crying afterwards. I was too busy wondering what Herbert must be thinking to fully engage at the time.

The technique feels a bit like patting your head and rubbing your stomach at the same time: just for starters, you have to breathe in a certain way, clench your pelvic-floor muscles and rock your pelvis. It takes me a while to get the hang of this, and I keep having to pause and start again. I suspect I am just under-rehearsed. Then I have to visualise energy circulating around my chakras, progressing up my body.

I lie there, huffing and puffing and squeezing my pelvic floor, thinking, *Oh well, this probably means I can skip tonight's meditation at least.* The rocking and the clenching feel rather nice, and I console myself with that.

But then something rather strange happens. As the visualisation gets nearer the top of my body, I begin to get the sense that I'm not imagining it any more. The energy seems to be flowing upwards on its own. It reaches the top of my head, and I hold my breath, clench every muscle in my body and then let go . . .

For a few moments, I feel an upwards rushing in my head, and colours flash before my eyes: pulsing blues and greens. The soles of my feet tingle. Then everything is black and empty and timeless. I surface feeling sleepy and serene, sort of switched on everywhere. Impossibly, an hour has passed since I started.

I am amazed, startled and a bit confounded. I have no idea what happened, but I can't wait to try it again.

Maybe a seduction on my own doesn't count, but it occurred to me, sitting in the afterglow of this bizarre encounter, that we must learn to seduce ourselves before we can hope to seduce another person.

Seduction #32
Mars Attacks

I have been reading *Men Are From Mars, Women Are From Venus*, and resenting every second of it. I so want it to be wrong; I so want to live in a post-gender world in which we are not men or women, but just people. Nope. Turns out Herbert is a perfect Mars, and I am a perfect Venus, albeit a particularly combative strain.

Take, for example, this weekend. H has been claiming that he's too ill for sex, and yet seems surprisingly perky outside the bedroom. My suggestions that we practise our tantric breathing instead are met with a martyred sigh. By Monday, I am heartily sick of this. It feels like he's not co-operating, and I'm doing all the running.

Now, usually this would lead to a row. But that afternoon I take *Mars & Venus* with me to a coffee shop, and find it disappointingly insightful. Herbert, it appears, is feeling like his competence is being challenged by all the new, technique-y stuff I've been trying to drag him through. He's passively resisting, and has retreated to his cave to sulk. I mean *think*, sorry.

Like the Venutian I am, I'm allowing all my emotions to hinge on his responses, and failing to set boundaries about how much I'm willing to work towards the seductions before it makes me cross. Well, there's the theory anyway. But what on earth does this mean in practice?

That evening, I decide to put a bit of *Mars & Venus* theory to the test. I make sure I'm out when he gets home. In fact, I take a nice long walk along the seafront, which goes some way to making me a bit less cross. When I get in, I skip straight into a shower after a quick hello. H isn't used to this. I usually pounce on him when he gets home and demand to know every detail of his day. He's reduced to following me into the bathroom and saying, 'I did some weight training when I got home and then had a shower.' Translation: 'Where were you?'

'Well done!' I say, brightly.

Then I make chicken sandwiches for dinner. No fuss, no cutlery. I confess, I possibly make dinner into hard work most nights; I love to cook, and sometimes my standards get a bit above themselves. Not tonight. We eat the sandwiches, I clear up, H does the laundry, and then I go to my study to read a book. For the second time, it is he who comes and finds me.

'Have we got any plans?' he asks.

'Nope,' I say. I get up and cuddle up to him. 'We could have sex?'

'What did you have in mind?'

'Nothing. No plans. No seductions. Let's just have sex, like the good old days, hmm?'

H looks uncomfortable. 'Non-penetrative though.'

I had forgotten about this. I have recently suggested to Herbert that I might feel a bit more enthusiastic about sex if I didn't have the nagging suspicion that it might injure me. I would rather ration penetrative sex than get rid of it altogether.

'Does that worry you?' I say.

'No.'

'Because I'm led to believe there are quite a few things you enjoy about that sort of sex.'

'It's not me,' he says, 'it's you.'

He's right. I'm usually the one petitioning for penetrative sex. I love the feeling of being filled up, and I love the orgasms it gives me. I feel like I can lose myself in it. Up until recently, of course, this has made me positively good company. Now, though, I can see why it might leave H feeling a bit incompetent.

'Hey,' I say, 'I think I'll survive. But we do need to think of a sexier term than non-penetrative sex.'

'NPS,' he says.

'Right,' I say, 'let's go and have NPS. Or do you "perform" NPS?'

I'm sure I don't need to tell you the variety of things that might constitute NPS, so we'll skip to the end. We are both lying in a slightly dazed post-orgasmic state, and I have an idea.

'Herbert,' I say, 'here's a seduction for you. I'll let you take a photo of my fanny on your new phone, but in return you have to masturbate over it in public tomorrow, and then tell me what it was like.'

'Riiight,' says H. 'How public do you mean?'

'Oh, I just mean out of the house. In the toilets somewhere. Not in the middle of a shopping centre.'

'But I've got work tomorrow. I'm not doing it there.'

'Don't you have a lunch hour?'

'Yes, but I'm going to the pub with J . . . oh . . .'

'Great. You can do it there.'

Herbert thinks for a while, not looking astonishingly enthusiastic at the prospect. 'Well, seeing as I've got the technology, it would be a shame not to take a video.'

I can't very well argue with that, can I? He hurries downstairs to get his phone, and before I know it, I am following a series of instructions to put this leg here, to hold my lips apart, to move my fingers down towards my vagina. Not for the first time, I am amused at how specific the male imagination is when it comes to viewing a woman. His camera feels like a lustful gaze over my body. I like it.

Afterwards, he lies beside me and plays back the film. I don't have my glasses on, so it's all a blur, but I can see white flesh with a darker streak in the middle, and then the camera pans back to reveal my naked shape against our turquoise sheets. I am beyond flattered that he wanted the whole of me in the frame.

Around lunchtime the next day, I get a text from H.

Come I have.

It takes me a few moments to work out what he's on about.

You're informing me in the style of Yoda? I text back.

Yes. It adds an extra frisson.

No, Herbert, it really doesn't.

When he gets home that evening, I ask him how it went.

'Well, I had a wank in the toilets at the pub, what is there to say?'

'Was it nice?'

'Yes.'

'And . . .'

Herbert sighs.

'It was a bit loud. I was in one of those little cubicles, so I had to be bloody careful. Also, I accidentally set my phone to play through all the videos on it, rather than just yours. I ended up watching the trailer for *Kick Ass* for a while. Then I had to stop and re-set it so it looped the film of you. Then I nearly dropped it down the toilet. Then I realised I needed some lubrication, so I, you know, spat on my hand . . .'

Me: 'Ha! So *Brokeback Mountain* was right!'

H (ignoring me): '. . . but then that made too much noise, so I had to dry off again.'

'So a bit rubbish overall?'

'No. I had a great orgasm, actually. It was just that J looked at me ever so funny when I got back from the loo.'

On Friday night I got so drunk I had to spend most of Saturday in bed.

I am not, you understand, telling you this in a state of glowing pride. I should have switched to tea at midnight rather than sloshing ever more wine into people's glasses. I have a well-established way of telling I've had too much: I compulsively play 'Journey of the Sorcerer' by The Eagles to my assembled guests. I ignored this warning sign, and followed it with that other hangover pit canary 'Egyptian Reggae'. When will I learn?

The point of telling you this is not to wallow in liverish guilt. It's just that the whole experience made me think about the ways in which, sometimes, we choose illness over health.

As I am lying in bed on Saturday afternoon, trying to stay still enough to avoid being sick, I think about how hangovers aren't really as accidental as they feel. They are not a failure of restraint, but a choice against it, a deliberate surrender to the night. They are a way of accessing your younger self again, those times when you didn't have anything much to do on a Saturday afternoon anyway, and so could afford some extra time in bed. They are, in effect, a request for some time off the adult treadmill. They are a request, for a while, to forget you're thirty-three, functionally infertile, waiting for the results of more cervical biopsies, and frankly clueless about what happens next.

I would love to have a more emotionally intelligent way of dealing with life's transitional moments, but this is the best I've got. By relinquishing a bit of my adult control, I suppose I externalise the disruption I'm feeling. I turn an emotional crisis into a much more tangible, manageable physical crisis. And that, in turn, means I take better care of myself for a few days.

Seduction #33
Time and Tide

Herbert is quite determined about this one.

'But it's raining,' I say. 'We'll just have to put it off until the weather's better.'

'The BBC website says there'll be no cloud cover at all by 1 a.m.'

'I'm not waiting until 1 a.m.'

'Clouds don't suddenly vanish. They gradually go away.'

'Well, as long as you don't mind me in wellies and a cagoule.'

'Sounds ravishing.'

Damn him. That was supposed to put him off. Instead, I find myself contemplating my wardrobe, wondering what might be the most appropriate outfit for sex on a rainy beach. 'Shall I get the picnic blanket out of the loft?' yells H from downstairs.

'I'm not bloody lying down!' Whatever happens will have to happen standing up, no doubt leaning against one of the damp wooden groynes that break up the beach. This, at least, makes it easier to select an outfit. Long skirt, no knickers, thick stockings (it's nippy out there), boots and, yes, the cagoule. I wasn't joking.

It is dark when we get in the car, but the rain has stopped. As we drive along the coast, we see that the sun hasn't quite yet fully set. The horizon glows red, thick black clouds above. We catch glimpses of the shore flashing between houses. The sea is lit up by the retreating sun. It is so beautiful that I gasp, and H catches sight of it at the same time, swerving the car. I put my hand on his thigh, and he clutches it. There is something arousing about this dark, portentous beach, despite the cagoule.

We drive until the houses thin out and park in an empty lay-by. The sea is hidden behind a steep bank now, and we clamber up slippery wooden steps until we reach the top. Below us, the sea-breaks are silhouetted black against a thin strip of blue and orange sky. The tide is out, revealing a seabed covered in shallow, reflecting pools, each one mirroring the sunset. It's extraordinary, a mackerel shore and a mackerel sky. We both run down on to the shingle and stand silently, listening to the minute trickle of the water before us, the birds calling on the marsh behind us. The air is electric, awaiting another storm.

I lean back against a ragged wooden post and pull H towards me. We kiss, and he pulls up my skirt, and then places his hardening penis between my thighs. It bobs up to meet me. I feel as though I have absorbed some of the static from the air.

Tonight, I know that H would like a repeat performance of his favourite memory, the night we had sex on the beach after our delayed wedding, but it is not to be. As we are kissing, we hear distant voices and two figures appear on the footpath at the top of the bank. H hurriedly zips up his jeans, and I say, 'Well, maybe we're better off retiring home to bed. We'll call it the best foreplay ever.'

We turn towards the sea to catch one last sight before heading back to the car. Above us, the clouds have cleared to reveal a sky sparkling with stars.

September

First day back to work after the school holidays. I didn't want to be in this position. My work is publically funded, and we're braced for cuts this year. I had hoped to find another job by now, but there's nothing out there. I feel like a sitting duck.

Meeting first thing. My client arrives forty-five minutes late, even though I've driven an hour to his workplace. I'm livid. He doesn't even offer me a glass of water.

Then home to tackle the huge pile of paperwork that's building up already. The credit card bill is a surprise. I've got behind with the washing. My office floor is covered with bags of jumble for a sale I'm helping out with next week. My mum, who lives in Spain, has emailed to say that her spine condition has got so much worse since I last saw her that she struggles to get herself dressed in the morning. She's visiting next week, so I book her an appointment with a local physiotherapist, hoping she won't be cross. I worry about the bed I was planning to put her up in, and realise I need to buy a new one. I wish she didn't live so far away.

I start on my To Do list. My dentist has forgotten to write a referral letter to the dental surgeon about my jaw, which seems to be travelling to the left, painfully. I am assured she'll do it this Friday. I take a deep breath and call my gynaecologist's office, which has not been in touch after seven weeks to either give me my biopsy results or arrange a new appointment. 'His secretary left suddenly,'

I am told, 'and there's a black hole of paperwork. We're trying to get through it.' A timescale? 'Couldn't say.'

'Look,' I say, 'I'm waiting for my third biopsy for cervical cancer. Can't you just tell me the results?'

'No. It's in the system, probably being typed up. Chase at the end of next week.'

I launch into a diatribe about how long this has been going on, how I keep getting pushed from pillar to post and I'm sick of it, but I falter halfway through. The woman on the other end of the phone has gone quiet. 'I'm sorry,' I say, 'I know this hasn't got anything to do with you.'

'It's awful here,' she says quietly. 'We've just had so much dumped on us, and we can't cope.'

An email drops into my inbox from work, asking me to complete an evaluation for a project that hasn't happened yet. I query. My heartbeat is singing in my ears.

Several times over the last few months, I have entertained the fantasy of crawling under my desk and assuming the brace position.

Today, however, I think, *What the hell*. I take a breath, pull out my chair, and examine the space under the desk. It's small, but I think I can fit. I squeeze myself under there, resting my chin on my knees, and clamp my hands over my head. I wish I'd done this months ago. It's wonderful: muffled, dark, smelling of dry wood. I feel so silly it makes me smile. My ridiculous blood pressure sounds delightful down here, like the wind blustering across the beach.

I wonder how long it's acceptable to stay here. It's uncomfortable, but at least that's a challenge I can confront. I find the customary gathering of my eyebrows in the centre of my forehead, and smooth it out with my fingers. I counsel myself that I must not cry all over Herbert when he gets home.

Then, on the tabletop above me, I feel my phone buzzing to announce a new text. I tentatively reach out a hand and bring it down to my underworld. It's Herbert.

I'm just leaving work, so you need to prepare for my plan, hee hee.

I hope you're still wearing your short skirt, the same as this morning. Put on some long socks with it, and some white cotton knickers.

Can you get yourself wet and ready for me, maybe using your vibrator?

I will text you when I've parked outside. Go into the kitchen and bend over the work surface.

I will come in and, without speaking, I will start fucking you. We won't speak until that has happened.

Is that okay with you? I'm getting hard just writing it.

I stare at the text for a while, the light from my phone bright amid the gloom.

I'm giggling like a schoolgirl, I reply.

Seduction #34
Mystery Man

'm excited by the thought of this one. Occasionally, Herbert suggests a seduction that is so specific and unusual that it feels like I've glimpsed a part of his fantasy life. I wonder if I ever really invite him into my psyche in that way.

I don't own a single pair of white cotton knickers, though. It is sod's law that, in the light of my exemplary lingerie collection, my husband will crave plain white pants. I rifle through my tangled knicker drawer for something in the same ballpark, and come across a pair that have yellow and pink love-hearts all over them. They will have to do. Otherwise it's between my black sports knickers or my single pair of thermal harvest pants (all is safely gathered in), which I reserve for a once-a-year walk in the January snow. And then take them off as soon as I get home, in case anyone sees me in them.

Long socks, short skirt, love-heart knickers. It's a bit

like being fifteen again, except without the dodgy green hair dye. I set about clearing an appropriate kitchen surface, the only section that isn't overhung by cupboards. It is overhung by a magnetic knife-rack instead, but I can't help that. I unplug the kettle.

Happy as I am to oblige with the masturbation request (as I have remarked before, I work from home), I douse myself liberally with lube too. Then, when he texts to say he's parked outside, I apply some more. This zipless fuck thing takes some planning.

As the front door slams, I position myself over the kitchen unit. I hear H undress in the living room and then walk into the kitchen. He doesn't waste any time carrying out his promise, although it's a little fumbly at first, probably not as easy as he was imagining. But it's also wonderful. I can feel his penis grow as he enters me, and his bare legs brushing against mine. I have to tune in carefully so that I can get a sense of whether he's enjoying it, through the sounds he makes and his movements.

After a while, I begin to wonder if he's floundering a bit. To carry out this sort of fantasy effectively, I think you have to abandon your concerns about the female orgasm. This is not something that H likes to do without explicit permission. So I turn around, wrap my legs around him and clamp my mouth over his nipple. He groans, and we continue enthusiastically onwards.

A few minutes later, I see his eyes widen, and he grabs hold of my shoulders and gasps. *Spectacular orgasm*, I think. But no.

'Sorry to break the mood,' he gasps, 'and it's not that I don't like it that you've turned round, but you keep nearly headbutting the knife-rack, and I'm finding it hard to concentrate.' He removes the knives one by one, puts them in the sink, and we proceed: a little longer on the kitchen units, and then the kitchen floor.

After we've finished, he smiles, kisses me and says, 'So, how was your day?'

'Well, I had resorted to hiding under my desk when you texted,' I say, 'but I feel much better now.'

He looks at me through narrowed eyes for a moment, and then clearly decides I must surely be joking.

inally, a letter arrives from my consultant. The test results are clear.

I catch myself feeling relieved, and then curse myself for ever getting caught up in worrying about it. They are only testing because they've run out of other ideas. I have to stop letting this hijack my emotional state, especially when the NHS works to such geological time-scales.

I still manage to ring Herbert in tears, though.

'That's good news,' he says. 'Isn't it?'

'Yes,' I sniff, 'but the next appointment's two months away. It's all just endless waiting. And whenever I see him, he's forgotten what I'm there for in the first place.'

'Well, that's what the insurance is for. You've waited long enough by anyone's standards.'

Herbert and I are members of a health insurance scheme that you can only use if NHS waiting lists are too long. They don't ask any questions; if you consider your wait to be excessive, that's good enough for them. They trust you to make a fair decision. This inevitably makes me behave like an especially guilty child whenever I think about using it. If nothing's actively falling off, I find it hard to justify it.

But Herbert's got a point this time. I feel like I'm not getting the treatment I need on the NHS. I pick up the phone, ready to call the insurance company. And then, as the recorded menu kicks in, I find myself putting it down again.

I'm not even sure why. I just don't feel right about it. I make myself a cup of coffee so that I can think. Somehow, I just can't justify it. I don't actually feel ill any more; that's the problem. Certainly, I have a few symptoms, but I know how to control them myself. We have developed strategies.

If anything, I could do with being a little bit fitter, keeping a closer eye on what I eat, cutting down on the booze. These things are nothing to do with my doctor.

A year ago, I desperately needed medical attention; now I've had some. It's not offered the perfect cure, but it's given me enough to be getting on with. For as long as I'm reliant on these professionals to sort me out, I'm stuck in a cycle of wondering and waiting, a dependency that exhausts and frightens me. I want to be in control again. I want the right to see myself as fundamentally well.

I call Herbert back.

'I think I won't bother with the health insurance,' I say, ever so casually. 'I think I'll wait and see how I am in November.'

'You don't have to, you know,' he says, sounding somewhat perplexed.

'No, it's alright, I want to. It's my choice.'

Seduction #35
Call Centres

'I'm just going for a normal one,' says H decisively.
'Not Barely 21 or Mature Ladies?'
'No.'
'Dominant Mistress?'
'No.'
'Are you sure?'
'YES.'

It is, I suppose, slightly unfair to tease him over his choice of live chat line, when it's my fault he has to choose one at all. I have had, you see, a rather genius idea. Something to ratchet up the sense of jeopardy a little bit, add a little frisson. I have offered to give Herbert a blow job while he rings a sex chat line.

My reasoning runs thus: it's a monogamous way of almost having a threesome. Also, I have noted Herbert's enthusiasm for talking dirty, and wonder if this might be just the thing. Actually, scrub that, it's not entirely honest:

I am hoping to put him in a situation where he feels as awkward as I do around all this erotic conversation. There's a slightly vengeful part of me that wants to put him outside his comfort zone.

It is heartening, therefore, to see that he feels the need to down two beers before he can even open the back pages of *Time Out* to find a suitable phone number.

'Dutch courage?' I say, and he blushes. I'm not sure if I've ever seen him blush before.

I'm the one losing their nerve now. 'You don't have to do this if you don't want to,' I say. 'I mean, it's only worth it if you think it would be fun.'

He sighs. 'It does sound fun. It's fine. Just don't make me call anyone too specialist.'

'Fine,' I say, and go upstairs to put on some lipstick. When I come back down again, H is sitting naked in the armchair in my study, phone in hand. He's thoughtfully placed a cushion at his feet so that I can kneel on it. I am somehow rather touched by this.

He wastes no time in dialling, and so I begin to lick his still-soft penis in haste. H is capable of being overtaken by startling bouts of shyness, and so I'm convinced that we need to achieve an erection before he starts talking, or else there's no hope. But the opposite happens: as soon as the woman answers, his dick does a little jump for joy. I can hear his voice above me, strangely lost and breathy:

'Hello? Oh, hello, Erica. . . My name's Herbert . . . I'm thirty-eight . . . You're thirty? What colour hair do you have?'

What? I think, *Why is that relevant? She'll be blonde, I guarantee it.*

'Erica,' he says, 'I've got a naughty confession to make.' I glance up at him, hoping he will catch my eye and smirk, but it appears that he's saying this with no irony what-soever. 'My wife is with me. She's sucking my cock.'

Oh yuck, I think. I suppose I couldn't expect him not to tell her, but now I am wondering what on earth Erica thinks of me. It brings to mind the wife of the vile man in *There's Something About Mary*, who merrily fellates her husband while he watches the football.

'She's got brown eyes and mousy brown hair.' Mousy? He might as well tell her about the grey flecks as well.

'Oh, would you? Mmmm . . . Yes, I'd like to watch that.' Erica has, of course, now said she'd like to get it on with me. She knows her male fantasies, I'll give her that. 'Your favourite fantasy? Yes, tell me then . . . Mmmm . . . Mmmm . . . Mmmm . . . Three cocks . . .' *How would that even work in real life?* 'Yes, that does sound a bit greedy.' He keeps closing his eyes and groaning. I'm beginning to worry about the state of the phone bill. I suck harder, and start to mentally rehearse my 36p-per-minute times table. This soothes me among the 'Mmmms' and 'Ohs'.

He doesn't do any of his own dirty talking really; he mainly just listens. So this is what he wants when he requests dirty talk. I just couldn't bear to spew out that pile of clichés, and in any case, H knows me too well to believe them. Frankly, I am in awe of Erica for making them sound so convincing.

I consider for a moment whether I could learn some-thing from her, but then a much more delightful thought hits me: I'm outsourcing. The wonders of advanced capi-talism are making it possible for me to hive off a particularly tiresome element of my sexual duties. Excel-lent. Worth every penny of the fiver it's going to put on my phone bill.

The second bonus is that all this female attention moves

Herbert to orgasm with unusual speed. He announces it – twice – to both of us, and then thanks Erica politely for her time. I wonder if I should yell a 'Cheers, Erica!' towards the handset too, but I prefer to leave her wondering whether Herbert isn't faking his extremely compliant wife.

There is an argument.

In the manner of these things, it starts with something stupid, and expands to take in our whole universe. I accuse Herbert of being awkward about collecting my mother from the airport.

'I'm not being awkward,' he says, 'just trying to work out the logistics. Why are you blowing this out of all proportion?'

I express surprise that he thinks he has the right to snap at me like this, given that it was he who was being so awkward. You can see how the circle starts.

'Why do you always have to do this?' he says. 'Why do you always have to see the worst in me?'

We are walking along the seafront when this happens. 'Keep your voice down,' I say. 'You're making a fool of both of us.'

He shakes his head at me and storms on. 'Look,' I say, 'forget this. I'll pick her up. It's easier all round.'

'I haven't got a problem with picking her up,' he nearly shouts.

'Okay! Fine! You haven't got a problem. Whatever. I'll pick her up.'

We walk in silence. I grab for his hand. 'Herbert,' I say, 'I mean it. I'll pick her up. Don't worry about it.'

It's a genuine attempt to defuse the situation, but it doesn't come across that way. He shakes my hand away. We walk for another ten minutes before I say, 'I'm going home. There's no point carrying on with this walk if we're not talking.' I mean for him to come home with me, but he shakes his head and marches away from me. I walk home alone.

From then on, the whole day becomes a clashing pattern of the peaks and troughs of our anger. Herbert offers me a cup of tea and asks if I'll proofread the poster he's making, and I'm furious at him for acting as though nothing's happened. I go and sulk in my office. And then burst out later to shout at him for it. We battle over who should apologise. I am in the unfortunate position of being in the middle of cooking a lamb biryani, H's favourite dish, which has been marinating since the day before. I can't waste it, but it's a labour of love to cook the damned thing. I assume that this will all have blown over by the time it's ready.

It hasn't. It's 9 p.m. and I'm starving, but I'm damned if I'm going to serve him food. I spoon a portion out for myself, and call to the living room to say that there's food if he wants it. He doesn't come and get it. I fork a few pieces into my mouth, but I can't swallow. 'Are you not even going to eat my food?' I say.

'No.'

'God, you are so fucking cruel sometimes.'

The shouting starts again. I can't even remember what is said, but I end up doing something I've never done before: I walk out. I grab my handbag, make sure to close the door gently behind me so the neighbours don't hear, and head out into the darkness. I make a few confused steps at my own front gate, unsure even of what direction to go in, and then strike off for the sea. I know he won't follow me. Bob the cat trots after me down the road for a while, but I pretend I haven't seen her.

I feel as though I am made of soup, my skin barely containing the sloshing, uncontrollable, sickly tides. I pass a seafront bar and go inside to pick up a pint of strong cider in a plastic glass. Then I clamber on to the beach. The tide is far out, and the air is soft and humid. At night, the wooden breakers cast black shadows near the tideline, and you can be invisible in their darker reaches. I perch myself under a damp strut and drink my cider, feeling calmer than I have felt in a long time.

I don't want to go home. The stars spread across the sky in a milky array. A fox hunts through the shingle, thrillingly close. I check to see whether I have missed the last train to London. I wonder if it's possible to disappear in this day and age, to throw your iPhone into the sea and vanish. I realise I am laughing whenever the wind blows, hanging my mouth open to feel the gusts catch between my cheeks. Could I sleep on the beach tonight, a ridiculous hobo with an Orla Kiely handbag?

Herbert texts after an hour. *Please can you let me know where you are?* I don't care. I stay on the beach until midnight, after all the houses and restaurants have turned out their lights, and even the fox has gone away.

It occurs to me during this time that we argue like this in complete safety. When we were first together, each row carried the risk of a break-up, and I used to feel like I was fighting on two sides at once: to protect my own interests, and save our togetherness. Now, that danger's gone. We're not going to split up, not over this, not over anything. And that leaves us in a terrible bind. We're each fighting to retain our sense of self, really, and yet we're in no position to make any threats. Even if we refuse to change, neither of us will leave.

When we argue nowadays (which is mercifully rare) it feels as though we're trying to annihilate each other, to win for winning's sake. We do this knowing there are no wins at this stage; we're always going to be denied our moment of triumph because we are not fighting an entirely separate person.

Herbert is out looking for me when I get home. I text

him and he rushes back, and holds me like I'm the most precious thing in the world. We sit up and talk half the night, but we still don't really understand each other, not even after fifteen years of articulation. But then, love and understanding are two different things.

Seduction #36
TLC

After the horrible row, Herbert makes one of the nicest gestures I've ever known him to make: he takes the day off work to talk to me.

Amongst other things, we talk about the way the seductions have changed us, how the pace of innovation sometimes exhausts us, but also how they've given us both a sense of delicious conspiracy that we never had before. We want the year to be over, but we're scared of what will happen when it ends.

'The seductions have made me more ambitious about life,' I say. 'They've made me think that I don't have to accept an inevitable winding-down. They've made me feel at the height of my powers.'

'I just feel more relaxed about everything,' says H. 'I used to be a lot more worried about getting it right. Now I understand how wonky it's supposed to be.'

'That's so true. Before this started, you used to be offended if I used lube.'

A small, embarrassed smile. 'Maybe. I can't remember.'

We drive out to the next town for afternoon tea and strawberry tarts. 'I wonder if we sometimes forget the actual idea of seduction in all of this,' I say. 'We keep interpreting it as "a different thing to do every time". It shouldn't be like that. It should be "What would make my partner wild with desire tonight? What does he need?"'

'Give me an example,' says H.

'Okay, if I were to seduce you tonight, what would you need? What would turn you on the most?'

'I don't know,' he says. 'I'm exhausted. I don't feel much like sex at all.'

'Exactly. What you need is to be soothed. You want to feel safe again, and you want to rest.'

'You mean, what we've done today is a seduction?'

'I suppose so. But let me see if I can do better tonight.'

That evening, after dinner, I draw a bath and spend half an hour lying in the hot water, reading. Then I invite H to do the same.

While he's lolling there in his ridiculous floral shower cap (he has twice tried to persuade me to have sex with him when he's forgotten to take it off), I light candles all around the bedroom and make a pot of fresh mint tea.

'Shall I put some music on?' I ask.

'No,' he says. 'Peace and quiet.'

We lie back on pillows and cushions, and I say, 'So, what would soothe you the most right now?'

'Nothing,' he says. 'I'm nice and warm after my bath. What about you?'

'A back rub. My shoulders are sore.'

He massages my shoulders while I lean against him, and then runs his oily hands over my breasts. I used to hate it when he did this; I used to think it was intruding on my massage. Tonight, it feels warm and affectionate. 'I tell you what I'd like,' he whispers in my ear. 'I'd like a boob massage.'

'You want me to massage your moobs?' I giggle.

'No, I'd like you to massage me with your boobs. Really lightly. Sometimes your nipples brush against me by accident and it's lovely.'

I smirk at him, and proceed to attempt the requested boob massage, which is a more precise procedure than it sounds. Soon, though, I just lie on top of him so that our whole bodies are touching, and without even thinking about it I slide him inside me.

We have slow, oily, electrically sensitive sex, and then we blow out the candles and fall asleep.

Seduction #37
In-Car Entertainment

My mother is staying with us. For ten days.

Now, I like my mother as much as the next girl, but ten days is a long time to tolerate the presence of another human being in your house, even if they gave birth to you. However, given that my mother now lives a genteel life of boozing and smoking in Spain, extended parental visits are unavoidable. Herbert and I are simply not used to working around other people. We have our routines, goddamnit! I like to blame my complete lack of tolerance and flexibility on being raised an only child, which means that, in turn, I can blame it on my mother. Neat.

I have mentioned before that my mother is not averse to sex. In fact, she is an enthusiastic proponent of it. However, I assume that even she doesn't particularly want to be aware of the exact moment H and I are seducing each other. We need another plan.

'Well,' says H, 'I've been wondering about car sex for a while.'

'Right,' I say, without giving it much thought. 'Good idea.'

Come the appointed hour, though, I have caught the autumn cold that is going around, and am hacking like an old sailor. This is not attractive; and, from my point of view, neither is the pounding headache.

'Shall we leave this for another day?' asks H.

'No,' I say, somewhat heroically, 'we can't give up that easily.'

Around nine o'clock, we make an excuse to my mother about needing to witness some papers for a friend, and head out in the car.

'So, where are we going?' I ask.

'Dunno,' says H. 'I was hoping you had some thoughts.'

'I can't think of anywhere.'

'Well,' he says, 'what's the best sort of place? Car park?'

'Seems a bit too much like dogging. What if someone happens to park next to us?'

'Industrial estate?'

'CCTV. Security guards.'

'Country park?'

'Close at dusk. Dog-walkers.'

'Country lane?'

I think for a while. 'I don't know. Shall we just have a drive around and see?'

H turns up a road that we've never explored before, and for a while we find ourselves on a narrow lane lined with hedges, with only the occasional house.

'Here?' says H.

'That's someone's drive.'

He also suggests a lay-by (too much risk of passing

cars catching us in their headlights) and a track leading into a field (the overlooking houses would spot our head-lights and most likely call the police). I wonder if there's a single location in the south-east of England where it's quiet enough to have sex in your car, particularly if exhi-bitionism isn't your thing. What's more, the headache and the cough are making me feel increasingly like a woman who would rather be tucked up in bed. I am not in the least bit aroused.

'Can I suggest an alternative?' I say to Herbert, as we find ourselves on an increasingly residential road. 'How about I give you a hand-job while you drive us home?'

'Doesn't sound all that much fun for you.'

'The "getting home" part is my reward.'

He pulls over and undoes his jeans, and I reach across to him. We drive on in silence for a while.

'Is that nice?'

'More lovely than I even expected. It's a bit like listening to an audiobook while you drive; your body is working on autopilot, so your brain is freed up to concentrate.'

'Good,' I say. He reaches between my legs and begins to stroke me, but I say, 'No, it's fine. I'd rather you had both hands on the wheel if that's alright.'

Herbert takes the long route home, and we arrive back to find my mother completing the crossword on the sofa.

H scuttles up to the bathroom without saying hello. I swallow two Night Nurse and put myself to bed.

Seduction #38
Shhhh!

Herbert and I are sitting in my study. We are working on putting together a website for a friend's charity, something that I have rashly promised to do and which is now severely testing my levels of competence. Herbert, who builds databases for a living, is trying to help me, but is baffled by the sheer simplicity of the software. My mother is in the next room, playing Scrabble against herself. I have told her that this gives her a mild air of neediness, but she has ignored me.

I am trying to explain to H that I want to make a tag cloud of names, but given that he has never come across a tag cloud before, I am beginning to realise that this will take longer than I thought. We both fall silent for a while as I hunt around Google for a few examples. Then, Herbert takes my laptop from me, opens a new email, and starts typing.

You okay? He writes. *We don't get much time to talk while your mum's here.*

I'm fine, I type back. *Just a bit overwhelmed. Too much to do. Not enough time to do it in. Etc.*

I can babysit her tomorrow night while you go out, if you like?

Thanks, but I'll manage. Nearly the weekend.

Love you.

Love you too. Loving the typed conversation also.

;-)

It's delicious to be able to talk like this, in secret.

'Hey,' I say out loud, winking at him, 'I've thought of a website that'll show you what I mean.'

I type, *I think this site's a real turn-on. Such lovely pictures,* and open up a blog someone recommended to me. It's a compilation of pictures of people actually enjoying having sex, rather than posing or looking exploited. Some of them are clearly just enjoying being naked. I scroll down the page for H to see.

'Ah!' he says. 'That's exactly the kind of tag cloud we need.'

We giggle, quietly. 'Which ones are your favourites?' I ask.

I go back to the top of the page and move my cursor down, picture by picture. H puts a thumb up at the first, and then lets it rise or fall, depending on his response to each picture. I'm delighted to see that the pictures he likes the most are the ones where people are smiling, relaxed and slightly dishevelled. His thumb drops despondently at any hint of gloss or pose, or anything too serious.

I used to be afraid of looking at porn with him because I was scared that I'd find out that he had secretly been harbouring an exploitative male gaze. Quite the opposite.

His thumb spikes up the most enthusiastically for a woman sitting on a bed, her large stomach forming rolls.

'Why that one?' I mouth at him.

'She's got a lovely, knowing smile,' he whispers back.

By 11 p.m. I am exhausted, but somehow I have agreed to have sex with Herbert on the sofa all the same. It's amazing what you can achieve if you're really motivated.

In my case tonight, motivation is coming from my ability to access my teenage rebellious streak, even at my age. Ridiculous, I know. But there's something compelling about canoodling downstairs while your mother sleeps upstairs.

Actually, it's just like old times. It's uncomfortable, rushed and inconvenient, and requires near-impossible levels of quiet on our part. There has been a tense wait for her to go to bed, during which we have exchanged covert glances and suppressed yawns. At one point, I even managed to stroke Herbert's nipples while she had her back turned in the kitchen. But now, after she's pottered around in the bathroom for what seems like an eternity, and called Bob the cat to join her in bed (Bob is a traitor. She wouldn't dream of climbing into bed with me), we are finally alone.

At this point, what I want more than anything is to watch *The Inbetweeners* in peace, without anyone saying, repeatedly, 'And this counts as funny these days?' However, it is not to be. Herbert has already removed his pyjamas.

We leave the TV on, though, which means that every few minutes H dissolves into laughter at a particularly funny joke. My concentration is less than perfect too: I've got one ear on the landing, listening for footsteps. Meanwhile, H has decided to answer everything I say with 'Shhhh!' In my experience, distant conversation is indistinct, but 'shhhh' travels. It is a dead giveaway.

But I suppose the pleasure of a seduction like this is nine-tenths nostalgia anyway. It takes me back to the times when sex had to be carefully concealed from parents and housemates, which also happened to be a time when sex was at its most light-headedly compelling. Now that sex is readily available in a nice, comfortable bedroom, it's harder to truly desire it. Maybe the truth is that our formative experiences of sex are hushed and risky; we don't quite believe that a languorous, unhurried encounter is the real deal.

Perhaps the seductions are nothing more than a symbolic mother in bed upstairs. Perhaps they are nothing more than a reason to say: 'Here. Now.'

Seduction #39
An Awfully Big Adventure

I said once before that monogamous love is nothing more than a choice amongst other choices.

Today, I want to say the opposite. Today, I want to say that love can neatly side-step your ability to make decisions. Today, I want to say that love is compulsive.

Both things are true: love is both a choice and an uncontrollable urge, an act of will and an imposition. When I first met Herbert, I didn't choose to fall in love with him; I just did. If you'd have asked me, ten minutes before we met, what it felt like to fall in love, I wouldn't have known the answer. But he appeared on the chair next to me, and there it was: this unnerving feeling of complete adoration that I've never quite lost.

By the time I started these seductions – almost a year ago now – that breathtaking flare of love had mellowed into something a little tamer. We had been through a fair few sticky moments by then, and I was inclined to see love as something a little more mechanical, at least in the long term. We definitely loved each other, but it was choice that had stuck us together when life got difficult. I felt that the compromises – the fading of sex, the limiting of one's own choices so that your lives fit together – were inevitable, but worth it.

Now that addictive form of love seems to be back again. One minute I was thinking, *I wonder if these seductions will actually make any difference to our lives at all?* And then, quite suddenly, I realised that I couldn't stop looking at him. I have noticed lately that my eyes like to drink in his face. It's restful, soothing, endlessly fascinating. And I'm more certain about it than I ever was before. In the early days, I used to wonder whether I would one day wake up and find that attraction had worn off, like pain seeping through morphine. Now I know that it hasn't happened, and won't happen.

I say all of this because while my mother was staying, I missed him. I saw him every day and shared a bed with him every night, but I missed him all the same. I was desperate for some time alone, just the chance to check in with him and be together, quietly.

By Friday, I am quite beside myself with something that feels like sexual frustration, but which is actually love frustration. In addition, it's Herbert's birthday on Monday, and was mine last week. I hate missing the chance to celebrate.

I text him at work: *Can you get the day off on Monday? Booking it now*, comes the reply.

Okay, I say, *I'm going to take you on a Grand Day Out.*

Come Monday, with my mother dropped safely off at the airport the night before, I pack Herbert on to a train to London. For lunch, we eat a biryani with dhal and reminisce about our trip to India two years ago. Then we head over to London Zoo to admire the sleeping tigers and coo over the penguins. After a spot of tea and cake in Primrose Hill, I let H browse the record shops in Camden while I drink coffee and refrain from complaining.

Today's seduction, then, is not about sex, but about romance. We kiss in the street and walk to our destinations holding hands. By the end of the day, we are good for nothing more than snuggling into bed together and falling asleep.

The seductions may not have made sex compulsive again, or at least not in the same way it was when we were first together. But they have drawn love to the surface, blooming and giddy. It's hard to imagine that a mere year ago I felt as though I'd put aside those childish things of sex and romance. It's hard to imagine the intensity with which I fantasised about sex with other people, and how desolate that felt.

And now, sex and romance are not only back, but they are bringing with them strange new feelings of change and possibility. Gone is my image of Herbert as unchanging and complacent (or, as I once threw at him during a row, 'just killing time before death'); gone is my image of our relationship as having somehow found its fixed state. Here we both are, able to make any life we choose.

We walk through Exmouth Market on the way to Moro for our supper. 'Do you think you could live here?' I say.

H looks around him. 'Yes,' he says. 'Maybe.'

October

When I met Herbert, I was appalled by the idea of having children, and so was he. But then, I changed. Early in my twenties, I became unspeakably desperate for a baby. Herbert's view didn't change. He just didn't want one. There were rows. There were attempts at persuasion. Eventually, it came down to this: why should Herbert's 'no' outweigh my 'yes'? H is a reasonable man. He agreed that it wasn't fair.

We made a deal. He was allowed five more years of freedom – until my twenty-eighth birthday – and then I was allowed my baby. This squared nicely with me; it was the age at which my mother had me. Five years came and went. It was luxurious to dismiss the insistent baby-making part of my brain for a while. Friends began to reproduce. I held gazing infants and played with toddlers. I listened to defensive justifications of maternal choices: breast or bottle, parental bed or nursery cot. It seemed to me that a range of children were happy in a range of situations. I wondered if I'd ever be able to make those choices myself.

More than anything, I saw how deeply children cut into my friends' lives – the women and the men – and realised how much devotion I'd need to dig up in order to tolerate that lifestyle.

By the time twenty-eight arrived, I wasn't sure at all. I couldn't honestly say that I felt like I'd done all I'd wanted to do and was ready to settle down. But more than that, I could no longer see parenthood as something I could casually toss towards Herbert on the back of some hostile deal I'd brokered at twenty-three.

We hear a lot about the overriding power of women's body clocks and how they must not be denied. Since the beginning of my marriage, countless women have advised me to ignore Herbert's wishes and to just 'get myself pregnant'. This fills me with horror. Imagine women receiving the same treatment in return, the triple-bind of being denied your choice, having your lifestyle seriously curtailed, and then invoking the chorused disapproval of massed society should you then fail to fully adore that child. Perhaps I have a more wobbly body clock than other women, but this unstoppable urge to be a mother sounds suspiciously like the (mercifully) now-defunct assertion that men cannot help but to rape.

I am told, over and over again, that when presented with the fruit of his loins, Herbert will come round. He has told me this himself, after ringing around all his friends to interrogate them about their own attitudes to fatherhood. He's even tried to talk me out of my wariness of IVF, despite the fact that I know very well that he holds the same objections. And I suppose, one day, I may take him up on the offer. I also wish that one day I will fall magically, accidentally pregnant and that all this decision-making will be taken away from me.

But here and now, I'm happy to be a slightly unfashionable voice and say that I love H too much to force him into parenthood against his will. It's a good life, and I'm not willing to gamble it for the love of a person that doesn't exist yet. But I think, also, that being a grown-up is the process of learning to live in the fork between two roads. We should stop being surprised that there's more than one good way of doing things. We are fortunate to have the choice.

Seduction #40
Show and Tell

Herbert and I have never really shared our fantasies. I'm sure that sharing a fantasy is the ultimate act of intimacy, but that's just the problem. Long-term relationships offer a glut of intimacy. I want to hold a bit back for myself, and building a wall around my fantasy life is the best way I can think of achieving this. My fantasies offer me a modicum of sexual privacy.

More than this, my fantasies don't necessarily represent what I want to do in real life. I relish the unreality of them. I am afraid that they will turn brown, like the flesh of an apple, if I expose them to air.

But looking at pictures with Herbert last week made me think that good porn mediates our fantasies for us, letting us express tastes and preferences without exposing too much of our own psychic flesh. Watching Herbert's responses taught me so much about him that I wanted to not only learn more, but share more too. I wondered how I could build a seduction around sharing our turn-ons in this way.

The one thing I know a lot about is books. I have quite a few of them. Sometimes I read them, but mostly I like to gather them around me. In our house, there are two downstairs rooms. Herbert has filled the back one with records (we had to reinforce the joists underneath them), and I have filled the front one with books. When we throw parties, all the guests congregate around the records rather than the books. That suits me just fine.

When I thought about sharing fantasies, books came to mind immediately. From the moment I found my grandma's stash of Jackie Collins novels buried in the spare-room drawer, through *The English Patient* and *The Unbearable Lightness of Being* in my teens, to *The Crimson Petal and the White* this year, books have always fuelled my erotic imagination. Many's the time I have found my hand creeping under the waistband of my jeans as I read.

I suggest it to Herbert: 'We'll share the passages in books that have turned us on,' I say. 'The aim is to give each other a glimpse into our fantasy lives.'

Herbert looks worried for a while; he's dyslexic and a slow reader, and probably reads four or five books a year. But then he goes diving into his small section of the bookshelves, and pulls out four books without hesitation. I, meanwhile, am left dithering over my own book collection, wondering what on earth could have turned me on so much in the past. Whatever it was, I must have lent it to someone else.

'Hurry up!' says H. 'Don't give yourself time to get anxious about it.' Ah, there's the rub. I am pulling my usual trick of over-thinking. I am wondering whether I really want H to know about the fantasies in each book I pull from the shelf. Still, I hover.

'What are you looking for?' he asks. 'Something specific?'

'I know I had an idea yesterday, but I can't think of it right now.'

'Forget that one then.'

'Fine. I also think I've given away my copy of *The Story of O.*'

'I'll download it on to my phone. Not a problem.'

'You've picked out more than me.'

'Also not an issue. I didn't have so many to choose from. It was easier for me.'

It pains me that he has to ease me through my own seduction like this. I swipe a couple of books from the shelf, and we head for the bedroom.

Herbert opens one of his choices first. It is a book I have also read, but it never occurred to me that it might be erotic – *Jude: Level 1* by Julian Gough. It's a piece of wonderful Irish comic absurdity, and Herbert finds his desired section with surprising speed. I thought that he would talk to me about it and then pass the book to me, but no: he begins to read. Our hero, Jude, who has two penises (one of which is also his nose), is riding into battle on a horse with the object of his desire perched in front of him. Inevitably, his more normally placed member becomes erect, and they end up having sex on the horse amid their baying crowd of supporters.

'Well,' I say, 'I didn't think about it in that way.'

'But don't you think it sounds brilliant? Not just the having two penises thing either.'

'I suppose so,' I say. I confess, it does sound kind of fun. More fun than my first choice, the part in *Midnight's Children* where the doctor is seduced by examining a young woman only through a hole in a sheet, piece by piece. It's not written to thrill you, to be honest; I had forgotten this. H is unmoved. He selects in turn an excerpt from *American Gods* by Neil Gaiman, in which a man is having sex with a prostitute who seems to be dressed as Wonder Woman, and who, after asking him to worship her, engulfs his whole body in her vagina.

'Herbert,' I say, 'would it be rude to suggest that your choices are weird?'

'Yeah,' he says, 'but look how much fun he was having before she swallowed him up.'

I turn to safer ground: *The Story of O* on H's phone. I first came across it when I was seventeen, in an anthology of erotic stories on a friend's bookshelf. It only contained the first few pages, and I was a little disappointed when I read the whole thing and gradually had to watch O submit more and more. Still, the first few pages remain potent for me as I read them aloud. H seems to like them too.

'So, you like the idea of being told what to do?'

'Don't get any ideas. The thing I like about it is the sensual detail; the idea of her becoming naked under her clothes.'

'Mmm,' says H, looking dreamy.

He turns to *My Secret Garden* by Nancy Friday, where he's chosen the fantasy of a woman who dreams of an unseen lover performing cunnilingus on her under the table of a swish restaurant. 'I like the idea of no one else knowing,' he says.

I fumble through my copy of *The Sexual Life of Catherine M*, but can find no one passage that works for me. 'I think I just liked the overall idea of her insatiability,' I say. I should have added, *And the idea of being taken by hordes of unknown men*, but I didn't. Maybe I still quite relish that wall of privacy around my fantasy life.

'Shall we give up on books?' says H. 'It's late.' He turns out the light, and I am left feeling as if I've failed. Clearly this hasn't aroused him. Perhaps I've not given enough of myself.

But then, in the darkness, he climbs on top of me, and begins to kiss me frantically. The feeling of his erect penis spiking my thigh makes me gasp.

'I've remembered the other book!' I say.

'Mmm,' says H, whose mind is now on other things.

'It's the bit in *Cleaving* where her lover can't wait to get her upstairs, so they do it up against the wall in the hallway of his flats. I love the idea of someone being that desperate for me.'

H isn't really listening.

Seduction #41
Upside Down

Recently, apropos of absolutely nothing at all, Herbert said, 'Do you know what? I think we've learned to have sex without being drunk first.'

I don't think this is entirely fair. In the far-distant past, I'm sure we must have had sex sober. It's just that in recent years, being drunk was the only way we could get around our cringing embarrassment at making the first move. What's more, many's the time this year that I've had to down a steadying drink in order to tackle a seduction. We may have got more relaxed about admitting to being in the mood, but in many ways the seductions have made me reach for the Bombay Sapphire like never before.

In the case of today's example, however, it's difficult to imagine how it happened at all without a fair amount of inebriated bravado. Oh yes, I know: Herbert actually thought it was a good idea. That's right.

I'm not a huge fan of the 69. It's for teenagers (or at least ones whose parents go out sometimes). It's the kind of thing that sounds amazing – *We both get oral sex! At the same time! Woohoo!* – but that, in practice, is considerably less than the sum of its parts. The positioning is not particularly comfortable, whichever way you swing it (more of which later), but that's not the worst bit. No, the real problem is neural overload. I may be about to blow the myth of the multitasking woman out of the water here, but I can't concentrate on giving a blow job and receiving cunnilingus at the same time. I can only focus on one or the other, either my pleasure (in which case, sloppy blow job) or his (in which case, complete obliviousness to his hard work).

'What's the point?' I say to Herbert.

'Ah,' he replies sagely, 'but you always come when we 69. You just sometimes don't know what you like.'

He is both right and wrong here. I do orgasm, certainly, but it's a small, mechanical sort of an orgasm, polite and perfunctory. It's as if only my clitoris knows what's going on. Which is all very well. But, to be honest, I'd much rather take it in turns.

Now, as you may have guessed, Herbert is a huge fan of the 69. He would revert to it every time we have sex if I let him. That element of distraction that I so detest is exactly what he likes about it. It lets him turn off his conscious brain, the bit that often over-thinks everything. He is engaging in two things that he likes to do at once. He doesn't understand why I make such a fuss about it.

So when he suggests a 69-based seduction, I am not surprised. What raises my eyebrows a little, though, is his choice of format. 'I want to do that thing where you hang yourself upside down from my shoulders with your legs,' he says.

I stare at him.

'I mean, obviously, neither of us could do that.'

'Riiight.'

'So I've worked out a way of nearly getting there using the chair in the front room.'

'I don't see how that can work.'

'Don't worry.' He taps his skull. 'All figured out.'

Cometh the hour, and we are both standing naked in the front room, stone-cold sober. H has pushed the armchair into the middle of the floor, and we are both circling it. 'What you need to do,' he is saying, 'is bend your legs over the back to keep upside down.'

'I'm supposed to hang over the back of the chair like a bat?' I say. 'And where do I suddenly acquire the thigh muscles for that?'

'No!' he says. 'The other way round. Look, I'll show you.'

What he does, essentially, is to sit on the chair backwards, with his back on the seat and his legs propped up against the back.

'Oh,' I say, 'you're not really upside down, are you? You've just got your legs in the air.'

At this point, H begins to giggle. He can't stop. His face is turning beetroot. 'I must admit,' he says between gasps, 'it was a bit more upside down in my head.'

I begin to laugh too, and edge towards him to demonstrate just how impossible his position is. His head is so near the floor that I'd need to be an expert limbo dancer to be in with any chance of making contact with his tongue. Meanwhile, his testicles are flopping forwards over his penis, and I have a much more detailed view of his bum crack than I would prefer.

'Okay!' he says. 'Regroup!' And he attempts to dismount from the chair, but only succeeds in flipping his legs over his head, so that he is stranded like an upturned beetle. He waves his huge feet in the air and laughs so hard that I fear he will pass out. 'Help!' he puffs.

Once we have (inelegantly) set him upright, he's unde-terred. 'Okay,' he says, 'the problem was that the chair was too low. Let's try the sofa. Your turn.'

Making a great show of my patience, I lie backwards across the seat of the sofa.

'Hang on.' H grabs my legs and hoiks me upwards so that my bottom is on the top of the back-rest. 'That's better,' he says, and proceeds to crawl on top of me.

Well, his face may well be in my crotch, but in all other aspects we are hideously out of line. His penis is several miles away from my mouth, and his testicles are resting neatly on my forehead, like a warm compress. Now I am the one who's giggling uncontrollably. It must be related to all the blood rushing to my head. Herbert is laughing too. 'If you just sway your head from side to side, it's really quite nice,' he says.

I turn myself the right side up. 'Never mind,' I say supportively.

'No, we're not giving up yet. I've got another idea.'

I follow him to the spare room, where he presents me with the spare bed, covered in cat hair. 'You can do a headstand on the bed, leaning against the wall,' he says, as if this is the most simple, obvious thing in the world.

'No, Herbert, I cannot do a headstand. That is not a possibility.'

'It's okay, I'll help you.'

I don't know why I agree to this, but I obediently place my hands on either side of my head, like I learned in yoga class. H grabs my ankles and tries to lift them up to his shoulders, but at this point my head collapses sideways, and I fall, landing first on the bed, and then sliding down the back of it.

'No more,' I say.

'If you could just keep your neck a bit more steady?'

'NO. MORE.'

Herbert juts out his bottom lip. 'It was so perfect in my imagination.'

'Good,' I say. 'Keep it there.'

If this was all a ploy to make me adopt the more standard version of the 69 with enthusiasm, it worked.

*H*ow would you feel if I brought a kitten home with me tonight?

Other women may go wild for babies, but with me, it's kittens. Herbert must have been bracing himself for this text all his life. Coming from a four-cat family, he must have known that one would never be enough.

Do you want my honest answer? he replies.

Of course.

No.

I'm sure he can't mean that. And, in any case, he hasn't seen the little bundle in question, or heard its back-story. I am at a conference in a hotel, and there are seven identical black kittens scampering around the car park and generally getting under the wheels of every passing car. According to the gardener, one has been run over already. They're feral, apparently, and the hotel doesn't feel responsible for them.

'In a few weeks,' I say to a colleague, 'they'll all start breeding with each other, and then there will be hundreds of little black kittens.'

'All of them deaf and blind,' she says.

I am picking pieces of tuna out of my lunchtime sandwich and tossing them to the kittens, who skirt nervously around my feet.

'It would be cruel not to take one,' I say. I wonder if Herbert might feel differently if only he could see them. I hurriedly text him a picture.

Yes, cute, comes the reply, *but what will Bob do?*

Bob will love having a kitten around! I text, not entirely honestly. Bob is the most insanely highly strung cat I have ever encountered. She is as likely to eat the new kitten as to nurture it into tameness.

Look, says H, *I know nothing I say will stop you. I am just registering my opinion.*

Well, that's carte blanche, isn't it? I reach out to stroke one of the kittens and it hisses and runs away.

'Don't worry,' says my colleague, 'I'll catch one for you at home time. I'm good with wild cats.'

Do I spend the subsequent afternoon wondering whether I'm doing the right thing? Not a bit of it. I spend it pretending to work and furtively searching for a suitable box to take the kitten home in.

When the time comes, though, I am overcome with nerves. The kittens are all about eight weeks old, and I have seen them eating solid food (this is a polite way of saying, 'stripping a pigeon carcass'), but I am suddenly conscious that I am about to take one of them away from its mother. This seems like a mean thing to do, if only in the short term. I wait in the car while my colleague captures the kitten for me, and then, presented with a box with copious air-holes, I drive off without peeking.

Back home, I set the box on the floor of my study, and gingerly peel off the Sellotape. Inside, a small black mass of fur blinks at me for a few moments, and then charges in five directions at once, eventually crashing her head against the window and coming to a standstill, glaring at me. I hurriedly take a photo and send it to Herbert.

Elsie the kitten, in her new home.

Aaah, he replies. *Is it a girl then?*

I have no idea. All kittens are girls, right?

By the time Herbert gets home, Elsie has wedged herself under my filing cabinet, from which she doesn't emerge – at least while we're looking – for quite some time.

Seduction #42
The CAT

At this stage in the game – with only ten seductions to go – I feel that we should have developed some form of expertise.

We should be able to breeze into the bedroom, shake off our clothes, indulge in something mutually enticing, achieve monumental orgasms and then put our feet up for a post-coital cigarette (a metaphorical one, in our case) and a glass of wine. But no. Sometimes, even the basics elude us.

'Shall we try the CAT this week?' I say to Herbert.

'Sure,' he says. 'Remind me of the point of it again?' We've discussed the Coital Alignment Technique before, and never quite got round to it. You start off in the missionary position, and then the man shifts his whole body upwards, so that his penis is only just inside the woman, with the length of it sitting against her vulva. She tilts her pelvis upwards, and together they rock in what's often described as a see-saw motion. H has always maintained that this sounds too complicated to be worth it.

'Well,' I say, 'it's recommended for women who struggle to orgasm, so I reckon it must be brilliant if you can orgasm anyway.'

Sometimes, though, two and two do not make four. I blame *The Inbetweeners*. Before we head to the bedroom, we watch an episode in which Simon attempts to lose his virginity to his girlfriend, but can't get an erection. How we roared with laughter as the hapless Simon was reduced to slapping and shouting at his cock in a vain attempt to stir it into action.

Cut to half an hour later, and Herbert seems to be suffering from some televisual contagion. There's not a lot going on down there.

'Are you perhaps not in the mood?' I say as delicately as possible. 'We can go and have a cup of tea and come back later?'

'Gah! Don't talk about it! You'll make it worse! Oh, look what you've done!'

He's right. What little progress we have made has very definitely been reversed. I scoot sideways and put it in my mouth, and gradually we reach some semblance of an erection, albeit slightly lethargic. Meanwhile, Herbert reaches down and attempts to rub my labia. 'Ouch!' I yelp. Completely dry.

'Use some lube!' I say, and if I'm honest there's probably a slight snap in my voice.

H smears some lube on me, and we get into position. We are not, after all, going to pass up an opportunity like this, the synchronising of an erect penis and a moist, if disinterested, vagina.

Now, when it comes to sex, I'm a great believer in the

adage 'fake it till you feel it'. Many's the time that I have trundled along without much desire until my body finally catches on. The problem is, when you're both approaching sex with a workmanlike sigh, it's pretty hard for your body to find anything much to enthuse over.

The mechanics are fine. We get into missionary position, H shifts upwards, and after a couple of false starts, we think we've done it. I wrap my legs around his calves and we begin to rock. It's funny how, without arousal, sex can feel like a body part rubbing against a body part, nothing else. There is no magic spark. I wonder, if I concentrate hard enough, if my clitoris will eventually respond. After five minutes of wondering, I say to H, 'Is this doing anything for you?'

'Nope,' he says. 'You?'

'Nothing.'

'I'm not sure if it's even still in.'

'Oh, it is. It's just not doing anything interesting.'

'Right.'

'Shall we give up then?'

'If you wouldn't mind.'

Back in the safety of the living room, tea in hand, I say to Herbert, 'Would it be fair to say that you have an issue with technique?'

A sigh. 'What's wrong with my technique?'

'Oh God, I don't mean that. I mean you hate the idea of seductions that you need a technique for. It makes you nervous.'

'Maybe. I don't know.'

'Because, you know it's fine to make mistakes when you try new things, don't you? You just have to laugh it off and try again.'

Herbert is staring resolutely forwards.

I know when I'm beat.

Seduction #43
The Reverse Cowgirl Rides Again

Seduction #42 leaves a sour taste in our mouths. There is something particularly affecting about failed sex; it leaves a trail behind it that follows you into the next day. Fragile egos, I suppose. My instinct is to grin and bear it rather than give up halfway through like that, but that doesn't work when both of you are grinning and bearing.

We are in need of a little redemption. We are in need of an uncomplicated orgasm. On Sunday morning I am presented with what, under the circumstances, feels like divine inspiration.

I awake from a dream, the details of which are hazy to me now, but which found Herbert and me in the basement bar of a beautiful hotel, surrounded by the cast of a circus. Not to put too fine a point on it, they were all getting it on. Two aerialists were swinging from a trapeze above us, their bodies entwined. Over H's shoulder, I could see the ringmaster spanking a ballerina, her bottom like a huge rosette, framed by her tutu. The dream ended just as we were debating whether to join them.

I get up and stumble dry-mouthed into the bathroom, where I inhale a glass of water and then climb into a shower. Even as I'm drying myself, I'm still aroused; I find myself lamenting the fact that Sunday morning sex is not really what we do.

But we used to. It used to practically be part of our routine. I think that all changed when we bought our own house and Sundays turned into a cacophony of drilling and painting, early mornings, loud radios and fish and chips for lunch. But today, I wonder . . .

I put my head around the bedroom door. H has, as is his custom, moved his head on to my pillow, so that his body is spread diagonally across the bed. He does this every morning, as soon as I get up. I tickle his feet.

'Fancy a shag?' I say.

A deep breath. A pause. 'No.'

'Oh go on! I'll make you a cup of tea, and you can get in a shower to wake you up.'

H rubs his face. 'Okay,' he says, without much enthusiasm.

I pad downstairs and put the kettle on, and am heartened to hear the shower turn on upstairs. At least he hasn't just rolled over and fallen asleep again. By the time the tea is ready, I can hear him pottering around the bathroom, so I slip, naked, into bed.

Before long, he gets in beside me, and takes a big draw on his tea. I snuggle in so that my back is pressing against him. 'Wait,' he says, 'I haven't finished my tea yet.' This is not looking promising.

But he drains the cup of tea, and then immediately dives under the covers. He runs his tongue down the base of my spine and then along the cleft between my buttocks. Then he lifts my leg over his shoulder and continues to lap at me with his tongue. I lie on my side and put the pillow over my face. I wasn't expecting this. Clearly it is worth catching him before he's woken up too much.

Things proceed, and I find myself happily squirming about on top of him. 'Herbert,' I say, 'I've got a notion I'd like to try the Reverse Cowgirl again.'

A raised eyebrow from H. We have vowed never to go near it again. But, in the last couple of months, my body seems to be behaving itself. It's a long time since I bled after sex. I think it might all be getting better. And, besides, the devil in me wants to put it to the test. 'Sure,' says H. 'We'll just take it easy.'

H loves the Reverse Cowgirl. It's his idea of a good view, and it lets him orchestrate the proceedings. I find it marginally undignified, but I love the way it feels. I swivel round so that I'm facing his feet, and let him guide his penis into place. First of all, he chooses to let it rest between my legs, which is very pleasurable for both of us, and then he slides it into me. I lean forwards to get the full effect, and H parts my buttock cheeks and begins to massage my anus. He often does this, and I used to object on principle; I wasn't sure it was hygienic. But now, this year, I've got over myself. It feels fabulous.

This time, though, he goes a little further. I can hear him fumbling about on the bedside table, and before long I feel cold lube on my bottom, and then his finger slipping deep inside it. I gasp, but in pleasure, and smile to myself about how many inhibitions I've shed this year. It's a wonderful feeling, his finger and his cock inside me, every movement I make changing the intense sensations.

As I begin to feel an orgasm welling up inside me, I turn back to face him, and he holds on to my hips as I throw back my head and feel my whole being rush to my head. Underneath me, H's legs are scissoring as he matches my convulsions.

We both fall into laughter and then, overwhelmed, my laughter segues into tears.

'Not sad,' I say, between gasps, 'just . . . good . . . orgasm.'

H gazes up at me in wonder.

The masseuse looks alarmed at my scratches. I am reminded of the scene in *The Story of O*, in which our heroine is confronted about the welts on her body when she goes for a wax.

'Oh,' I say, 'that's just my new kitten. I tried to pick her up.'

She widens her eyes. Kittens are supposed to be small and playful, aren't they? Not Elsie. She is like a little lump of dark matter. She mostly lurks under the filing cabinet, and if we dare to even glance at her, she hisses. Yesterday, she wedged herself behind my printer, and I foolishly thought to take this opportunity to sex her. Let's just say that lifting her by the scruff of the neck did not have the calming effect that the kitten book claimed. She managed to swing round mid-air and set about my hand with her claws and teeth. Then, when I finally managed to detach her from my flesh, she hissed at me again, just to make her position clear. I never got as far as checking under her tail.

Meanwhile, Bob the cat has turned unaccountably friendly. In the rare moments that she is not keeping sentry outside my office door, sniffing and occasionally growling, she follows me around, demanding my attention. This is unheard of for Bob, who usually likes to give out the impression that I am her captor rather than her loving owner. Clearly a little jealousy is no bad thing. Treat 'em mean and keep 'em keen, that's what I say.

I am finding this kitten ownership business rather stressful. I confess that I assumed it would take Elsie a mere couple of days to start curling up on my lap and playing with my shoelaces. Instead, I feel as though I'm affecting a full-scale rehabilitation. To his credit, Herbert has not once said, 'I didn't want her in the first place.' On the other hand, he wasn't as sympathetic as I'd have liked when she used my knitting basket as a latrine.

Either way, I have earned this massage. It is something I'm doing more and more of late, booking myself a little treat that keeps my body feeling cared for. Once, I'd have considered it a heinous waste of money, but now it feels like the best kind of indulgence – the kind that doesn't leave you feeling guilty afterwards. I have even got in the habit of exfoliating twice a week, which leaves the bottom of the shower gritty underfoot, but means that my elbows are a great deal less crusty.

I'd have seen it all as a pointless vanity before. I was clean and (occasionally) shaven-legged; what more did I need? And besides, Herbert has never made the slightest effort in that direction. He thinks that metrosexual is a magazine supplement. I have to remind him to trim his beard and cut his toenails, and even then there is generally a lag before he actually does this. Why should I primp myself up when he doesn't care about my grooming or his?

However, just like buying good lingerie, I've learned that I do this for me, not him. I feel absolutely no yearning to be stick-thin and perfect, but on the other hand, I am no longer convinced when I tell myself that I don't feel any need to be beautiful. Over the years, I have been horrified by the way that my body has stowed away deposits of fat and caches of grey skin. It is as if my mental image of myself has been gradually shaded in with black patches, signifying the bits I can no longer bear to contemplate, let alone show in public. The problem was, there were few remaining parts that weren't shaded black.

I think I might have mistaken 'accepting my own body' for 'turning a blind eye to it'. I wanted to be confident and self-affirming enough to not obsess about things I couldn't change. Instead, I forced myself to swallow a notion of bodily decline that made me feel desolate and unattractive. And, crucially, I told myself that it was vain to feel this way.

I'm beginning to shine a light into those dark zones that I'd tried to persuade my brain to forget. I'm taking a yoga class and building up strength with power-plate exercises. I'm eating better and drinking less. And I've even taken up running, although, in fairness, this currently means that I shuffle, gasping, for a minute at a time, followed by a two-minute walk. I'm not sure that really counts.

All of this feels different to vanity. Instead, it's part of the behaviour of a lover; it's not about seeking perfection, just satisfaction, and the ability to feel free and comfortable in my own flesh.

Seduction #44
The Food of Love

Herbert grimaces, swallows hard, and then swills fizzy wine around his mouth to wash the taste away.

'Well,' he says, 'that was an . . . *indifferent* experience.'

'I'm so proud of you!' I say. 'You hardly made any fuss about that.'

Herbert, you see, has just consumed his first oyster. Raw. To put this in context, I have never seen him eat seafood before – ever – expect for moments when some wag has snuck some shrimps into his Singapore noodles and he is obliged to spit them out.

All the more surprisingly, he has done this of his own volition. I am willing to pressgang H into a wide range of activities, but I draw the line at making him eat fish. I tried it early on in our relationship, and it led to hysteria. I have learned my lesson.

Herbert's seduction tonight, then, is food. Specifically,

he's researched a list of foodstuffs with aphrodisiac prop-
erties. Most of the items on his list, he tells me, were
debunked elsewhere on the internet, but he's willing to
give them a go.

His list contains: almonds, aniseed, asparagus,
avocado, bananas, chilli peppers, chocolate, coffee,
fennel, figs, garlic, ginger, honey, mustard, nutmeg, pine-
apple, pine nuts, raw oysters, rocket, truffles, vanilla and
wine.

'Which are we eating then?' I ask.

'I want to eat all of them, to be honest.'

Right. Of course. 'I take it you have a concept?'

'Well,' he says, 'oysters on their own, obviously. What's
that stuff you normally eat them with?'

'Shallot vinegar.'

'Lots of that then. How do you get hold of truffles?'

'Trust me, we can't afford them.'

'Oh.'

'I think you can get truffle oil though.'

'That'll do. I was thinking of having it on asparagus.'

'Asparagus is out of season.'

'You're going to have to live with that for today.'

'Fair enough. Main course?'

'A molé sort of a thing. I reckon I can bung a lot of
those ingredients in there, get it all over and done with.'

'And the fruit? You don't eat fruit.'

'Yes I do!'

'Name me the last time you voluntarily ate fruit.'

'I dunno. In a crumble?'

'That doesn't count.'

H sighs at me. I am not appreciating the effort he's
going to.

'How about we grill the fruit,' I say, 'and get some ginger

ice cream to go with it? I could make a honey and butter sauce to pour over the top.'

We spend the afternoon shopping and cooking. H lays the table with the tablecloth we bought on holiday and my charity-shop champagne bowls. There are candles and silver cutlery. He even remembers napkins, although I confess that I refold them from triangles to oblongs while his back's turned.

We start with the oysters, and then move on to asparagus with truffle butter and Parmesan. Out of season, it's slightly watery, but lovely all the same.

'Are you feeling anything yet?' I ask him.

'Maybe a bit light-headed?'

'That's just the lingering fear from the oysters.'

We take a break before the main course, and we pass the time sitting around the filing cabinet in my study, pushing bits of leftover chicken towards Elsie the kitten. She occasionally hisses in response. H wonders aloud whether she would have enjoyed his oyster more than he did.

The molé, which has stewed down to a thick, meaty paste, is divine, an odd combination of sweet and spicy, and very hot. We temper it with avocado and fennel salad, and huge blobs of sour cream. Afterwards, we mean to take another break before dessert, but we end up falling on to the sofa together, and from there we progress to bed. Dessert is all but forgotten.

Did the food have an aphrodisiac effect?

Well, from my point of view, I think perhaps it did. I was definitely in the mood by the time the main course was over, and my orgasm seemed to come tumbling out of me without much encouragement. Whether this was the result of the romantic evening or the food, I don't know And if it was the food, I wonder which particular ingredient worked its magic?

For H, though, it was less successful. There was no doubt that he was also in the mood, but such was his enthusiasm that he tipped himself upside down early on, nearly fainted because all his blood was, um, elsewhere, and then lost his erection because his circulatory system over-compensated and sent all his blood to his head.

At least, that's his excuse. My theory is that the box of Viagra that he's ordered for a seduction later this week was working some kind of impotence-voodoo on him.

Seduction #45
The Blue Pill

There have been seductions with more auspicious starts.

Herbert, you see, has it in mind to carry out a consumer test of sorts: herbal Viagra versus the real thing. It was one of his first suggestions for a seduction, and he has continued to petition for it all through our year. I didn't even know you could buy the stuff without a prescription from your GP, but H found a website offering an online consultation, and after that there was no stopping him.

He comes home one night and breezily says over dinner, 'The Viagra's on its way.'

'Oh my God,' I say, 'did you actually pretend you had erectile dysfunction to a real doctor?'

'No,' he says, 'I told nothing but the truth. I said that sometimes I can't get an erection if I feel under pressure, or if I'm distracted. I said that I can't always have sex with my wife when she wants me to.'

'But I suspect you didn't mention that this only accounts for around 5 per cent of the time.'

'No. But then neither did I mention that this is all part of some bizarre sex project.'

Bizarre is such an ugly word. Still, those mythical little blue pills arrive promptly in the post, followed swiftly by their herbal cousins. H opts to take the latter first. He says he wants to build up to the main event. So, on Thursday night, he swallows two tablets, and shortly afterwards two friends drop by unexpectedly.

As I carefully offer them tea instead of wine and leave their cups unreplenished, I watch H closely. He's very quiet. I very much hope he's not trying to conceal a bump in his trousers.

As soon as they leave, he says, 'That was awful. Do you think they could tell?'

'Did it work then?'

'No. First my nose went numb, then the rest of my face. Now I've got a raging headache and I can't see straight.'

'Blimey.'

'Yeah. There's me thinking they wouldn't have any effect at all.'

An early night for Herbert then. And following that experience, he is understandably reluctant to try the real thing. But come Sunday night, his sense of adventure has recovered sufficiently for him to slip into the kitchen during *Antiques Roadshow* and take half a Viagra.

'It should take half an hour to work,' he says, so we settle down on the sofa to watch a fascinating segment on Agatha Christie's old safe. This elicits no stirrings, so we decide to wait a little longer. Half an hour passes. 'I think maybe I'll take the other half,' says H.

He does this, and we watch *Have I Got News for You*.

Neither Janet Street-Porter's cleavage nor Paul Merton's impish grin rouses H into action. I yawn.

'Well,' says H, 'that was a waste of time. Shall we go to bed?'

'We could just achieve an erection the old-fashioned way?'

'No. I'm sulking now.'

We go upstairs and, as I'm brushing my teeth, H reads the leaflet from the Viagra packet. 'Oh,' he says, 'apparently you have to actually be aroused for it to work. You don't just get a hard-on.'

'You didn't think to read that before you took it, no?'

'Whatever.'

'So basically it's just like normal then? What's the point of that?'

'Well, technically,' says H, 'it's for people with erectile dysfunction.'

We get into bed, and H suggests I stroke his penis. Frankly, my brain has now switched to 'going to sleep' mode, but I suppose there's no sense in wasting twelve quid's worth of Viagra. It doesn't take long for the wee fella to perk up, and soon it's rock solid.

'Erm, goodness,' I say, 'that's the Viagra difference, I suppose.'

H gazes down at it rather proudly.

'Does it feel any different?'

'No,' he says, 'not really.' Then he thinks for a moment. 'Actually, yes, maybe it does.'

'In what way?'

'I dunno. Just different.'

I refrain from asking him to be more specific, as too in-depth a discussion of our sexual congress tends to get us into the kind of situations that require Viagra in the first place. H climbs on top of me, and soon his weirdly hard penis is frolicking happily. Except that, from my end, it feels like a battering ram.

'Ow,' I say, 'that's actually quite uncomfortable.'

'Do you want me to stop?'

'No,' I say, 'but maybe we could just slide it between my legs?'

H is always keen on this particular manoeuvre; in fact, he really can't tell the difference between this and actual penetration. Normally, I'm pretty fond of it too, but tonight the sensation of his completely unyielding dick against my more delicate parts is none too comfortable.

'Maybe some lube?' I suggest.

We apply lube. It improves things somewhat, and I even manage a small orgasm myself, but I can't help feeling relief when he finally comes. He lies back on the pillows and sighs deeply. I glance down.

'Bloody hell,' I say, 'it's still going strong down there.'

We both stare at it in a kind of awe. I almost fancy that it's staring back at us, defiantly.

'Would you say,' I venture, 'that it looks different from normal?'

'I was just thinking that too.'

'Sort of shorter and fatter?'

'Yes! You're right.'

'How weird. It's a new shape of erection.'

'Hmm. I wasn't expecting that.'

'Well, what are you going to do with it now?'

'Go to sleep.'

'Won't it bother you? I mean, won't it demand your attention?'

'Betty,' says H, 'you have no idea what it's like to be a teenage boy, have you?'

And on that somewhat cryptic note, he conceals his straight-backed tyrant of a penis in his pyjamas and drifts off to sleep.

November

I am now four weeks into my running programme and can now just about manage to go for three minutes without dying.

But that is fine, because I am a runner in my heart. Everything about my running experience so far has told me to stop. This is, in fact, my fourth attempt to get started. The first attempt ended after I found my personal trainer so scary that I actually had a panic attack. The second time, I realised that being anaemic made it difficult to stay conscious and run at the same time. The third time, I developed agonising shin splints. No matter. I have waited patiently for all these things to pass, and now I am trying again.

It may be that something will happen that stops me this time too. My knees are feeling a little tired, I'll confess. But the problem is, my second ever run happened early one winter morning on sparkly black pavements. The air was thick with frost and even though I was gasping for breath, there was something addictive about that cold, quiet morning, the glittering tarmac and my feet pounding unsteadily upon it. I knew this was for me, however long it took.

I remember feeling exactly the same way about meditation. I knew that I needed it, and I tried various ways to get into it, but it nevertheless took me six years to make it stick to my life. Now, I'd feel like half a person without it. I find it impossible to attend clubs or to follow routines, but my twenty minutes, twice a day, are sacrosanct.

It's the same with the seductions. We've spent years wishing we had a better sex life but – the odd summer holiday aside – until now, nothing has stuck. I'm now so grateful that we didn't just give up altogether. It's a miracle that we still knew that sex was important, even when we couldn't be bothered to do it. Why did it rise to the surface again and again, even when we were trying hard to push it down?

I have a million answers to that question now (intimacy, biology, a shared sense of conspiracy), but the one that I return to the most is this: sex is an expression of robustness. It requires robust self-esteem and a robust relationship to wade through the morass of embarrassment and reach pleasure. And it also requires a robust conception of one's own body. In order to have sex, to really surrender to it, we must see ourselves as strong and well, capable of a little rough and tumble.

I did not feel like this when I began the seductions. But yesterday, I went for a long-scheduled appointment with my gynaecologist and was able to say, 'Do you know what? I'm absolutely fine.' He discharged me.

So, arguably, this year my medical treatment has worked, and I am now in a much better bodily position to enjoy sex again. But there's more to it than that. My self-image has changed. I have stopped suspecting that I am basically sickly. This is a belief I have carried from childhood, and this year I have realised that I no longer have any use for it.

It's not that my lady garden is a utopia. We still have to be careful sometimes (but then again, sometimes not). We've developed ways around all the problems. And more than anything, I've learned that my body belongs to me. It is no more Herbert's responsibility to find ways to please it than it is my doctor's responsibility to make it run smoothly. It is mine. I now see it as strong, fit and healthy. I take excellent care of it.

This time a year ago, I was wondering what was the most appropriate form of pubic hair-grooming for a doctor's appointment. Would they disapprove of a little tidying around the edges with a razor? Was a bikini wax too extreme? Yesterday, I turned up ready to present a completely bald pudenda. It is mine to do with as I wish. I find it hard to believe that I ever thought otherwise.

Seduction #46
Ticklish

I can't stand to be tickled. I do not see it as remotely fun. It doesn't make me laugh so much as growl like an animal. It just doesn't seem like a very nice thing to do to someone else.

Herbert learned this early on in our relationship, when he tried to playfully tickle me and I hit him full-on in the mouth.

'What was that for?' he said, clasping his face.

'I told you to stop, and you didn't.'

A horrified stare. 'But you're *supposed* to beg me to stop. It's all part of the game.'

'Don't like it.'

This conversation has been repeated, in various guises (although usually without the accompanying violence), at regular intervals throughout our marriage. Herbert is convinced that tickling is fun. I am convinced that it is creepy. Stalemate.

So I knew that, sooner or later, he would suggest it as a seduction.

'Oh God, no,' is my response.

'Come on. It'll be fine.'

'Do you know what the sensation of being ticklish means?'

'No, Betty, and it doesn't matter . . .'

'It's an evolutionary response. We learned to feel ticklish so that we can tell when insects are crawling on us. In case they're poisonous.'

H shakes his head.

'Therefore,' I say, 'tickling should really count as a sadomasochistic practice.'

'You don't really mean that.'

'I do.'

'It's just tickling.'

'Fine,' I say, 'I'll tickle you.'

'And I'll tickle you back.'

'I'll need a safe word.'

This is the problem with the seductions: it's not entirely legitimate to say no to anything. In preparation, I comfort myself with the purchase of a feather tickler from Coco de Mer, which I hope will pose less of an affront to my personal space than the jabbing and writhing of another person's fingers.

When the appointed seduction-hour arrives, I decide to seize the initiative.

'Right,' I say, 'I'm going to tickle you.'

'No,' says H, 'you first.' I screw up my face. 'Don't worry, I'll stop if you ask me to.'

He asks me to undress and lie face down on the bed. I am probably the most excessively ticklish person alive. If, for example, H goes down on me before I'm properly warmed up, I will spend the first five minutes squealing in ticklish agony and pushing his face away. I suppose I should count myself lucky that he finds this endearing and persists.

Tonight, all he does is float the tickler down my back, and I am in convulsions. I do not giggle; I make a noise for which there is no name, but which sounds very much like 'Urrrrrrr'. Very loudly.

At this point, H decides that it's appropriate to talk to me as if I'm Elsie the psychotic new kitten. 'It's alright,' he says in a frankly camp voice. 'Just calm down. There.'

'Fuck off,' I say.

He rests the tickler on the very base of my spine, and I begin to kick and flail my legs around. It's hideously intense, the very definition of discomfort.

'You just have to breathe through it. It's like taking pain.'

'Right,' I say, 'I'm not doing this. Let's see how you like it.'

He looks disappointed, but lies on his front all the same. I twirl the tickler down his legs and across his buttocks, then drag it slowly up his spine. Nothing. 'Can't you even feel that?' I ask.

'Of course I can. It's lovely.'

'Freak,' I say. 'Turn over.'

He likes it even more across his nipples and over his testicles. He's not even giggling. I'm sure he's showing off.

Eventually, I get bored. If he's not going to find this even vaguely torturous, I'm not interested.

'This isn't really a seduction, is it?' I say. 'It's just a chance for you to demonstrate how rubbish I am.'

He rolls over. 'That's not true!'

'Yes it is. You're deliberately trying not to laugh. You're

behaving like a six-year-old who's being tickled by one of his siblings. You're straining every muscle to avoid feeling anything.'

'No, I'm . . . Well, yes, alright, I suppose it's force of habit.' Herbert's elder sister, who, in adulthood, is a full foot shorter than him and incredibly sweet-tempered, was allegedly a tyrant in her youth.

'At least I'm actually engaging with it.'

'Okay, Betty, your moral superiority is asserted.'

'Good.'

'Good.'

'Well, shall I tickle you some more then?' I say. 'Only if you'll agree to laugh, obviously.'

'Okay. And after that, it's your turn.'

I don't think so. I'll just have to find other ways to distract him.

Seduction #47
I'm In Charge

As I stand in my bathroom trying to crowbar myself into a black PVC corset, I find myself reflecting on Jane Austen.

In particular, I am thinking that the feminine accomplishments that the young ladies in her books had to attain – singing, dancing, a smattering of French – are nothing compared to the accomplishments required of the modern woman. I have already tested my handcuffs, practised my whip-strokes and worked wonders on myself with a tube of lip gloss and some black eyeliner. I fear, however, that the corset may be a challenge too far.

Eventually, after zipping my flesh into it several times, and observing that even this garment is not enough to give me any sort of a cleavage, I declare myself satisfied. Actually, being a recovering teenage goth, I rather like the outfit. I would probably have worn it out clubbing fifteen years ago. Even the ridiculous PVC pencil skirt. And the elbow-length PVC gloves.

In the bedroom, I light some candles to create a dungeon vibe. Unsurprisingly, this doesn't work. The problem with playing out fantasies at home is that it's hard to escape the domesticity of the setting. I spend quite some time clearing discarded clothes away into drawers and removing empty tea mugs, but as soon as I call down to H to come and join me, I realise that my slippers are sitting neatly under my bedside table. I resolve to use the blindfold after all.

I can't say that this is particularly my fantasy, but I think it might at least partly resemble Herbert's. My guess has long been that he would really like to be dominated. The problem is, I have absolutely no idea where to start. I have already bottled out once on this seduction, and I feel just as ridiculous about my second attempt. Hence the costume, which I let H choose. Sometimes you have to go through the tacky phase to find your inner connoisseur.

And, actually, it's not the domination I mind, it's the submissive response. I get him to kneel naked on the bed and blindfold him, and then I attempt to handcuff his hands behind his back. This is not going to happen. The handcuffs that worked perfectly well on me don't even go around H's wrists. I giggle and he giggles too. With nothing else in sight, I reach for the elastic that held the handcuffs in their box. This holds out for about five minutes. After that, H just obediently holds his hands in place as if they are still tied together.

Meanwhile, I try out my various tools. I swish my suede flogger over his naked body, and use it to flick his nipples and testicles. I go a little harder on his buttocks and the backs of his thighs. I manhandle his penis with my gloved hands and bite his nipples. I run my feather tickler along his rib cage.

Then I get a bit bored. This is all a bit one-way for my liking. Seeking inspiration, my eye alights on the burning candle. We've all seen *Body of Evidence*, right? It seemed to go down well when Madonna did it.

'How about some candle wax?' I say to H in my best dominatrix voice.

'Um, okay,' he says in reply. Feeling brave, I drip a trail of hot wax along his stomach. H looks horrified. His skin turns a deep red underneath the wax.

'Would you like some more?' I say. I watch his erection wane.

'Err, yes, Mistress.' I know he doesn't mean this. I also wonder if it's okay to ban the use of the word 'mistress' at this late stage.

'You wouldn't lie to me, would you?' I say, trying not to break out of character. 'Do you really want it?'

H lets out a breath. 'You're right,' he says. 'No, I don't. Mistress.'

'Good boy,' I say. I'm feeling horribly guilty and am dying to see whether the wax has actually burnt him. 'You may remove the wax.'

He brushes it off with his fingers, revealing a line of crimson blotches on his skin. At least it hasn't blistered. I lean in and lick them, and then, by way of distraction, bite his nipples some more.

The problem with all this domination is that it's such a lonely job. With H behaving so passively, I'm not getting any of the cues I usually rely on to turn myself on. I think I just don't understand the point of the roles being so different. Why, for example, can't we take it in turns with the flogger? That would be much more interesting. I also have a notion that I'd make less of a fuss over the candle wax.

H, thankfully, notices I'm a bit lost. He asks to take off his blindfold to get a better view, and, after that, everything is fine. He claims that the corset brings about a cleavage, even if I can't see it. But later, I find myself wondering what the point of all that was.

'I felt like I was trying to have someone else's sex,' I say.

Herbert is lying in bed with a cold, and I am wondering when he'll be back on his feet. I want to have sex with him, you see, and not just because we're on a deadline here. My body wants it. Maybe I have finally jump-started my sex drive.

Actually, it turns out it was there all along. My sexual self feels the same as she always did, except that I'm not embarrassed by her any more. I used to think that this year would uncover something entirely new in me, a different set of desires. Perhaps I would find some kinks that would make me more interesting. But no. I always knew exactly who I was; I've just never given myself free rein before. I feel like I'm just beginning to get the hang of it.

Seduction #47 made me realise that part of my queasiness around sex comes from feeling the pressure to perform. I should have known better, but I have been suckered in by media sex, that parade of perfect bodies and branded eroticism. In the twenty-first century it just doesn't feel enough any more to have straightforward sex without any particular spin on it – or 'vanilla' sex, as it's sometimes rather sniffily called. If I am to be a modern, liberated woman, I feel as though I should be into something darker, dirtier, edgier.

I always did want to be the cool kid at the back of the classroom. I earned my teenage stripes by dying my hair green and extolling the virtues of records that even I found unlistenable. And a part of me yearns to be a cool kid sexually too, someone with tastes that are slightly curious and challenging. I have to accept, frankly, that this isn't true, and that it's irrelevant in any case.

If I ask myself, honestly, what I want out of sex, then I'd say I want astonishing sensations, intimate communication and the sense of being transported to another state of being for a while. But more than anything, I want authenticity. I don't want to be self-consciously play-acting the kind of sex I think I ought to be having. I want to be pursuing authentic desires and erotic hunches and generating my own genuine responses. This is the hardest thing to pull off, particularly when you're navigating your way around your partner's own set of desires and preconceptions.

Sticking to the seductions has not always been easy. Their structure has given me the motivation I needed to start a dialogue with Herbert about sex, but the constant push towards novelty that they entail is relentless. There's no scope in them to go back to the things we enjoyed and to explore them even further. Moreover, they have sometimes meant that we've tried our ideas – the CAT is a good example here – for the sake of it.

Yet, on the other hand, I'm worried that we'll go stale again without the seductions. It feels as though we'll need to broker an entirely new sexual settlement once they're gone.

Seduction #48
Boy Toy

Herbert is browsing the internet when I get home.

'I want one of these,' he says.

This is nothing unusual; H's online purchases are probably the only thing keeping Royal Mail afloat these days. But on closer inspection, he is not looking at a record or a DVD. He is showing me the Flip Hole, what is charmingly termed a 'male masturbator'.

'Ew,' I say.

'But it says it's the best sex toy for men ever!'

'Yes,' I say, 'single men.'

And that is that. Except that, soon afterwards, I begin to feel guilty. What right have I got to be so judgemental? After all, I'm more than comfortable with sex toys shaped as penises; why should I have a problem with sex toys that mimic vaginas?

There is, I think, a lingering stigma attached to men using sex toys. We women have done a good job of rebranding our masturbatory lives as liberating and health-giving; but male masturbation is in desperate need of a makeover. Perhaps we're still clinging to the idea of the stud who doesn't need to masturbate because he's got sex on tap; or perhaps we've been infected by the image of the furtive male masturbator who 'has a rummage' at the most inappropriate moments.

Either way, my sense is that, unlike their male counterparts, straight women are not in any hurry to watch their partners masturbate.

So, inevitably, I order Herbert a Flip Hole. In actual fact, I'm incredibly curious about what it entails. As soon as it arrives, and before H can even get a look-in, I have whipped it out of the packet and flipped it open.

It's a long plastic sleeve, lined with a kind of moulded jelly. Remember those sticky little creatures you had as a kid that you could throw at a window and watch them ooze down? It's made of that. It's very soft and is cast to roughly resemble a Klingon's forehead. According to the manufacturer's website, each bump and ridge serves a different function; there's even a handy space-age diagram. I close the thing up and poke my fingers in. I'm not sure if I can distinguish between the different parts, but I do concede it feels rather nice in there. Almost erotic.

H arrives home and spends some time reading the instructions. How difficult can it be? You just poke your knob in it, surely? I refrain from telling him this; it's nice that he appreciates his new toy.

'What are you going to do while I use it?' he asks.

'I dunno. Watch? Not watch? I'm easy either way.'

We leave it at that. But then, a little later, I hear music coming from the living room, and H calling, 'Hurry up then, I'm getting cold.'

He is sitting, naked, on the sofa, watching a Bettie Page

DVD that he bought in an art gallery a couple of weeks ago.

'Very retro,' I say.

H grins.

The Flip Hole comes with three varieties of lube, and H selects 'Wild' rather than 'Real' or 'Mellow'. This seems inevitable to me; selecting 'Mellow' would be like buying condoms in size 'Small'. Every man, surely, wants to have a 'Wild' experience rather than a 'Mellow' one?

In any case, the Flip Hole seems to certainly do its job. I try very hard not to find it comical, but it's difficult not to. I suppose the reason men like to see women using sex toys is because they enhance the view; with the Flip Hole, there's nothing to see, just a jogging motion.

'Can you feel all the different bits?' I ask. 'Do the buttons make any difference?'

'No, and no, but it's lovely all the same, and can you stop asking me questions? I'm trying to concentrate here.'

I am chastened. Instead, I try to take a leaf out of the male gaze handbook and simply watch. His legs are taut, but his face is relaxed and his breathing is slow. His eyes are closed; he's completely self-contained. I am being allowed to see something fragile and beautiful; it's intimate and trusting, not so much a turn-on as an act of love.

His head rolls back as he orgasms, and then he shivers and looks from me to the Flip Hole and then back again.

'Nice?' I say.

'Lovely. But I feel a bit silly now.'

'You shouldn't feel silly at all,' I say. I kiss him. 'And now I'll be able to picture what you're doing the next time I go out.'

Our little household is gradually finding its equilibrium again.

Elsie the kitten is showing signs of believing that we're not entirely pointless after all, courtesy of a feather on a stick that we bought from the local pet shop, which she will wrestle with contentedly after a little persuasion. The fact that it's impregnated with catnip helps, as does the cat pheromone plug-in that is supposed to fool her into thinking she's scent-marked everything. Yes, we are drugging our kitten into liking us, and we are not ashamed. She's still decidedly frosty about us touching her, though she'll nearly take your hand off for a scrap of smoked salmon.

It is during these games with the feather on a stick that we come to understand that Elsie is in fact more of an Elvis. He seems to take this change of gender with good grace. Bob remains appalled, but will occasionally consent to staging strikes on his food bowl. She has also taken to sleeping on my feet at night to assert her ownership of me.

It will all settle down; everything does in the end. Other things are settling too. At some point over the last few months – and I couldn't tell you when – I stopped seeing myself as a woman in the process of deciding whether to have children, and instead became a woman who doesn't want children yet. The difference is small but crucial. Rather than wringing my hands and trying to force a choice, I am settling for who I am now. I'm perfectly aware of all the dire warnings about declining female fertility after thirty, but that's not a good enough reason for me to reproduce. Sorry, life, you'll have to wait for me to get there in my own sweet time.

The problem is that the world suddenly seems too much fun. Herbert and I are safe. We are happy. We are damned near unassailable. That means that we don't have to cling to each other quite so tightly any more. We can pursue our own schemes now. If this sounds like a minor understanding to you, to me, it feels like my heart has been split open and the light is pouring in.

'If we're not having children,' I say to Herbert, 'then we don't need to live in the pattern of people who do any more, do we?'

'Um,' says H, 'no, I suppose not. What do you mean?'

'Well, we don't have to work full-time jobs and own a three-bedroom house,' I say. 'Just as an example.'

H looks appalled. 'I love this house. This house is great.'

'Okay, fine. I love this house too. But there's nothing stopping us from renting it out for a while, living somewhere else maybe. If we wanted to.'

'Well, no. But don't forget my job.'

'You could take a sabbatical. Or get a new one!'

H shoots me his wide-eyed, terrified look, the one that makes his words dry up.

'Alright, Herbert, don't panic. Nobody is forcing you to change. But maybe I can try some different things out instead. Maybe I can travel a bit, or rent myself the tiniest flat in London so that I can have my time living in a big city. Maybe you can come and visit me when I'm there, and we can pretend we're lovers again, rather than an old married couple.'

Herbert smiles. 'You'd better find a way to afford it first.'

I am just thinking, *Damn you, Herbert, and your wretched resistance to anything new*, when he says, 'I'd like some more time without you too. I'd like to go out with my friends without it having to be about couples, and I'd like to spend more time playing computer games without worrying whether you'll disapprove. There's a little group in London who meet up once a month to talk about records. I think I might start going along.'

That rather takes me aback for a few seconds. In all our time together, we've clung to each other like particularly desperate limpets, even when we're bored senseless. It wasn't that we were monitoring each other, or fearing the other would stray; it was just what we thought close couples ought to do. Now, when we feel closer than ever, we can afford to be a little bit further apart.

Seduction #49
Workout

There comes a time in every woman's life when she must take her pelvic-floor muscles in hand and give them a stern talking to. Or something like that.

Actually, it would be more honest to put it this way: there comes a point in every woman's life when she suspects that she no longer has the vagina of a sixteen-year-old.

This, for me, came when I had to buy a new Mooncup last year. Their website helpfully explained that women over thirty lose 'vaginal tone' and so have to buy the larger size. Thanks, Mooncup. I could have done without the perky little reminder that I am en route to the grave.

There was also An Incident in which I coughed and weed a bit. Quite a bit, actually. I began to suspect that my pelvic floor was subsiding.

I am not the sort of person to take these things lying down. A few months ago, I purchased a set of Lelo Luna

Beads, which are nice, pastel-coloured vaginal weights that look entirely innocent, even when you – ahem – forget you've left them by the bathroom sink when you have guests for dinner. They come in two sizes, and you can gradually increase the resistance by joining two balls together with a little collar.

Now, the first thing I'll mention is that there's nothing remotely erotic about wearing them, regardless of what it says on the packet. There is a moving ball bearing inside that is supposed to be stimulating, but actually feels rather like you've got wind. Every time I move, I can feel a sort of internal glug, as if I am a bottle of water that's been upended. This is not a problem once you've worked out what's going on – and, in all honesty, I'm a little bit grateful that I'm not in a permanent lather when they're in.

Also, it has taken me a while to learn to take them out before I use the toilet. The most minute push and they pop out of their own accord. I am still unsure whether this means I'm exceptionally toned or completely slack, and I think on balance I'd rather not know. But either way, I've already flushed one away altogether. This did not make me happy.

However, they are beginning to have a pretty good effect. I was sitting in a meeting a couple of days ago and, as I was rapidly losing interest, I decided to do a few PC clenches to pass the time. Oh my. It was as if my whole undercarriage came alive. Within thirty seconds, I was bounding towards an orgasm, right there under the meeting table. Hands-free. I had to rapidly apply the brakes before I did something embarrassing.

I decide to put this to the test on Herbert. Of course, being the woman I am, I'm completely unable to do this in a straightforward way. I decide to set it up as an experiment. I offer Herbert 'normal' (i.e. seduction-free) sex, and see if he notices any difference.

We start with him giving me oral sex. We nearly always start this way; Herbert is suspicious that I'll never really enter into the spirit of things if he doesn't put in some hard work upfront. Today, I wait until he slips a finger inside me, and then I begin a furious series of clenches.

I think he notices; at least, he giggles. I giggle back, to show him that I'm not having some sort of a fit. At this stage, the pelvic-floor contractions are clearly of no use to Herbert, but they help me along. Not only do they add to the sensation, but they keep me focused on my vagina, rather than letting my mind drift happily on to other matters, such as the shopping list.

After a while, he wipes his mouth on the duvet cover (that habit's my fault; I've instilled a modicum of post-oral-sex etiquette), and rolls on to his back. I straddle him and begin some slow, long strokes, squeezing my PC muscles as I go. This seems to elicit no particular response. Soon I stay still altogether, to see if my pelvic floor can do all the work on its own.

Herbert lies back with a look of patient expectation on his face.

'Can you feel that?' I say. 'I'm squeezing my pelvic-floor muscles?'

'Um, would it be rude to say no?'

'Oh. Alright then.' Yes, Herbert, it would be rude to say no. I am clenching like a madwoman down here.

'It's probably because it all feels so wonderful anyway that I can't tell the difference.' Ever the diplomat.

'It's okay. You can either feel it or you can't. I'm not taking it personally.'

We carry on. At least all those clenches lead to a nice

orgasm. Herbert comes just after me, and I lean down to rest my head on his chest. We breathe together for a while, and I try a last few speculative twitches, just in case.

'Ouch!' says Herbert. 'I can feel that!'

'Excellent,' I cackle, and exercise my new-found muscle a few more times. Just to make sure it works, you understand.

Seduction #50
Medicine

In our house, there is no such thing as man-flu. The very phrase makes Herbert wild with rage.

This is mostly because he troops on stoically when he catches a cold. I, on the other hand, routinely fail to locate my stiff upper lip. I whine and attention-seek for the first day of any illness, and then spend all subsequent days moaning that I'm bored and lamenting the terrible waste of my life that this represents.

However, lately he has not been stoical enough for my tastes. He recovered from his cold a fortnight ago, only to come down with another one this week. Yes, he's put himself to bed without grumbling, and has continued to work his way through the laundry basket and load the dishwasher, but he's also been somewhat unwilling to have sex with me. Now, I know that, technically, this isn't his fault, but we're on a deadline here. We have booked a weekend in Paris to celebrate the end of the seductions,

and that's at the beginning of December. Ergo, all seductions must be done and dusted by the end of November.
I am not budging on this one. Yet time is ticking.

Luckily, I have a cunning plan: a seduction that doubles
as a cold remedy. I have been tipped off, you see, that
Fisherman's Friend cough lozenges are the last word in
exciting oral sex.

I suggest this to Herbert.

'If nothing else,' I say, 'it will clear your nose.'

'Have they got aniseed in them?'

'Almost certainly.'

'I don't like them then.'

It is gently explained to Herbert that this is very much
not the point.

'Oh, alright then,' he sighs, 'but only if I can go first. I
won't be able to come if it means I'll have to put a Fisherman's Friend in my mouth afterwards.'

Fine. Whatever. We open the packet, and he manages
to suck on the weird little brown biscuit without flinching
too much.

The sensation takes a while to build. At first it's a very
mild tingle, but then it becomes something that feels both
hot and cold at the same time. Unlike the infernal mint
lube of Seduction #6, this makes me feel sparkly and ultra-
sensitive, like my vulva is continually demanding my
attention. When Herbert briefly takes his mouth away, the
feeling carries on, a kind of icy glow.

I begin to read the back of the packet.

'Oh, there's eucalyptus and capsicum in them,' I say.
'No wonder. Hot and cold, you see.'

Herbert ignores me.

'Didn't your friend once spray Deep Heat on his knob?'

'His balls.'

'And how did that work out?'

'Painfully. Shh.'

'Shall we swap over?'

We do. Herbert enjoys the FF effect too, which I find slightly surprising, but he adds a caveat: 'I think they might make it impossible to come,' he says.

Well, that makes them rather dual-purpose in my view. Sensitivity and longevity? Surely this is the Holy Grail.

'You didn't seem to mind the taste at all,' I say to him afterwards.

'Oh God, they were still disgusting,' he says, 'but even I know when I'm on to a good thing.'

Despite Herbert's cold, which is now threatening to become a chest infection, I drag him along to London's Erotica fair on a Friday night after work.

He is frightfully brave about the whole thing, which may or may not be connected to the fact that Dita von Teese is performing. I suspect that he has swallowed so much Day Nurse that he doesn't care either way.

I am hoping that Erotica will stoke our imaginations as we head towards our final seductions. I am seeking inspiration. What I find instead is mild puzzlement. It is as if someone has spread out a tablecloth at my feet, and laid out a banquet representing every area of contemporary sexuality for my perusal. There are the bits I disapprove of (a stand of *Sunday Sport* lovelies signing autographs), the bits I'm sniffy about (leopard-print satin sheets), the bits I don't really understand (human dog cages) and the bits I'm fascinated by (electro-stimulation sex toys).

At least I'm not intimidated by this stuff any more; once upon a time, I would have skittered through the aisles and out into the bar, trying to avoid eye contact. But instead my mind is blank. I want something special to jump out at me, but after a year of trying new things, I'm pretty hard to impress. Prostate toys? Meh. Under-bed restraints? Nothing new. Suede floggers? Someone else's fantasy, not mine.

I am enchanted, for a while, by the astonishing corsetry on display, intricate confections of lace and ribbon, but they're well beyond my price-range. In any case, I don't think they'd be enough to set the night on fire in and of themselves; they're more likely to be admired by my girl-friends than by Herbert. The sex furniture looks fun, but then so are the contours of our sofa. H is too delighted with his Flip Hole to ever consider another sex toy again.

It's great to be able to touch and examine toys I've only ever seen online before. I find myself looking more closely at things that I've previously written off as 'not for me'. H lets me lead him around, but without much interest. What he's always understood – and what I admire him for – is that sex boils down to only a few elements, however they're packaged. He doesn't seek novelty, just contact, communication, sensation. That authenticity I crave, he's quietly guarded that for years. This year, he's flourished into a comfortable sense of his own sexuality, while I've run in zigzags around my sexual core.

We are nearly losing interest, and are ready to head home.

'I suppose we'll just have to think of something for the last seduction ourselves,' says H.

'Well,' I say, 'there was something I *was* curious about.' My stomach flips. 'But I'm not sure what you'd think.'

'Show me,' he says.

'I mean, it's expensive and maybe not really our thing.'

'Don't talk yourself out of it. Just show me.'

I lead him to a stand that we'd merely glanced at before, and first of all it makes Herbert's eyebrows raise to say, *Really?* But soon we are both happily absorbed in its racks, and I am nervously holding up an item for H's inspection and whispering, 'Don't you think it's lovely?'

Seduction #51
Bad Girl

'Urrgh! Stay still. Ow. Ow. Retreat! Slowly! Slowly!'

'Was that not good?'

'I wasn't expecting you to put the whole bloody thing in at once on our first try, Herbert.'

'Oh, sorry. It just went in so easily.'

'That's the lube!'

'Oh. Yeah. Sorry.'

'I might need to have a little think for a while before we start again.'

When I started the seductions, I wondered if sex had changed since I was last really engaged in it. And, actually, I think that anal sex is one way in which it has. In my day (says the old lady of thirty-three), only really bad girls did it. I can remember a whispered conversation between one ex-boyfriend and his mates, in which they discussed a friend known as 'Dirt-box Sarah' without any semblance of self-awareness that one of them had put his penis into that very place and had avoided gaining a nickname, derogatory or otherwise.

Were I eighteen now, and entering a new relationship, I think that anal sex would probably be very much on the cards. But when I met Herbert, it wasn't. Over the years, I've noticed a peculiar obsession with it amongst our male friends, most of whom admit to never having had the opportunity. Meanwhile, the notion of anal sex receives a studied indifference from our female friends – not to mention a fair amount of mythologising. The consensus seems to be that nice girls don't, and that those who do get piles.

And the problem for me, over the course of this year, is that I've begun to find that latent disapproval tempting. I tend to think that if thirty-five-year-old women disapprove of something, it's likely to be quite fun. I came to like the idea of transgression that it encompasses, that freedom from bodily hang-ups that it demands. Anal sex is a truly shameless thing to do. In my mind, it began to embody disinhibition.

Nevertheless, I was coy about approaching the issue with Herbert. More than anything else we'd done, it felt like a U-turn. I hoped for a while that he'd suggest it himself, but he didn't. Was this through fear of offending me? Either way, when I finally broached the issue ('I suppose we really ought to do anal sex, for the sake of completion'), he simply said, 'Sure.'

And then we left it. For ages. The seductions rolled on. We mentioned it a few times, but neither of us seemed to really want to initiate it. Until tonight. With two seductions left, and something already purchased for Seduction #52, there is no more room for manoeuvre. Herbert arrives home, we have a glass of wine and, without discussing our plans, we head for the bedroom.

Things proceed very well. Truth be told, I'm quite turned on at the thought of doing something so risqué, and there is a moment when I wonder if we'll skip the anal sex altogether because we're having so much fun. But then Herbert asks where I'm keeping the lube these days, and I find myself negotiating the merits of all-fours versus face-to-face. All-fours seems to offer me a bit more privacy to arrange my face, and adds to the animal nature of the whole thing, I think.

However, as you will already have discerned, H's first attempt is a little more robust than I expected. It's not horrific, but it certainly burns. I turn to face him, and we kiss for a while, as I wonder whether I'll feel equal to giving it another go. Five minutes later, I do. Nothing has fallen off, as far as I can tell. No harm done. I fetch my vibrator from the top of the wardrobe to see if I can't enjoy myself a little more this time.

I assume the position again, and H takes things a bit steadier. He pushes just the tip of his penis into me, and then stays still while I acclimatise. It feels fine – not especially painful, but certainly tight and a little resistant. It is, in fact, a bit like losing your virginity, although I am less perplexed this time around. The vibrator helps a great deal. I hold it against my clitoris until the soles of my feet tingle, and do my best to relax into the whole thing, to surrender. Soon, I am absorbed in inhabiting my body, rather than thinking about the process. When I next come to awareness, I find myself rocking just slightly and Herbert taking in little gasps of air.

'How about I have a quick wash,' he says, 'and we finish off the more usual way?'

I'm happy to agree; it's nice to reconnect again, face to face. Afterwards, he says, 'I couldn't tell whether you were enjoying that.'

'Yes,' I say, 'I think I was,' and I spend the rest of the evening trailing the special glow of the Bad Girl behind me.

Seduction #52
Through the Looking Glass

I turn on the bathroom light and gaze into the mirror. My cheeks are pink and my hair pokes out at many angles. What remains of my red lipstick is still on my mouth, but also my chin, my ear, my throat and my breasts. I suspect that Herbert is now wearing more of it than I am.

I pour some cleanser on to a pad of cotton wool, and set about wiping it off the rubber nurse outfit I am wearing. I want it to be pristine for the next time.

Herbert comes in. I take off my stockings, and he unzips my dress. I peel it off. For the last hour, it has felt like a miraculous second skin, peach-soft and arousing. But now, underneath, I am damp and slightly cold.

'I wonder how you wash it?' I say.

'Wipe it down with a cloth, I expect,' says H.

And then I catch our reflection in the mirror. Both of us naked and flushed, radiant. Herbert wearing my little rubber nurse's cap. He embraces me from behind, and we stand there for a moment, smiling as if the mirror is capturing our fleeting portrait.

'Will we ever have sex again after this?' I ask him.

'Of course!'

'We'll leave it a few days though, eh? For a rest?'

Herbert smiles and hands me my pyjamas. 'Actually,' he says, 'I just took a Viagra, so you've got about an hour.'

It's been a long year. There were moments when I wondered what I'd got myself into. There were moments when I thought that Herbert would mutiny. When I suggested the seductions, I thought that we would perhaps learn to have better sex. I didn't expect to have my whole sense of self rearranged.

I have been profoundly changed by this. By doing something as simple as forcing ourselves to have sex once a week (which, according to some surveys, doesn't even hit the average frequency), we seem to have dredged through every element of our lives together. At times, it's felt like an extended and particularly harrowing course of psychotherapy. We've been holding up a mirror to our lives, both individually and as a couple. There has been nowhere to hide.

Of course, it wasn't the sex itself that mattered; it was the need to address desire. When we started this, I thought that desire would be resurrected by the mere act of having more sex. It was not. Desire, I learned, is a wily little creature. It shifts and changes over time, and it demands our constant attention and understanding. In seducing each other, we've been making up for years of neglect, and coaxing the beast back to life has been agonising at times. But if we can't be honest about *what* we truly desire, how can we expect to truly *feel* desire?

Take, for example, this final seduction. It was constructed of things that neither of us could have admitted we wanted a year ago. Me in my teeny-tiny (*Aren't I too fat for teeny-tiny?*) rubber (*Rubber? Isn't that for perverts?*) nurse outfit (*Oh please! What a dated, sexist stereotype that is!*), with its deep-cut neckline (*I do not need to poke my breasts uncomfortably out of an outfit in order to have sex*). Herbert being finally allowed to appreciate me in a costume like that, rather than being terrified that it's not politically correct for him to do so (H: 'We'll start with you kneeling over my face, please. It's such a great view'). Both of us agreeing that we'd like to have another try at anal sex, because we enjoyed it last time.

I don't think I ever realised before just how confused I felt about sex. My liberal views mean that I've always believed that people should be allowed to do what they choose in bed. My feminist views told me that women were often exploited and degraded by sex. I never noticed the contradiction until this year. I was effectively telling myself that other people were free to go out there and have all the fun they could take, but I'd better not, just in case I accidentally oppressed myself in the process. I now realise that's nonsense. Sex is a morally neutral act, not a dark force, and, as long as we're consenting, we can't be oppressed by the things we choose to do in the bedroom. Unequal relationships do not merely emerge from the roles we play during sex, and it's reductive to think that they do.

At the beginning of the seductions, I said, 'I just don't see sex as remotely spicy.' I don't believe that any more. I had to learn all over again what gives sex its edge. Half of me needed to make it feel emotionally safe, but the other half needed to feel the risk and the danger of sex. That has nothing to do with being physically threatened; it is instead based on your willingness to truly engage with your partner, to let them glimpse the secret parts of your soul. It's scary to reveal the passion that writhes underneath your sensible, predictable self, but it's exhilarating too. The beauty of that revelation is that it cuts through the cosiness of marriage, and means that sex can continue to be exciting long after the first flush. We just both have to be willing to surrender, to look each other in the eye. That is true intimacy.

I still feel as though we have miles to go. There are layers of desire we have yet to uncover. The relentless logic of the seductions meant that we had little chance to give anything a second try. Now we will have time to develop a little more competence, without the pressure of the project. We're both exhausted and slightly shell-shocked, but I, for one, can't wait to dive in.

Epilogue

erbert and I are sitting in a café in the Marais, drinking Kirs.

'Don't look now, but the couple behind you are snogging across the table! Oh, she's got up . . . She's sitting on his lap . . . Oh my God, she's straddling him! I said DON'T look, Herbert!'

Herbert ignores me and cranes his head over his shoulder to stare. Luckily, the man and woman behind us are oblivious.

'Maybe we should do that too,' says Herbert.

'I'm just not French enough.'

'We used to do it all the time.'

'I was eighteen. I don't know what your excuse was.'

'I was just grateful you wanted to snog me.'

'Anyway, our friends started to comment. It got embarrassing.'

'True.'

We have returned to Paris to celebrate the end of the seductions, leaving Elvis and Bob behind to sort out their differences in the capable hands of some good friends. It seemed right when we booked it; I remember last year's Parisian seduction as the moment I began to glimpse my own sexuality again. But at that point, I didn't know how odd I'd feel at the end of the seductions, how bereft. The project that has consumed me all year has suddenly vanished, just as we were getting the hang of it. On the one hand, I'm beginning to think that I might have time to occasionally weed the garden again; on the other, I feel like my road map has been snatched from my hands. Without the structure of the seductions, will we fall into our old, bad habits?

Herbert is unhelpful on this matter. 'We will or we won't, there's no way of telling,' he says. In all fairness, I have asked him the question while we're sitting on the Eurostar, so it probably isn't the best moment. But nevertheless, this sounds worryingly like we haven't learned our lesson to me. If there is any scrap of knowledge that we can keep from this year, surely it is that good sex requires some level of effort, or at least forethought.

It doesn't help that I have booked us a room with separate beds. This is not as eccentric as it sounds. Herbert is 6'3", and I am 6'. We just don't fit into a standard double bed, particularly not if we want to actually sleep. When I was making the arrangements, this felt like a sensible, grown-up decision: being intimate and sharing a bed are not the same thing. On arrival at the hotel, though, it seems like a desolate choice to have made. We roll into Paris, go out for dinner and then curl up chastely in our separate beds and go to sleep.

The next morning, we wander down the road to an antiques market, where I am disappointed to find that there are a great deal of records. As Herbert loses himself in the stacks, I drift through the stalls, burying my face in my scarf to keep warm. A few snowflakes begin to fall. I rush back and tell Herbert. He smiles, distracted.

Within fifteen minutes, the snow is setting in. The stall-holders curse the weather and begin to pack up. Herbert insists on going through one last box of records before I can drag him into a café for a warming coffee. We are both cold and have damp feet. We agree that it's best to return to our hotel room for better shoes and more layers. Then we head out again, bulked up in so many clothes that it feels difficult to move. This is not sexy.

Paris is very beautiful in the snow. Shop canopies and pavements are dusted white, and the low buildings take on a sober beauty. After another freezing walk, we head into a restaurant for lunch, and emerge a couple of hours later, sleepy with wine and duck confit. The cold weather outside makes walking feel like hard work. Herbert tries to liven me up with a trip to the Pompidou Centre, but its neon lights and enormous queues just make me feel more exhausted. I persuade him to take me back to the hotel for an afternoon nap.

I strip off my boots, two pairs of socks, jeans, leggings, jumper, shirt and three T-shirts, and get into bed. Herbert curls in behind me. One moment, I am on the very border of sleep, and the next I find Herbert is kissing the back of my neck and I am running the soles of my feet along his shins.

On Sunday, we have sex, with me bridging my body between our two beds. Then we head out to Belleville for our evening meal. I am wearing my best shoes, which are frankly ridiculous on pavements this icy: black suede courts with a leopard-skin wedge. I should be in wellies. But then, high-heeled shoes are a bit like sex; you have to make your own opportunities to wear them. This, at least, is what I tell Herbert, as I cling to his arm whilst tottering down the steep steps of the Metro.

Herbert drinks Mojitos and I stick to wine. We talk about next year's holiday, our plans for Christmas, whether we'll ever manage to socialise Elvis the kitten. I raise the subject of the seductions again.

'Do you think we'll manage without them? Do you think we've actually changed?'

'Yes,' says Herbert, 'I do. Don't you?'

'I don't know. At the beginning, I wanted to get back that feeling we had when we were first together, when we couldn't leave each other alone. I wanted butterflies in my stomach again. Now I know that won't happen. It takes more effort and planning than that. But do I think it's worth it? Definitely.'

'That's life, Betty. It's not like a romantic novel. Nothing happens by magic.'

'You're right, of course. But I want to know that I won't be the only one making the effort. I want to know that, sometimes, I'll be seduced without asking first.'

Herbert shrugs, and I know I'm asking too much. I want it both ways, really: to be practical and independent, and romanced and cosseted. Piece by piece, I've constructed a relationship that's sincere, equal and balanced and yet sometimes a rebel part of me craves to be swept off my feet, to be plied with roses and grand gestures. Such things baffle Herbert, and I wouldn't have him any other way. Love and sex boil down to the same essence: connection. We have that in spades, and I am grateful for it.

'Well,' says Herbert, 'how about I move over and sit next to you, and then we can snog like Parisians for a while?'

That night, as we drift to sleep in our separate beds, I say, 'I love you.'

'What's "I love you" in French?'

'Je t'aime.'

'Okay then. Je t'aime vous.'

'No, just "je t'aime". We're well past "vous" in any case.'

'That's what I said. Je t'aime vous.'

'Alright, Herbert, je t'aime vous aussi. Night night.'

Acknowledgements

First and foremost, my profound thanks and adoration must go to Herbert, who generously volunteered his body for a year of sexual experimentation. As ever, he has astonished me with his trust, support and kindness. He's definitely a keeper.

Huge thanks to the people who made this book possible: super-agent Felicity Blunt and the team at Curtis Brown; Carly Cook, Rhea Halford, Helena Towers, Vicky Cowell and Jo Whitford at Headline; Katie McGowan and Lucy Abrahams for going global.

I wouldn't have got through the year without the following people: Andrea Gibb, Barbara Carrellas, my partner in crime Peggy Riley, and Beccy Shaw, Sarah Williams, Amy Barker, Marnie Summerfield-Smith, Rosa Ainley, Sue Jones, Tracey Falcon and Imogen Noble, all of whom have absorbed my obsessive need to talk about the project. Thanks should also go to my mum for not having kittens over the whole thing.

Finally, I'm deeply indebted to my friends on Twitter and the readers of my blog (I'm afraid you're too numerous to mention here), who have variously urged on, supported, celebrated, commiserated, shared experience and offered impressive expertise throughout the whole process. The blog would have been nothing without you. Thank you.